STRUCTURALISM OR CRITICISM?
THOUGHTS ON HOW WE READ

For Nicholas and Peter

STRUCTURALISM OR CRITICISM?

THOUGHTS ON HOW WE READ

GEOFFREY STRICKLAND

CAMBRIDGE UNIVERSITY PRESS

CAMBRIDGE

LONDON   NEW YORK   NEW ROCHELLE

MELBOURNE   SYDNEY

Published by the Press Syndicate of the University of Cambridge
The Pitt Building, Trumpington Street, Cambridge CB2 1RP
32 East 57th Street, New York, NY 10022, USA
296 Beaconsfield Parade, Middle Park, Melbourne 3206, Australia

First published 1981

Printed in Great Britain by
Western Printing Services Ltd, Bristol

British Library Cataloguing in Publication Data
Strickland, Geoffrey
Structuralism or criticism?
1. French Literature – History and criticism
2. Criticism
3. English Literature – History and criticism
I. Title
840'.9   PQ71   80-40721
ISBN 0 521 23184 1

CONTENTS

Acknowledgments   *page* vii
A note on the quotations   viii

Part I

1 Introduction. Reading as distinct from talking or writing
   about books   3
2 Benveniste and semiology: or where structuralism
   doesn't work   12

Part II

3 Thoughts on how we read   35
   1 All that we say or think about a particular utterance or
      piece of writing presupposes an assumption on our
      part, correct or otherwise, concerning the intention of
      the speaker or writer   36
   2 Which is why we can say certain things about what
      we read which are true but never deny the possibility
      that we may be wrong   55
   3 But a true understanding of what is written or said
      does not and could not possibly imply a complete
      sharing of the writer's or speaker's experience; which
      is why a true understanding of those whose experi-
      ence differs from our own, including writers from a
      distant past, is always possible   67
   4 We cannot possibly understand what is written or said
      unless we understand its interest and importance for
      the writer or speaker; which affects inevitably its inter-
      est and importance for us. Evaluation, in this sense,
      and interpretation are the same   83
   5 The student of literature is a student of history   109

Part III

4 The Utopianism of Roland Barthes   127

v

5   The criticism of F. R. Leavis   145

Notes   176
Bibliography   196
Index   203

ACKNOWLEDGMENTS

This book began to take shape during a series of weekly discussions in the University of Reading in 1974 among students of literature in various departments. We called our meetings an 'inter-departmental course on criticism' and they were meant to air problems of common concern. Few of those who came would, I imagine, say they were an unqualified success. The claims of various 'isms', including what was known for convenience as 'traditionalism', were debated for hours on end. And though good feeling prevailed and people seemed to want to agree or at least persuade others to see their own point of view, many meetings ended with our having nothing to take away but an agreement to differ. We weren't using words in the same way.

My conviction – which I certainly wasn't alone in holding – that there was something wrong with such a situation and that a remedy ought to be found led me to set out the reflections which follow. I have done so in the possibly quixotic belief that, despite our frequent failure to identify them, there must be certain things on which those who read and talk about what they read can agree, for all their often salutary differences; that certain common assumptions are possible and hence a common language in which even the differences can be expressed. My first acknowledgment must therefore be to colleagues and students who, unintentionally, convinced me that the book was worth writing.

Two colleagues in particular helped me to rewrite the first drafts by telling me at length what they thought of them: Michael Proudfoot of the Department of Philosophy, who also gave me valuable advice for further reading, and Walter Redfern of the Department of French. I have also received help and advice from Professor E. D. Hirsch, from Dr Jan Horvat and from Professor W. W. Robson. For painstaking and valuable assistance in rewriting and planning the final drafts, I am indebted to Mr Michael Black of the Cambridge University Press. For typing this and previous versions

I must thank Mrs Mava Quinlan, who has had to see her beautiful typing vandalised several times, and Mrs Erika Stockbridge.

Much of Chapter 2 appeared originally in *The Cambridge Quarterly* and whole paragraphs in the concluding chapter of the book are taken from a broadcast lecture I gave on the criticism of F. R. Leavis in 1976 for the Open University. Permission to reproduce these is gratefully acknowledged here.

Finally, I should express my gratitude to the Leverhulme Foundation for a Fellowship which enabled me to spend a year writing the book in its present form.

GEOFFREY STRICKLAND

Department of French
University of Reading
November 1979

A NOTE ON THE QUOTATIONS

Many quotations from French authors are given here in my own translation. Page references are to the French originals. Where page references are to an English translation of a foreign work, the translation is not my own.

PART I

Chapter 1

INTRODUCTION
READING AS DISTINCT FROM
TALKING OR WRITING ABOUT BOOKS

Understanding is silent, interpretation extremely garrulous.

(E. D. Hirsch)

It is generally assumed that there is what has been called an art –
some would say a science – of reading that can be acquired over
many years of training in schools and universities and is exemplified
in good criticism. Reading, of course, in a restricted sense. It is
something more highly developed than the elementary skills of
literacy, yet, at the same time, no one would claim that it is a matter
of interpreting any piece of writing with expertise. The good critic,
it is acknowledged, may be a poor linguist and capable of reading
fewer foreign languages and understanding them less well than a
professional interpreter, an air hostess or a German politician. Nor
will he be expected to understand a manual of electronics or even a
piece of ordinary technical philosophy. His skill will be apparent in
what he says or writes about poetry, fiction, drama and those works
of history or philosophy which call for no specialised knowledge and
no other kind of skill for their interpretation. It may be apparent too,
according to those who have been influenced by the writings of
F. R. Leavis and Denys Thompson in England or Roland Barthes in
France, in his reading of newspapers, advertisements, politicians'
rhetoric and the catch-phrases of popular culture.

It would be absurd to deny that such a skill could exist or that
different people might possess it in varying degrees. But what is
difficult, on any level of sophistication, is to answer the question:
how do you know it is being exercised and that a particular reading
of the words on the page is correct, especially if by 'the words on the
page' we mean the words understood as the author intended them
to be? It is true that disagreements as to how one should read them
are often resolved to the satisfaction of all concerned, and one may
be grateful to a teacher, a friend or the work of a critic for having
opened one's eyes to what one now sees as the true or full meaning
of a poem. But it is unlikely that anyone who has enjoyed this

3

experience will be able to say what general principle or rule he happened to violate when he misread the poem in the first place, and how he might avoid making such a mistake again. This is probably why, though many attempts have been made to formulate such rules and principles, there is none, apart from simple caveats such as Plutarch's reminder that poets tell deliberate lies, which has commanded for long any general assent.[1]

Something else that is difficult – in fact, practically impossible – is to know whether the academic study of literature has proved, on balance, a blessing or a curse.[2] A blessing of course, it would be said by many of the academics themselves and by those who assume that people in their position must know what they're talking about. Yet is there any way in which this is obvious? At least, it might be said, it has ensured that the great poets and novelists of the past continue to be read, just as the schools of the Greek and Roman *grammatikoi* helped to preserve the reputation of a canon of poets, dramatists, orators and historians. Possibly. But the reputation of Shakespeare in England spread and became established centuries before he became the object of 'commentary' and 'appreciation' in universities and schools. That of Dickens was made by his unschooled readers, and it was not to university or adult education audiences that he delivered his public readings.[3] The idea of a canon of literary classics is, in any case, becoming increasingly unfashionable in schools and universities themselves. Literature is coming more and more to be regarded as a branch of sociology or linguistics. Writings of avowedly ephemeral interest are coming to dominate the syllabus, to the point where in America, according to E. D. Hirsch (*The aims of interpretation*, p. 136), 'little remains that the underground can call its own'. In some universities, it is now possible for a student to take a good degree in French without having read either Racine or Flaubert. Even among those who profess to take the idea of the literary classic seriously, there is an understandable tendency to question established reputations or to want to add to the list, and it would be outrageous to wish that things should be otherwise. As a result, the list of 'major authors' now far exceeds any possible syllabus, and the idea of the 'well-read' man or woman comes to seem increasingly unreal as the years go by. It may be impossible to revive the customs and pieties of antiquity, but there was a purely practical advantage in the creation of a canon which included only ten works in every genre. It ensured, if nothing else, the existence of a common culture among the literate classes of the Hellenistic and Roman worlds and one extending over many generations.

The question whether the so-called teaching of literature has been of general benefit to humanity is, of course, impossible to answer. There is no conceivable form of investigation that would enable us to weigh the cost against the advantages and only a biased or un-questioning mind will reply unhesitatingly in the negative or – dare I say? – affirmative. Someone may ask, of course, 'What harm can it do?' And the question needs to be asked, but if anyone doubts that it can do harm, he ought perhaps to read John Newton's article in *The Cambridge Quarterly*, 'Literary criticism, universities, mur-der'. Newton points out, with copious illustrations, how much better, from any point of view, a first-year undergraduate can write on the poetry of Donne than his or her elders and betters, reputed academic critics for whom the prolonged study of literature seems to have become only a conventional chore. Matthew Arnold says somewhere that one can read too much poetry, and anyone who believes that enforced exposure to literature is, at the worst, harmless should con-sider how often intelligent young people are dismayed by its apparent effect on the minds of those who have been exposed to it for years; also how often a normally sensitive boy or girl has been made to hate poetry by being made to write or talk about it in words which have then been held up for kindly or unkind ridicule. The love of poetry can be an intensely private affair.[4] Glibness is not the guarantee of either insight or sensitivity.

However, it is not with the possible consequences of the universal and compulsory study of literature during the last hundred years that this book is concerned, valuable though it might be to know more than we do of the history of that particular educational reform. My purpose is rather to suggest what, by the nature of things and at any time, reading and critical discussion is able and unable to achieve.

Among the objects which critical discussion is unable to achieve, we are often told, is the communication to someone else of anything resembling a fact or a precept; that is, an addition to knowledge to be taken on trust. This has been said with some firmness by, for example, Roland Barthes, in his *Leçon inaugurale prononcée au Collège de France*; F. R. Leavis, who happened for this reason to dislike even referring to himself as a 'teacher' and John Newton in the article I have already mentioned. Newton writes:

Poetry can be studied, but the study of it can't be taught. So it had better *not* be taught. Some people would say that in that case it has no place in a university. I'm inclined to say that, on the contrary, it is therefore an ideal study for a university. The idea of a university that is being taken for granted by those people who think the opposite is a widespread one but seems to me barbaric . . .   ('Literary criticism, universities, murder', p. 348)

That 'study', one may agree, involves constant discussion and exchange. Otherwise, the university would only be what it often is in reality, a university merely in name. Yet is discussion and exchange of what one has seen and understood *indispensable* to understanding? Newton doesn't assume this, nor can I think of any reason why one should.

Jane Austen or John Clare would not have needed to be told that the ability to read well has nothing necessarily to do with anything one writes or says or anything else one does, apart from reading. If this is not always obvious in our age of compulsory literary appreciation, it is because of the tenacity of the view I am questioning: that the study of literature in schools and universities is, *ipso facto*, worthwhile in that it consists in something more than mere solitary reading. A student of chemistry, it is assumed, can only become proficient by performing experiments, a mathematician by solving mathematical problems and a student of literature by writing critical commentaries and essays.

Yet for the student of literature, the equivalent – if one can talk of an equivalent at all – of solving the problem is the act of reading itself. As E. D. Hirsch has argued (cf. pp. 27–8 below), there is a sense in which the often effortless deciphering of the words on the page entails the solving of problems, even if these are solved instantaneously and unselfconsciously. We hear a great deal, especially in the rubric of examination papers, about something called literary 'analysis'. But analysis here is something very different from analysis in other academic disciplines and the reason seems to lie in what Roland Barthes has spoken of ('Ecrivains, intellectuels, professeurs', p. 9) as a characteristic of the human as distinct from the physical sciences: the impossibility of a 'method' to which one could attribute a 'result'. Barthes slightly over-simplifies the matter and seems to forget that there are such things as statistical surveys and word-counts. These, however, can only be used to answer certain types of question, questions of characteristic usage and authorship notably. Where the analysis of a text does not involve counting, the answer to any question one asks about it is a matter of simple confirmation or otherwise – yes, there is ambiguity here; no, this reading is syntactically impossible – and this seems to be true of literary analysis even at its most searching and subtle. In F. R. Leavis's commentary on Thomas Hardy's 'After a journey', for example (*The living principle*, pp. 127–34 and pp. 174–5 below), we are shown how all the elements in the poem combine to give reality to an experience of a remarkable kind, the remarkableness lying in the effective presence of the intelligence and character of a man reliving his past. I know of no piece of criticism which shows with such precision the complexity and coherence of effect which characterise the reading of a major poem. When I deny that criticism of this kind resembles in any way the performance of an experiment, I am not trying to say that Leavis merely tells us what he happened, without search or reflection, to notice when he was reading Hardy's poem. He himself reminds us constantly how much discussion and exchange are part of 'what we call analysis' (e.g. *English literature in our time and the university*, p. 48) and those who knew him may agree that his best thoughts seemed to come to him when he was thinking and reading aloud in discussion with a congenial audience. I have sometimes been asked to explain the Leavisian 'method', but Leavis himself never claimed that his way of expounding something, with its constant implicit appeal for confirmation, even if 'deliberate' and sustained by a concern for what he called 'relevance', was either methodical or systematic.

There are, of course, other kinds of literary 'analysis'. It may be a matter of pedagogic drill, a way of ensuring that no one in the classroom is left behind, as in the reading of a passage in a Greek or Roman school, calling for the establishment and correction of a common written text; the recitation of the passage; the *exegesis* or explanation of etymologies, learned and technical allusions and the genealogies of gods and heroes; the *krisis* or drawing of a moral from the tale. Something similar has survived into our own lifetimes in the French *explication de texte*, again a schoolroom exercise whose continued practice in the university can be partly explained by the fact that the conclusion of a student's university career is the oral examination of the *agrégation*, in which his examiners include school inspectors and he is judged for his pedagogic as well as intellectual gifts. Analysis here too is (explicitly) a matter of explanation rather than discovery and the rules of the exercise a matter of convention.

It would be absurd to pretend that they are any more than conventions and as absurd to object to them as such as to quarrel with the conventions of polite behaviour that enable strangers to know where they are with one another, to feel at ease and communicate freely.

It is, however, with reading that may or may not give rise to critical discussion that the reflections which follow are concerned. I prefer to leave open the question whether or how the ability to read can be taught and I do not presume to offer any method of criticism. I hope simply that what I am saying will help to clear away some of the current misconceptions surrounding the uniquely human gift for communicating over space and time.

It may be noticed that I have avoided using the word 'literature' in the title of this book, though the reading of novels, poetry and drama is what I mainly discuss and though it will interest mainly those who like myself are students of literature. The word is indispensable. We all know, broadly speaking, what it means in its various contexts, including that of the last lines of Verlaine's *Art poétique*. And misunderstanding only arises when we try to define it more precisely than anyone else: when we try to discover some necessary and sufficient condition which is met by, say, Shelley's 'Masque of Anarchy' or Gorki's autobiography and not by the national anthem or the memoirs of Sir Harold Wilson.

It is debatable whether, strictly speaking – that is from the point of view of philosophy – literature exists. It certainly has not existed for some of the greatest philosophers. This is why attempts to delimit rigorously a realm of what has been described as 'literary understanding' or 'literary communication' have generally failed to carry conviction, command general assent or achieve anything comparable to a breakthrough in molecular biology. How we understand what we read is the concern of philosophy but it is a matter here of what we understand in general. I shall not be arguing therefore as if I thought that the study of literature gave rise to philosophical problems not encountered when considering other, non-literary, kinds of writing or utterance; just as I shall not be assuming that the study of literature is a specialised study calling for specialised skills. The belief that it is such a study and that the ability to understand and appreciate one author – say Racine – necessarily implies an ability to read others – say Shakespeare – has been, as we know, in the past, one of the main causes of blindness and pedantry. This can be seen from the way Shakespeare was criticised by Voltaire or Lawrence's *Rainbow* by Arnold Bennett. 'Tell Arnold Bennett', Lawrence wrote to an acquaintance (16 December 1915), 'that all rules of construction hold good only for novels which are copies of other novels. A book which is not a copy of other books has its own construction, and what he calls faults. . .I call characteristics.'

Today the various misconceptions that have arisen concerning the act of reading arise partly from the sheer diversity and number of the theories of criticism that are being canvassed. The expansion of literary studies in Britain, North America and France in the last few decades has certainly not been accompanied by any commonly accepted notion of what the discipline entails. It is as if a corresponding expansion had taken place in physics and chemistry (significantly, it has not; in England especially, literary studies have, unfortunately, acquired the reputation of one of the 'soft options') before any agreement had been reached about what was meant by an experiment and at a time when the molecular theory was in conflict, or coexisting comfortably, with the claims of alchemy.

Perhaps the main source of confusion, however, lies in the prevalence of one particular view among those who have added to the welter of theory and the confusion here extends well beyond departments of literature. In Germany, certainly, it has its origins in existentialist philosophy and modern sceptical theology. This is the view that when we read writers of the past – for example, the authors of the Gospels – we read a text whose meaning is the reflection of our own presumptions and values and has no ascertainable bearing on what they actually wanted to say. The view that the intentions of the writer are a will-o'-the-wisp which it is foolish to pursue, even if the writer is a contemporary, has become commonplace among academic critics of literature. It has also tended to justify the assumption that the reading of literature is only a serious intellectual activity if it gives rise to the interpretation or theorising which is its only possible *raison d'être*.

Two writers on the theory of criticism have helped me to see what is wrong with this view. One is E. D. Hirsch, to whom I am indebted for, among many other things, the notion (developed on pages 36–55 below) of the inescapability of the attribution (whether mistaken or otherwise) of an intention to the author of any text one reads and how this is intrinsic to meaning. Hirsch also avoids the pitfalls of nineteenth-century German hermeneutics (of Schleiermacher and Dilthey notably) by distinguishing deliberately between an author's meaning and the significance it holds for us (*Validity in interpretation*, pp. 57–61 and pp. 212–29; *The aims of interpretation*, pp. 74–92). He thus enables us to avoid the error that understanding a writer's meaning is, to the extent that one succeeds at all, a matter of sharing some past experience. Those who have treated with scorn the notion that a writer's intention can in any way be known (and known to be known) have usually assumed that the implied knowledge entailed some impossible spiritual adventure of this kind.

My debt to Paul Ricœur's *La métaphore vive* is perhaps less obvious, since I have chosen neither to summarise nor to adapt his systematic account of the creative use of language. Ricœur's work here, as in his long study of Freud, is, in the best sense, tentative and ambitious, whereas my own book is intended as far as possible to be philosophically unexceptionable. I may be more indebted, none the less, to Ricœur's arguments than I realise; though I have no illusions as to how much I owe to his erudition. To read Ricœur is, apart from anything else, to receive an education in the history of ideas, and, specifically, those which bear on the problems of hermeneutics and the theory of language. If it had not been for *La métaphore vive*, I might easily, for example, have missed reading or noticing the writings of Emile Benveniste on semiology and semantics, writings which, as I argue in the following chapter, offer one of the most telling possible accounts of the scope and limitations of what is known as 'structuralism'.

Structuralism, though it can mean a great many different things, and in spite of the disavowals of many of its former adherents, is still invested with a prestige which justifies one's questioning publicly its own claims for itself. And someone who, as I do, remains unconvinced by their claims owes his readers an alternative account of how we read. This is what I have attempted in the second part of this book; though the thoughts I offer here are neither a complete nor a systematic account of what reading entails. A complete account (one that anticipates all that reading could possibly entail) and a systematic account (i.e. that meets every conceivable objection) may be ideally possible. It is an ideal I have not attempted to fulfil and I have confined myself strictly to problems and preoccupations which seem to me of special concern today. It is the hope of being able to say something timely as well (or in the Nietzschean sense untimely,

Unzeitgemässe Betrachtungen) which has led me to discuss also the work of two of the most influential writers on literature of our time, writers who, the question of nationality apart, are dissimilar in the extreme: Roland Barthes and F. R. Leavis.

The public for which this book is intended is primarily an academic one and, within the university, the very large public comprising students of literature of various ages and degrees of seniority. This does not mean that I have any reason to think of the academic study of literature as indispensable or that I am writing for students of literature alone. My subject, inevitably, raises philosophical issues, that is, issues of justified perennial debate; though it seeks, as far as possible, to remain within the realm of what is self-evident. I say self-evident, not indisputable or unquestionable. Little or nothing that we say is unquestionable and I am assuming that my own claims (including the claim that there are things which are self-evident) will be questioned and tested at every point. Problems of epistemology arise at every stage of reflection on or discussion of what we read. 'How do you know that you have understood?' 'How do you know this book is good? Do you mean you just like it?' Such questions are asked with genuine puzzlement by people of all degrees of learning and sophistication. And far from helping us to answer them, the welter of competing contemporary theory tends to serve, within the university itself, to confuse and discourage the honest student and provide the dishonest one with a pretext for glibness and sophistry. What I hope to show is that there are false problems, or to put it another way, problems which can be solved and forgotten; and genuine ones, which, because they are genuine, belong, properly speaking, to philosophy. Neither the ordinary reader nor the student of literature needs to be a philosopher in order to know what he is doing. He does, however, need to know which of the many doubts he may have about the nature of what he is doing can be resolved and which remain a matter of speculation and wonder. I hope that this book will contribute towards making the distinction clear.

Chapter 2

BENVENISTE AND SEMIOLOGY: OR WHERE STRUCTURALISM DOESN'T WORK

(1)

Anyone today who asks the question: 'What happens when we read?' is bound to consider the many answers that have been proposed in recent years by those who call themselves 'structuralists', and to ask how far these answers take us towards a clearer understanding of what we are doing, or at least how far they shake our confidence in what we had hitherto mistakenly assumed.

There are, of course, many kinds of structuralism. At the present moment, the 'genetic structuralism' of Lucien Goldmann seems to be less influential than in the years before his death in 1971, though any student of Racine, Pascal or the seventeenth-century Jansenists is still likely to take seriously the thesis of his *Dieu caché* of 1955. The belief that the great work of philosophy or literature owes its greatness to the power and coherence with which it 'extrapolates conceptually' the 'affective, intellectual and even motivating tendencies' of a particular group at a particular point in history (p. 349) is attractive in so far as it avoids crude literalism and the equally crude reductionism of an unsophisticated Marxist approach. The claim that the tragic view of life of Racine and Pascal is an expression of the near-despair of the class of jurists and *parlementaires* to which they belonged and whose power, during their lifetime, was passing into the hands of administrators appointed directly by the king (the actual 'hidden god') is one that, at least, makes sense of many disparate pieces of evidence. Goldmann's approach, however, was explicitly historical and I prefer to come back to it in a later Chapter (Chapter 3, Part 5.3). It owes little or nothing to modern linguistics and to the modern linguistician's preoccupation with structures that are 'synchronic', that is, considered explicitly outside the dimension of time.

Much of the most influential structuralist writing today derives, as its authors tell us, from the work of the great Swiss linguistician, Ferdinand de Saussure. When I talk of 'structuralism', therefore,

I shall be referring to the many attempts to bring about what Saussure envisaged as a necessary preliminary to any truly scientific study of language: namely, an understanding of human communication in general, verbal and non-verbal alike; the elaboration, that is, of a science of 'signs' or, Saussure's own term, 'semiology'.

What is it that Saussure actually wanted to see? Briefly, from what we can tell from his notebooks and from his lectures, as transcribed by Bally and Séchehaye, it was an explanation of what for the linguistician is the unpredictable and unclassifiable behaviour of the natural languages, a 'principle of classification' and a clear understanding of a 'natural order' (*Cours de linguistique générale*, p. 25). Yet to consider spoken and written languages alone is to limit arbitrarily the known possibilities of language, for

Language is a system of signs expressing ideas, and, thereby, comparable to writing, to the deaf-and-dumb alphabet, to symbolic rites, forms of politeness, military signals, etc., etc. It is merely the most important of these systems.

One can therefore imagine A SCIENCE WHICH STUDIES THE LIFE OF SIGNS IN THE HEART OF THE LIFE OF SOCIETY, which would form part of social psychology and hence psychology in general: we will call it SEMIOLOGY (from the Greek *sēmeîon* or 'sign'). It would tell us in what signs consist and what laws govern them. Since it doesn't yet exist, one can't say what it will be; but it has a right to existence, its place is determined in advance. Linguistics is only a part of this general science, the laws that semiology will discover will apply to linguistics and the latter will find itself thus attached to a well defined domain among human facts as a whole. (pp. 33–4)

Saussure's reason for believing such a science was possible was that he regarded all forms of human communication as systems of what are, at first, arbitrarily adopted signs, having only a conventional relationship, even in cases of mimesis and onomatopoeia, to their referents in the natural world. Signs define one another mutually by means of their differences from one another. 'The' and 'this' are meaningful only in so far as they are implicitly distinct from 'a' and 'that'. And much of the work of the two most eminent modern structuralists is concerned with the ways in which people dress, prepare their food and conceive their most intimate family relationships and with the possibilities that a particular choice in one of these matters excludes.[1] It is the apparent arbitrariness of such conventions and what can seem like an endless web of mutually defining relationships that makes it possible for us to think of language, in the widest sense of the word, as a system governed by its own laws and, since our explanations are verbal, to envisage a theory which will provide a wholly adequate theoretical explanation of itself.[2] Not only possible but necessary, for the linguistician primarily, since there is no other conceivable linguistic order which provides the basis for any kind of classification, according to Saussure at least; necessary also, according to more recent semiologists, for any man or woman since, without such a theory, we are liable to dangerous delusions as to what we can meaningfully say and hence as to who and what we are. The revolutionary implications of this way of thinking include, according to Jean-Marie Benoist, the abandonment of a 'humanism' which has proved as superstitious as the theism it has come to replace. For not only is God dead; so also is Man:

By what did man find himself replaced? By structure and by a disturbance of language (*une inquiétude du langage*). All these enterprises were taking place on a new continent, which had been opened up to knowledge by the problematic of the sign and of the structural systems conceived by Saussurean and post-Saussurean linguistics. Man, the donor of meanings and living source of significance, gradually effaced himself before the differential, structural and semiotic relationship which articulates the signs that are produced among themselves and presides over their meaningful production: among them, man was revealed as no less *spoken* than *speaking*. Everything was changed.   (*La révolution structuraliste*, p. 13)

It is possible that even Benoist today would agree that what he was describing was not so much a revolution as a riot, a magnificent riot, it is true, including the repeating of a number of excellent slogans and in which some of the best minds of our time have been engaged. Whatever we call it, it would be difficult to deny that it has served a number of useful purposes, in so far as it may have reminded us that humanism can be as idolatrous as the supernatural belief it claims to supersede and in so far as it may have shaken us into questioning the authority of the individual subject and its power to create meaning.[3] But to question the authority of the individual subject is different from denying it any authority at all. That would, if it were possible, be a real revolution and Benoist himself confesses that to banish Man from the world is more easily said than done.[4] It emerges from his book that what he is welcoming is, strictly speaking, an attempt to carry out a revolutionary programme.

There are reasons, however, for doubting whether the revolution is ever going to get beyond the manifesto stage, or whether Saussure's dream of a completely self-explanatory theory making explicit invariable laws of language and hence not merely of logic but of thought itself (which would indeed put Man in his place) will ever take shape in reality.

(ii)

The best reasons I know for taking this sceptical view are to be found in the work of a linguistician who is respected nowhere more than among the devotees of semiology, the late Emile Benveniste. Benveniste is, however, a very dubious ally of those who are seeking to give reality to the Saussurean dream and it is understandable if certain of his most consistently maintained beliefs should have been passed over somewhat lightly by his admirers and friends.[5] Passed over but certainly not ignored. It seems more than likely that the evolution of semiology during the last ten years into its professedly 'post-Saussurean' phase is due, to a great extent, to Benveniste's influence. (See Chapter 4, pp. 134–5 below.)

Benveniste's criticisms of Saussure are incidental to his sense of indebtedness, both as a theorist and as a fellow historian of Indo-European languages. The Saussure to whom he pays tribute in his 'Saussure après un demi-siècle' (*Problèmes de linguistique générale*, pp. 32–45) is the author of the highly original and, when it first appeared, little understood *Mémoire sur le système des voyelles dans les langues indo-européennes* – published when Saussure was 21 – and of the notebooks in which, increasingly incapable of expressing himself in the current language of philology, he anticipated the work of Jakobson and Trubetzkoy and the basic principles of phonology. Of the value of these discoveries and of the investigations they have made possible Benveniste seems to be in no doubt at all.

A relatively minor criticism of one of the key notions in the *Cours de linguistique générale* is made in a paper of 1939 in which Benveniste asks whether the 'acoustic image' in which the linguistic 'signifier' consists is, as Saussure argues, arbitrarily chosen in relation to the concept for which it stands; or whether the arbitrariness doesn't lie solely in the relation of both to their referent; in the fact that it is this meaning rather than another that is given to a thing, creature or event. Benveniste sees here

a distinctive trait of the historical and relativistic thinking of the end of the nineteenth century, a habitual step in that form of philosophical reflection which can be described as *l'intelligence comparative*. First, the different reactions to the same phenomenon among different peoples are observed: after this, the infinite diversity of attitudes and judgments leads the observer to conclude that nothing, apparently, is necessary at all. This universal dissemblance is taken for a state of universal contingency. The Saussurian conception [of the arbitrariness governing the relation of 'signifier' to 'referent'] belongs, still, to some extent, to this way of thinking. To say that the linguistic sign is arbitrary because the same animal is called *bœuf* in one country and *Ochs* elsewhere is like saying that the notion of 'mourning' is 'arbitrary' because its symbol in Europe is black, and white in China. Arbitrary, yes, but only to the impassive gaze of Sirius or for someone who is content to observe from outside the relation established between an objective reality and a form of human behaviour and who is thus condemned to find in it contingency alone. (*Problèmes de linguistique générale*, pp. 50–1)

The distinction between the concept and the acoustic image may be crucial for analysis as well as obvious (once pointed out), but it is a theoretical distinction only. An image is what we make of it,[6] and what we make of an acoustic image is determined by the concept for which it stands.

Between the signifier and the signified, the link is not arbitrary, on the contrary, it is *necessary*. The 'concept' ('what is signified') '*bœuf*' is necessarily identical in my consciousness to the phonic group ('signifier') *böf*. How could it be otherwise? The two have been imprinted together on my mind; they are evoked together in all circumstances. There is between them a symbiosis so close that the concept '*bœuf*' is like the very soul of the acoustic image *böf*. The mind has no room for empty forms or for concepts without a name.
(*Problèmes de linguistique générale*, p. 51)

This essay is a corrective to the kind of linguistics which regards the acoustic image as arbitrary in the sense of wholly unimportant in itself, like the choice of symbols in algebra or the shape of the pieces in chess, though the essay does not radically undermine or seek to undermine Saussure's general arguments in forms of semiology. It is a corrective, in other words, to the extreme view of the arbitrariness governing the choice of sounds in a language stated by Hjelmslev in his *Prolegomena to a theory of language*.[7]

A more radical departure from Saussure is to be found in the essay of 1969, 'Sémiologie de la langue', in which Benveniste asks whether it is true that the non-verbal forms of communication have a structure equivalent to that of the spoken language and are in equivalent ways expressive. Benveniste's conclusions are that they do not. But it is in the paper on 'Les niveaux de l'analyse linguistique' of 1962, to which he refers back explicitly in 'Sémiologie de la langue' and other more recent essays that the scope and inevitable limits to the scope of the semiotic theory of language are defined. A brief summary of the argument fails to do justice to the care with which it anticipates and meets possible objections and to the author's sophistication and learning, but its conclusions are unambiguous and to summarise it in simple terms is not necessarily to misrepresent it.

The smallest entity revealed to linguistic analysis is the phoneme, the /i/ of 'lip', for instance, distinguishing it from 'leap' to the surprise of Frenchmen learning English and in whose language this phoneme doesn't exist. The phoneme owes its existence to what distinguishes it from other phonemes in the same language (its distinctive *mérismes*, as Benveniste calls them) and also to the fact that it is an indispensable constituent of meaning. It is the function of linguistic entities in contributing to the constitution of meaning that, according to Benveniste, determines whether or not they exist. The only question we need to ask of any linguistic sign is whether it exists as part of any meaningful language, and this can be answered by a simple yes or no. How such a sign, in combination with (and contra-distinction from) others, constitutes meaning is a question about linguistic 'forms'. And this is true at any level of analysis:

The *form* of a linguistic unit can be defined as its capacity to dissociate itself into constituents of an inferior order.

The *meaning* ('*sens*') of a linguistic unit can be defined as its capacity to form an integral part of a unit of a higher order.

Form and meaning appear as given, necessary and simultaneous conjunct properties which are inseparable in the functioning of language.

(*Problèmes de linguistique générale*, pp. 126–7)

The kind of analysis that is possible depends on the level of analysis, and it is here that Benveniste distinguishes radically between what is possible up to and below the level of the sentence (or what he calls 'the categorematic level') and what is possible (and impossible) beyond it. For when we come to the sentence, 'a limit is passed, we enter a new domain',[8]

It follows from the fact that the sentence does not constitute a class of distinctive units which are virtual members of units on a higher level (as are phonemes or morphemes) that it is basically distinct from the other linguistic entities. The ground of this distinction is that the sentence contains signs, but is not itself a sign. Once this has been recognised, the contrast becomes clear between the groups of signs we have encountered on the lower levels and the entities of the level we are considering now.

The phonemes, morphemes, words (lexemes) can be counted; they are finite in number. Sentences are not.

The phonemes, morphemes, words (lexemes) have a certain distribution on their respective levels and a certain function on a higher level. Sentences have neither distribution nor function.

An inventory of the different uses of a word might never end; an inventory of the different uses of a sentence couldn't even begin.

The sentence, which is a matter of indefinite creation and limitless variety, is the very life of a functioning language. We can conclude then that, with the sentence, we leave the domain of language as a system of signs and enter another world, that of language as an instrument of communication, whose expression is discourse.

These are, truly, two different worlds, even though they embrace the same reality and they give rise to different levels of linguistics, although their paths cross at all times. On the one hand, there is language, a combination of formal signs, which can be disengaged by rigorous procedures, set out in classes and combined in structures and systems; on the other, the manifestation of language as living communication.

                    (*Problèmes de linguistique générale*, pp. 129–30)

In his later essays, Benveniste refers often to the two necessarily distinct approaches to these two different worlds as the 'semiotic' and the 'semantic'.

The implications of this argument seem to me to go to the heart of the issue dividing those who are and those who are not convinced by the claims of semiology. Benveniste himself pursues certain of these in a paper on 'La forme et le sens dans le langage' (in *Problèmes de linguistique générale II*), in which he outlines certain necessary conditions of any approach to language which is 'semantic'.

The semiotic sign can be characterised as a property of language, semantics arises from an activity of the speaker who puts language into action. The semiotic sign exists in itself, and establishes the reality of the language, but it has no particular application; the sentence, an expression of the semantic, can *only* be particular. With the sign, we come to the intrinsic reality of the language; with the sentence, one is in contact with what lies outside language; and just as the sign is partly constituted by the signified, which is inherent within it, so the meaning of the sentence implies reference to the situation of the discourse and the attitude of the speaker ... A sentence participates always in the 'here and now'; certain units of discourse come together within it to translate a particular idea concerning the particular present moment of a particular speaker. Every verbal form, without exception, is always related to a certain moment in time (*'un certain présent'*) and thus to a group of circumstances, which is each time unique, that language enunciates by means of a specific morphology.   (pp. 225–6)

One could say that it is his real as well as professed interest in the 'here and now' of language and in the uniqueness of the circumstances in which a particular expression is used that has made

Benveniste so remarkable a historian of the language and, as such, of civilisation and literature as well. A practical demonstration of the principles set out in his essays is his *Vocabulaire des institutions indo-européennes*.

(III)

It would be quite wrong, of course, to think of Benveniste as a polemical writer seeking to *discredit* structuralism of the post-Saussurean kind; and if the structuralists speak of him with respect, this is also because they claim to derive from him certain key notions and because he has subscribed to certain theories which are central to structuralism; for instance that all 'thought' necessarily pre-supposes 'language'.[9] The compliments, moreover, have been re-turned. Benveniste has expressed, for example, considerable respect for the anthropological writings of Claude Lévi-Strauss and he has applauded the various attempts to construct a 'semiology' of social 'signs'. It seems clear from the writings I have already quoted, how-ever, that he regarded this semiology as one that would require fundamentally different assumptions and focus on a different kind of object from the semiology whose limit is marked by the phrase. One method of analysis appropriate to one set of phenomena will often, of course, provide a starting point, at least, for the study of phenomena of a totally different kind. Saussure's explanation, for example, of the evolution of languages – the loss of and need to recover the equilibrium within a system – has its origin in classical economics. This is perhaps why Benveniste has never, as far as I know, openly questioned the right of Roland Barthes to transpose *telles quelles* the Saussurean categories of the 'syntagmatic' and the 'paradigmatic' to the study of literature (see Chapter 3, pp. 132–3 below), or A.-J. Greimas's attempts to analyse novels as structured arrangements of 'semes' and 'classemes', by analogy with 'phonemes' and 'morphemes' (*Sémantique structurale*).[10] It could be argued that it in no way follows that because the 'semantic' and the 'semiotic' constitute two distinct realms, the former can't be studied in a systematic way. The very history of the term 'structure', as Giulio Lepschy has argued, whether in the natural sciences or linguistics, shows that a structure or system is not necessarily to be thought of as conforming to a single universal model or taxonomy, which can only be seen for what it is outside the dimension of time ('Osservazioni sul termine "struttura"'). Both linguistics and the natural sciences have sought to discuss in various systematic ways the history and growth of individual forms.

There are, at the very least, three possible ways in which the realm of the semantic could be examined systematically and which have been exemplified in the work of those associated with structuralism in recent years. The first and most influential in France at least – also the most devastating in its implications – is the approach of the philosopher Jacques Derrida. For Derrida, Saussure's simple distinction between what a term *signifies*, what it refers to, and its function as *signifier* is untenable, together with the merely commonsensical notions of the world and of language which were necessary if the distinction was to have any justification at all. Common sense of this kind can only be justified by what Derrida calls 'the metaphysics of intuition and presence', that is, by a question-begging reference to other presuppositions. It is in what he calls '*la différance*' – an untranslatable coinage – that is, in the dynamic relationship between the terms of a language, each one of which is in itself a relation between other terms and so on *ad infinitum*, that Derrida sees the only possibility of an undeluded view of language. The word '*différance*' derives from the verb '*différer*' meaning both 'to be different' and 'to defer'.

Derrida's critique of Saussure amounts, in fact, to a *reductio ad absurdum*, though learning to live with the absurd has, in France especially, been thought of for many years as the only conceivable wisdom. To say that we cannot conduct our lives as if he were right or even agree with him without thereby contradicting what he is saying may well seem beside the point. Derrida obviously knows this and is undismayed by the thought that the elaboration of a truly self-sufficient and all-embracing theory of language is a task both 'immense and interminable' (*Positions*, p. 48). Not, however, 'impracticable'. Derrida, like other contemporary 'structuralists', sees not only Saussure but Marx as a precursor of the structuralist revolution or, to use Bachelard's term, 'epistemological break' with the past. 'Praxis', what is actually done in the world, is, he agrees with Marx, what actually matters, unresolvable though the problem may be of who or what does the actual doing or in what the doing consists. In the Marxist notion of 'matter', as in the Saussurean definition of the 'sign', there remain what, from a certain point of view, seem like 'metaphysical' presuppositions, unexplained within the ostensibly self-explanatory system. Everything depends, however,

on the use made of the terms, that is, on the ways in which the
system is re-applied; and terms which seem, in one context, like an
'obstacle' to critical enquiry, provide in another context a valuable
critical tool. Saussure, for example, saw through the illusion that
the linguistic sign is the reflection or imitation of phenomena in the
natural world and described, without naming it, the *différance* of all
terms. He was unable, none the less, to justify his intuitive understanding of the arbitrariness of all language. Like the mediaeval
schoolmen who, similarly, distinguished between the *signans* and
the *signatum*, he was obliged to fall back lamely on the implausible
notion of concepts independent of language (*Positions*, pp. 29–30)
yet communicated by means of sounds whose meaning is preserved
in the memory. The way out of this impasse lies, for Derrida, in
rejecting this 'logocentric' and 'phonocentric' view of the world
and in accepting, with Nietzschean gaiety, the contradictions such a
step entails.[11] It means also, as far as this is possible or conceivable,
respecting the letter rather than the dubious spirit of language.
(Saussure, he claims, failed to recognise the profound philosophical
implications of the distinction between writing and speech.) It means
elaborating, in fact, not a 'semiology' but what Derrida calls a
'grammatology'.

Derrida's writings on language are, in other words, those of a
certain type of philosophical sceptic, and it is not surprising that
much of what he has written has consisted of criticisms of the presuppositions of other writers on language: Husserl most notably
(*La voix et le phénomène*), Hegel ('the first semiologist') and
Rousseau as well as Saussure. The question how or whether we are
compelled to accept what he is saying is the question how or whether
we can know we are right when we say we understand what someone is writing or saying (see pp. 55–67 below). A less radically
sceptical approach to the realm of the semantic is exemplified by
John Lyons in his *Structural semantics* of 1963. Lyons, like Derrida,
seeks to avoid the logical circularity of explaining what is meant by
certain terms by reference to others which themselves remain unexplained – among them, according to Lyons, the 'disposition to
respond', of behavioural linguistics (pp. 2–4). One of the most
successful attempts so far, according to Lyons, to offer a genuine
explanation of the way language functions in the semantic realm is
the work of Jost Trier. To put it very briefly, Trier contrasts the
vocabulary of colour in eighteenth-century German with the same

vocabulary today. *Braun* in the eighteenth century embraced shades of colour which today have different names such as *violet*. All languages clearly differ in this respect, among themselves and in different ways at different stages of development, so that the actual physical spectrum is subtended to a different extent and at different points by the 'spectrum' of colour names. Which set of colour terms corresponds most closely to the shades of the actual spectrum? In any set, this closeness of correspondence can be an approximation only. The true precision of the terms lies in the way they exclude and in excluding define one another.

With colour terms, a reference to something else is possible, something else that can be observed and analysed: the spectrum itself. Yet there are other groups of mutually defining terms of which this can't be true. Trier studies the vocabulary of the early thirteenth century in German referring to various kinds of knowledge: what *we* would describe as courtly and merely practical. By the beginning of the following century, the precise meaning of the terms and their social connotations have changed. The 'conceptual field' is divided differently. But there is no possible reference, as with the colour spectrum, to other observable differences to which both sets of terms refer. (See Lyons, pp. 44–9, Ullmann, *The principles of semantics*, p. 166 and Trier, 'Das sprachliche Feld. Eine Auseinandersetzung'.) Professor Lyons rejects what he regards as certain 'metaphysical implications' in Trier's approach, the assumption that there is 'an *a priori* unformed medium of "content" or "reality" which is differently determined by different languages' (pp. 47–8) and, in a way reminiscent of Derrida, sees this as comparable to the (inadequately explained) Saussurean view of the association of thought and sound. But he acknowledges his debt to Trier for his discovery of 'conceptual' or 'lexical' 'fields', 'intermediate between the individual lexical items and the totality of the vocabulary' (*Structural semantics*, p. 45). His own analysis of the vocabulary of Plato is a careful study of mutually defining 'meanings', as distinct from 'references'; both notions, he claims, being essential to the theory of semantics.

Professor Lyons's structural semantics falls expressly far short of an all-embracing semiology. At least, this is what I assume he means when he rejects the idea of the semantic structure of the language as an 'overall closed system' (*Structural semantics*, p. 50). Despite his scrupulous weighing of all possibly relevant considerations, including the relation of syntax to semantics, his model does not appear to be incompatible with other, methodologically far simpler investigations of contrasting lexical fields: that, for example, surrounding the word '*noblesse*' in eighteenth-century France, which, as Tocqueville points out (*L'ancien régime*, pp. 36–7), has different connotations from that of the English 'aristocracy'; or Benveniste's comparison between the modern French vocabulary of the divine and the Homeric '*hiéros*' and '*hágios*', which distinguish clearly 'that which is animated by a holy power and agitation and that which is forbidden and with which contact is prohibited' (*Le vocabulaire des institutions indo-européennes*, p. 207). Learning any foreign language, for that matter, entails learning to make the same kind of distinctions: the lexical field occupied by '*joli*' and '*beau*' is by no means identical with that occupied by 'pretty' and 'beautiful'. 'Good' is not always the right translation of '*bon*'. This is not to minimise the value of the scrupulous investigation of concepts whose differentiation is far from obvious. But Professor Lyons's structural semantics offers no encouragement at all to the view that a single conceptual field or a single semiological theory could at any time embrace a single natural language or embrace the field of language as a whole.

A third justification of a 'structuralist' approach to the realm of the semantic is the one elaborated by Philip Pettit in his *Concept of structuralism*. This approach is entirely compatible with that of Professor Lyons, at least in principle, and Pettit is equally un-impressed by the grand design of Saussurean semiology and the 'fundamentalism' of Jacques Derrida (e.g. pp. 30 and 45). The value of the structuralist approach to human language and behaviour lies, for Professor Pettit, not in any presuppositions concerning the nature of truth or reality but in the method of inquiry it exemplifies. And here Pettit sees an exact analogy between the human and physical sciences. The structuralist approach lies, characteristically, in the adoption of a certain model; not a model in which the subject of the model is its source, as in the case of a baby's doll or a model Parliament; but one in which subject and source differ, like the 'double helix' which represents the DNA molecule but is itself modelled on a simple mechanical structure; or like the economic model used by Saussure to account for the loss and regaining of equilibrium within a language, which in turn explains its evolution. This type of model, the 'paramorph' defined by Rom Harré in his study *Philosophies of science*, is a kind of metaphor, but one which can be used as a means of discovery as well as of explanation.

The analogy with science is, however, obviously one which Pettit sees as holding good only to a certain point. And in his discussion of the structural anthropology of Lévi-Strauss, he makes the fairly common objection that its hypotheses may be true but are scientifically unverifiable in that they cannot be falsified. It may be answered that they will be falsified (and notably the hypothesis of the primacy of binary structures in all myth and kinship relations) if and when they are confirmed, as Lévi-Strauss claims they may be, by discoveries in neuro-physiology. Until this happens, however, Pettit may be right to doubt their truth and to deny that they belong, for all the wealth of corroboration Lévi-Strauss's learning provides, to the realm of experimental science.[12]

This, I think, affects Pettit's arguments in favour of the structuralist approach more radically than he himself admits. The analogy with science may be useful in that it points the way to more fruitful investigations of language and behaviour than any conducted in the past. But it is by no means certain that the use of 'models' in science itself is an indispensable device, as some philosophers claim. This has been denied, for instance, by those who argue that in quantum physics no intelligible model is possible. The question remains unresolved, we are told by Mary Hesse in her *Models and analogies in science*; it will presumably be settled, if at all, by what happens in practice. To show that the use of models is indispensable in literary criticism or sociology, one would have to show that this was a requirement of science in general, which is far from certain. One would have to show too that their procedures and goals were the same, which no one, least of all Professor Pettit, pretends.

If the systematic application of models is not essential to the study of human behaviour and language, what justification has it at all? Here Pettit's apology, coming as it does at the end of a survey which offers so discouraging a view of the achievements of structuralism so far, carries surprisingly little conviction. 'The structuralist framework certainly allows questions to be asked which look more interesting than everyday concepts might suggest' (*The concept of structuralism*, p. 113). Which everyday concepts, one is bound to ask, and in what way more interesting? 'The disappointing thing about the structuralist framework', he confesses on the same page, 'is that the answers to its questions do not seem capable of being assumed within a theory in any area outside language itself.' This is both vague and an underestimation of what 'structuralism', as he defines it, has achieved on various occasions in the past. Very little that one says about 'language' refers merely to language – according to Benveniste nothing at all, if we are talking about the realm of the semantic. And of the many theories that have been propounded over the millennia concerning the different ways in which people use words, some are interesting and can be shown to be probably true; either because of the weighing of alternative possibilities, as in the more intensely scrupulous applications of structural semantics, or because of the particular confirmation of a preconceived idea. William Empson's *Seven types of ambiguity* and Roman Jakobson's various writings on poetry[13] might be taken as typical of the latter type of enquiry. Each is based on a theory of the way poetry works, and each attempts to show that what can be found in some poems (the seemingly deliberate ambiguities of some Shakespeare sonnets, for example, or the symmetrical patterns of sound and recurring syntactic features that Jakobson finds in both Shakespeare and Baudelaire) might be found in the work of other poets as well. The reader's feeling that the theory has worked on this occasion, or has not on another, is no more or less reliable than his feelings concerning the unsystematic comments on Shakespeare or Baudelaire that are made by a critic or a friend. Nothing that Professor Pettit says shows that reference to a theory or a model is indispensable if the friend or critic is to say something true or interesting.

It is difficult, however, to object to the method of enquiry Pettit recommends and calls 'differential semantics'. For it is difficult to think of any other way in which we could understand what was written or said. It derives explicitly from Pettit's 'story', as he puts it, about 'the ordinary hearer' and how he succeeds in making sense of what he hears, even when listening to a statement in the form of a long sentence containing subordinate clauses and parentheses:

To attend to what someone says is to wait or hang on his words. It presupposes some idea of what to expect in any word, but not an assured idea: to lack the first is to get lost, to fail to lack the second is to get bored. Knowledge of the categorial and subcategorial constraints on the words [i.e. the kinds of general and particular context in which they normally occur] means in the normal case that this presupposed condition is realised and

attention is possible. For any word in the speaker's sentence, most significantly for the focal word, it guarantees that the hearer will find it neither
absolutely preposterous nor absolutely predictable.

(*The concept of structuralism*, p. 25)[14]

'Differential semantics' is not incompatible with the theories of
syntax propounded by Noam Chomsky or the semantic theories
these have in turn inspired. Nor does it depend on them, however:

we do not have to rely on the possibility of a syntax assigning a deep structure
to every sentence; we only require a grasp of the surface structure, and that
grasp need only be intuitive.   (*ibid*, p. 28)

It is something more than an account of how we normally listen or
read only to the extent that it proposes a new way of translating into
the language of formal logic certain essential features of ordinary
complex sentences and it is in that context that its likelihood of
success must be judged.[15]

(IV)

To summarise my argument so far, Saussure's notion of an
all-embracing and self-explanatory theory of signs is one that, after
more than half a century, remains no more than a theoretical goal.
In the writings of Benveniste, moreover, we are given excellent
reasons for doubting whether it can even be this, though there is still
an influential school of thought, that of Jacques Derrida, which tells
us that any alternative view of language is equally untenable and all
the more so if it fails to acknowledge its (inevitably) unjustified presuppositions. Among the many possible ways of coming to terms
with the situation that Benveniste describes, there is the approach of
those who try, as far as possible, to identify isolated self-explanatory
systems (Lyons), and that which sees certain advantages but not any
actual necessity in the consistent application of 'paramorphic'
models.

The alternative which I wish to mention in conclusion and at the
same time to defend, and whose presuppositions I discuss in the
following chapter, is not inconsistent with either of these last
approaches. Too often, even sometimes in the best (and *ad nauseam*
in the worst) 'structuralist' writing,[16] it is assumed that talking and,
more particularly, writing about books is a necessary condition of
thinking about them. This form of academic vulgarity explains at
least some of the prestige of structuralism, especially among aspiring
academics who find in its theories and methods promising new ways

of approaching subjects that have been approached all too often before; though it would be wrong to say that this was its only appeal or that structuralism alone, or even primarily, was responsible for this *déformation professionnelle*.

What structuralists, in any case, tend to overlook and what Professor Pettit rightly points out is the subtlety and skill of the ordinary listener and reader. The overvaluing of writing and talking about books goes with an underestimation of the intelligence that may only rarely be apparent to the ordinary reader's listeners, his own readers or himself. Professor E. D. Hirsch has argued, in *The aims of interpretation*, that it is this first and all-important stage in the interpretation of what we read that constitutes its actual validation; in other words, that the question: 'How do I know that I'm reading this correctly?' is both asked and answered in effect (satisfactorily or otherwise) as the act of reading takes place. Hirsch's account of this process resembles Pettit's in essentials, though he extends the description to show the ways in which reading or listening resemble other ways of learning to live in the world. Where Pettit talks of our having some idea of what to expect when we listen or read and yet not an 'assured' idea, Hirsch talks of 'corrigible schemata', a phrase he takes from Piaget: that is, a preconceived view of things which becomes less constricting with experience and yet remains essential at every stage, if we are to be aware of anything at all. Our very capacity for being surprised depends, after all, on our having some idea of what we will find:

What Heidegger called the priority of pre-understanding is described by experimental psychologists as the primacy of the schema; by Gombrich, in art history, as the primacy of the genre; by cognitive theorists (particularly those concerned with scientific knowledge) as the primacy of the hypothesis ... It is true that the term validation suggests a public activity, an objective marshaling of evidence in the cause of an interpretative hypothesis. Nonetheless, the private processes of verbal understanding have the same character, even if they are not similarly systematic and public. For that which we are understanding is itself a hypothesis constructed by ourselves, a schema, or genre, or type which provokes expectations that are confirmed by our linguistic experience, or when they are not confirmed, cause us to adjust our hypothesis or schema.   (*The aims of interpretation*, pp. 32–4)

Like any other unselfconscious activity, it is true, the act of reading can only be described in terms of what, presumably, is true and not what is self-evident. Seeing the bird hop on the gravel path and thinking about seeing the bird hopping are, obviously, not the same.

And Hirsch confesses that his description of reading is tentative and subject to 'empirical confirmation' from psychology. It is also, for the same reason, sufficiently general and imprecise to appear, as far as possible, unexceptionable.

This is, of course, an objection to unselfconscious reading as a form of knowledge which is often made or at least taken for granted. The kind of knowledge claimed by structuralism, it is often assumed, is at least systematic and as such able to offer an honest account of itself. The unselfconscious reader we all are when we read anything at all cannot even describe, let alone defend himself. It ought perhaps then to be said on his behalf that his very inability to say what theory he is obeying or what model he is taking pains to observe is simply the price he pays for freedom from the constrictions of any one conceptual scheme. That ability to form expectations about what we are to read and yet to alter these expectations when they are not fulfilled – to accept changes, in other words, in the rules of the language game – is what makes the understanding of language possible, since no natural language observes any single set of rules, except hypothetically at the level of 'deep structure' and this is debatable and has so far never been shown.[17] Our ability to recognise the unexpected and to alter in doing so our expectations is the condition, moreover, of our discovering anything at all. Michael Polanyi speaks of it with the authority of a natural scientist, though his terminology and examples are again taken from Piaget:

Jean Piaget has drawn a striking distinction between a sensorimotor act and an explicit inference. Explicit inference is reversible: we can go back to its premises and go forward again to its conclusions, rehearse the whole process as often as we like. This is not true for the sensorimotor act: for example, once we have seen through a puzzle, we cannot return to an ignorance of its solution.   ('The structure of consciousness', p. 316)

It is this success in making particular discoveries which we are unable to describe, since to recall what it was like would mean returning to our former state of ignorance. Similarly, we are told (Popper, *Objective knowledge*, and Medawar, *The art of the soluble*), the forming of hypotheses in science takes place through a process which is more aptly called psychological than logical. This is why 'analysis' in literary criticism, except in the rare cases of statistical word-counts, can only be a process of explanation and not one of discovery. For the discoveries are already made when the reader has solved the puzzle constituted by even the simplest message or test, and this is true whether we talk of reading which is solitary and unreflective or of what is discovered in the course of close reading in discussion, in say a seminar devoted to 'practical criticism'. Here the process of discovery may coincide with and be indistinguishable from some-one's finding the words to describe what is there in the text; and the process may be continued as qualifications are made or further corroboration adduced. It is never, however, what Polanyi calls a process of 'explicit inference', never, in other words, the equivalent of a calculation in arithmetic or an analytical test in chemistry. This is also, presumably, why, when we find we have misread something, we usually find it impossible, if we think about it, to say what general principle or rule we happened to violate or how we might avoid making the same mistake again; why too, though many attempts have been made to formulate such rules, there are remark-ably few that have commanded for long any general assent.

The issue dividing self-styled 'structuralists' from those who believe that structuralism works only in certain well-defined areas of study such as phonology is the issue of *evidence*, and what we are witnessing today is merely another phase of the debate about what we can know concerning what has been written and said which goes back to the last century and the writings of Taine. The value of the structuralist assault on what the structuralists call 'humanism' lies in the challenge it offers (unfortunately, often in a language too equivocal to be as challenging as it should be) to the critic, historian and sociologist who have forgotten the source and nature of their authority, who think of it as God-like or God-given. The value of its assault on 'empiricism' lies in the challenge it offers to a false ideal of science, to a naïve view of the nature of evidence. This kind of empiricism and humanism is exemplified triumphantly in the late Professor Raymond Picard's denunciation of Barthes (*Nouvelle critique ou nouvelle imposture*, see pp. 76–80 below). In literary criticism and literary history certainly, there is no evidence that could be used to justify the claim that we understood what someone else had said which could ever be conclusive. There are no *'certitudes de langage'*, in Professor Picard's phrase or *'zones d'objectivité'* from which 'the patient and modest researcher...can – very prudently – seek to form interpretations' (p. 69). Benveniste provides what seem like excellent reasons for thinking that certain key terms in Homer are read in a certain way (*Le vocabulaire des institutions indo-européennes*), excellent in the sense that it may be difficult for any

Homeric scholar to refute them. It would be absurd to deny that such a refutation is possible, just as it would be to deny that he could possibly be right. There is no reason at all for believing that an empirical observation is untrue simply because it's empirical and no reason for believing that what we say is *merely*, as many structuralists would have us believe, determined by the language we are condemned by history to use. Man is indeed, in Benoist's words, as much 'spoken' as 'speaking', and the language he inherits or borrows is obviously *one of the determining factors* in what he says. But there is a 'singular dialectic' by which language

offers the speakers the same system of personal references which each one appropriates through the act of language and which in each instance of its use, as soon as it is assumed by its enunciator, becomes unique and unlike any other, incapable of being realised even twice in the same way.

(Benveniste, *Problèmes de linguistique générale II*, p. 68)

(The most obvious instance of this is the personal pronoun, 'I'.) A language in which this is not true, in which nothing *new* can be said, is inconceivable.

To accept the *fallibility* of our attempts to understand one another is completely different from thinking we can never be right. We do, it is true, commit ourselves totally (though in ways of which we are usually unaware) in anything we do or avoid doing and in any claim to knowledge we make. We commit ourselves in that our behaviour has, by definition, moral implications which may well, in the last analysis, be philosophical and political as well. There is no non-moral point of view in the sense of a point of view which has no implications of this kind, though the universal acceptance of a heliocentric astronomy may have led us to forget what Galileo learned to his cost. It still doesn't follow that what we discover or say cannot be true, whether we are talking of astronomy or literary criticism – this is one of the few respects in which they are comparable – and a true observation may have political implications just as much as a false one.

'How do you know that?' or 'What right have you to say that?' are questions which anyone has the right to ask. But it may be often necessary to answer: 'I can't tell you unless you say what objections you have in mind.' One cannot defend oneself before one knows from what quarter one is liable to be attacked or what circumstances might render one's position vulnerable in the future. This is why it is impossible also to expect anyone to give an explicit account of all that his point of view implies, though it is customary now to require this show of putting all one's cards on the table, 'making all one's presuppositions explicit'.[18] An effective challenge is a real challenge, real in the sense that it suggests an alternative view and enables the one who is challenged, even if he is unconvinced by the alternative, to learn something more about what his own belief implies. This is true of many, possibly all kinds of knowledge, but true especially of understanding other people's words.

In the following chapter, I attempt, as far as I am able, to answer objections that have been made to the way in which we ordinarily and (I shall be claiming) inevitably read, as distinct from rationalising subsequently what we think we have seen in a text. The point of view from which I am writing has, I think, the advantages of neither pretending to guarantee itself against possible refutation nor assuming that one day it is bound itself to be invalidated by the unfolding of a dialectic.[19] One might say it is simply open to the unpredictable.[20] It is not a point of view for which I claim any originality, except in so far as my defence of it is my own. I hope therefore I will not be accused of arrogance if I say that there is no better viewpoint from which to contemplate Benveniste's realm of the semantic – or what amounts to the same thing – to read poetry and respond to living speech.

PART II

Chapter 3

THOUGHTS ON HOW WE READ

No one could predict what we are likely to find when we read. The possibilities are endless. But reading itself, like speaking or writing, is an unique activity and gift and has certain necessary conditions and consequences. To say that one reads presupposes that one does other things as well, such as examining a number of visible or tangible signs (which no one disputes) or attempting to understand what someone wishes to convey (which has been disputed a great deal in the last few decades) or forming a judgment of this (which has been disputed as well).

Today, anyone who tries to read to some purpose and to learn through reading is likely to find the disagreements among professional philosophers – and, more especially, among academic writers on literature as to what reading entails – an impediment to both learning and enjoyment. This is both regrettable and absurd, since many of the problems that are raised in the course of these dissensions are false problems not only distracting the serious reader from the direct pursuit of learning through the literature and history he reads, but also preventing him from seeing the genuine problems – that is, the authentic philosophical problems – which the pursuit of learning through reading entails. In the hope therefore that this will help to dissipate unnecessary confusion and anxiety and strengthen confidence and purpose where confidence and purpose are justified, I should like to set out and defend what I see as some of the inescapable presuppositions of the fact that anyone reads anything at all.

(1) All that we say or think about a particular utterance or piece of writing presupposes an assumption on our part, correct or otherwise, concerning the intention of the speaker or writer.

(2) Which is why we can say certain things about what we read which are true but never deny the possibility that we may be wrong.

(3) But a true understanding of what is written or said does not and could not possibly imply a complete sharing of the writer's or speaker's experience; which is why a true understanding of those

whose experience differs from our own, including writers from a distant past, is always possible.

(4) We cannot possibly understand what is written or said unless we understand its interest and importance for the writer or speaker; which affects inevitably its interest and importance for us. Evaluation, in this sense, and interpretation are the same.

(5) The student of literature is a student of history.

1 *All that we say or think about a particular utterance or piece of writing presupposes an assumption on our part, correct or otherwise, concerning the intention of the speaker or writer.*

1.1   The assumption itself may or may not be correct. Clearly, we often misunderstand. We also sometimes delude ourselves that we've understood when we've understood nothing at all. And when this is pointed out to us or we go back to the text, in order, say, to translate it into another language, we realise that our belief that it made sense was like one of the illusions of a dream.

Sometimes people speak or write meaning every word they say, especially when they have something they need to communicate urgently. Sometimes, *on parle pour ne rien dire.* Language, according to a French cynic, was given to man to conceal his thoughts. What passes for literature or eloquence is often little more than verbosity. There is an hour to fill. The audience has come to listen. A tutor or publisher is expecting by a certain date a certain number of words and meeting this requirement is foremost in one's mind. So one forms sentences with a recognisable syntax and cadence. One deludes one's readers, one's audience or oneself that one is conveying thoughts and feelings that one wishes them to share.

The reader or listener may or may not realise what we are up to when we do this. He may experience the dream- or trance-like illusion that he understands. Or he may understand what we are really doing as we talk or what we were really doing when we wrote the words he now reads. Take Leavis on C. P. Snow, for instance:

We think of cliché commonly as a matter of style. But style is a habit of expression, and a habit of expression that runs to cliché tells us something adverse about the quality of the thought expressed. 'History is merciless to failure': Snow makes play with a good many propositions of that kind – if 'proposition' is the right word. We call them clichés because, though Snow clearly feels that he is expressing thought, the thought, considered even for a moment, is seen to be a mere phantom, and Snow's illusion is due to the fact that he is *not* thinking, but resting inertly (though with a sense of power) on vague memories of the way in which he has heard (or seen) such phrases used. They carry for him – he belonging to what he calls a 'culture' – a charge of currency-value which is independent of first-hand, that is, actual, thinking. He would be surprised if he were told they are clichés.

(*Nor shall my sword*, pp. 50–1)

We have to distinguish here between 'intention' and 'meaning'. Leavis is saying that Snow's clichés, because they are clichés, lack meaning. He is not denying that Snow is responsible for them. Whether or not Leavis is right about Snow, or fair, scarcely affects the argument here. What he finds in Snow's writing is surrender to a common temptation (which is why he also insists that Snow is not 'distinguished'), a temptation common, particularly, among those of us who have to write or talk for a living.

1.2 But how can we know what the writer's intention was? How can we hope to 'see into other people's minds', in the way Leavis claims he is able to see into Snow's? If we cannot, then we, presumably, can't possibly know when people are *undeluded* in using words as they do, when they mean every word they say. And this is, in fact, the position that has been adopted for some time by a number of philosophers, theologians and literary critics. Not that anyone normally suggests that we can't tell, for immediate practical purposes, whether people know or mean what they say. There are various simple tests like asking people the way or reading the instructions on a bottle of medicine or a box of explosives. Nor do the sceptics I'm referring to write habitually as if what they themselves meant to say is something their readers couldn't hope to know. We are, after all, close to them in time and share many of their immediate assumptions about the world. Our view of the world is, none the less, very different, as the theologians remind us, from that of the authors of the New Testament. And though we can translate much of it into our own language or terms we can more or less understand, the act of translation and commentary distorts beyond recognition, it is often claimed, the meanings they originally conveyed. This has been said also by critics like Roland Barthes (*Sur Racine*) of the work of a far more recent period, and in particular of the tragedies of Racine which were written in a language which seems to have changed

very little up to the present day. And it has come to be taken as true
of all works of imaginative literature, even those of our own time,
especially those plays and poems which have a mask-like impersonality and in which language has come, in Sartre's words (*Qu 'est-ce
que la littérature?*), to seem more like an object, familiar yet strange,
than a recognisable form of communication between a particular
writer and oneself.[1]

I should like to come back (see section 2 below) to the question
whether or how we can know what other people's intentions are
when they write or speak and how or whether we can understand
the true (i.e. original) meaning of texts written in a period of history
very different from our own (section 4). Meanwhile, I should like to
suggest one thing only and that is that, *irrespective of whether we
can be right or wrong about the intentions of those we read, in
particular instances or as a general rule*, we cannot read a text, that
is, we cannot 'make sense of it' if it is discursive prose and cannot
respond to its effect otherwise, unless we read it *as if* we understand
to some extent, at least, the intentions of the author we read.

Let me give as an example some lines in which the immediate
effect of the words, what the language does, is obviously no less
important than what is said. It is clearly poetry in Sartre's and
Roman Jakobson's sense of the word. It comes from Stuart
Montgomery's *Circe*, published in 1969:

With a low voice	Circe
with a low voice	I called to the Goddess
outside the house	I see
her open doors	I see
the marble floors	dreading her eyes
dreading her face	I see
she led me in	I follow her feet
to sit me down	on a silver throne
I hold the arms	embossed and carved
she kissed my feet	caressed my limbs
she mixed her musk	in a cup of gold
Drink it down	I held the throne
Drink she said	in a low command
Drink it down	I drink I drink
I drowned my heart	I felt it groan
against the tide	I felt my feet
my feet are mine	touching the ground

I would say myself that Ulysses' determination to confront Circe
and resist her charm is conveyed to the reader in these lines as an

experience he can share. And this is because of the unusual spacing and rhythm of these lines: the controlled deliberateness, as it were, resisting the movement towards a hypnotic (litany-like and devoutly submissive) incantation. It is also because of their curiously dislocating effect, which induces (in a mild form, obviously, but induces none the less) an effect on the nervous system similar to that which one experiences when, like Ulysses, one finds it hard to 'coordinate' one's reactions and has to remind oneself that one's arms and legs are one's own. It is interesting too that the deliberately matter-of-fact utterances which resist the movement towards incantation seem in the end, though less obviously, incantatory too. Montgomery's Ulysses seems to resist the spell by casting an even more profound spell than hers over not only Circe but also himself.

It is quite possible, however, that my reading of these lines will seem eccentric or far-fetched and that this was not the effect which Montgomery intended, in the process of writing them, to convey. Yet a more plausible or faithful reading would resemble this at least to the extent that they offered an explanation of why Montgomery's words are as they are, in that particular sequence and order, and hence of why they may have been written as they were.

There was some amusing correspondence some years ago about the possible interpretations of a poem (whose author I don't recall) which included the words, 'Emily-coloured hands'. Here surely, it was argued, is an example of meaning which is private and inaccessible. It is, of course, a philosophical question of considerable interest whether private languages are possible, even if they only consist of three words. But, philosophy apart, it is obvious, at least, that whoever reads this phrase will have some ideas as to its possible meaning at least and that where two readings differ they will vary in precisely contrasting ways: according, for instance, to whether we take Emily to be the name of a negress, a Caucasian or a household pet and whether the hands are human hands or the hands of a clock.

Could there not, however, be two alternatively or simultaneously grasped meanings? What about puns?

> Where Bentley late tempestuous wont to sport
> In troubled waters, but now sleeps in port.

What about Empson's seven types of ambiguity or Cleanth Brooks's irony? Or Roland Barthes's deliberate 'mistreatment' of a text (*S/Z*), his wrenching apart of the 'univocal' novel or story of previous exegesis and liberation of the text into a number of simultaneous 'codes' and indefinitely varied readings? What happens when we grasp more than one meaning or one level of meaning in the same passage of a text is an interesting psychological question. Do we, for example, when we encounter Pope's pun on 'port' grasp both meanings at once? Does our mind register in swift alternation each meaning in turn? Are we disconcerted or amused or excited or impressed because we know we can read the word 'port' and hence the whole of Pope's couplet in two ways?

This doesn't affect the issue here. Even if we can genuinely grasp the separate meanings conveyed by a pun or an ambiguity or irony at the same time (which seems likely; we, after all, perform similar feats of divided attention when we read a long sentence, such as this) it is still a meaning or meanings which we grasp and hence an intention we attribute to the supposed author of the words we read. One may know that what reads like a pun or an ambiguous meaning may not have been intended. School-children are expert at finding comic possibilities in solemn verses. The following example is, of course, untranslatable:

> Arrestons un moment. La pompe de ces Lieux,
> Je le vois bien, Arsace, est nouvelle à tes yeux.
> Souvent ce Cabinet superbe et solitaire,
> Des secrets de Titus est le dépositaire.

> (*Bérénice*, i, i)

But the fun lies not only in the alternative meanings but in the gleeful substitution in imagination of a comically disreputable for the usually respected Racine. One may also read anachronistic meanings into the works of classical antiquity in the manner of mediaeval Christian commentators or certain contemporary structuralists, but this is again simply the conscious substitution of an author who is fictitious for one who is real.

1.3   I have been talking so far about what we assume the real or purely imaginary author of the words we read to have intended at the moment at which he wrote them down. This may or may not, of course, in the case of the real author, be what he meant to convey before writing them or what he afterwards told us his intentions were. Authors are often poor guides to their own writings. We do, after all, whether we are authors or not, sometimes actually want to forget what we meant when we said or wrote down certain things.

Sometimes, after a quarrel, we wish we could 'bite our tongue off' and since we can't, we try to make out in desperation that we have been misunderstood. Sometimes an author says, in the language of fiction, things that he would normally never think of saying. An example of this, according to D. H. Lawrence, is the kind of early American art represented by Hawthorne:

On the top it is as nice as pie, goody-goody and lovey-dovey. Like Hawthorne being such a blue-eyed darling, in life, and Longfellow and the rest such sucking doves. Hawthorne's wife says she 'never saw him in time', which doesn't mean she saw him too late. But always in the 'frail effulgence of eternity'.
   Serpents they were. Look at the inner meaning of their art and see what demons they were.
                    (*Studies in classic American literature*, pp. 92–3)

It is, presumably, this kind of inconsistency that Lawrence has in mind when he tells us never 'to trust the artist. Trust the tale'.

If the artist can never be taken as a necessarily reliable witness as to the 'inner meaning' of his art, when he talks about it afterwards, what difference then does it make whether or not we claim to be reading our own meanings into the words he used? What difference, that is, does it make in practice?

What we *claim* to be understanding may make no difference at all. An inspired guess, which is offered as nothing more than a guess, may be much better and also closer to the author's intentions than a laborious reduction of the text to the level of significance of its known sources, one of the commonest effects of pedantry. Roland Barthes is sometimes a better reader of Racine than Raymond Picard, for all the latter's scholarship. At the same time, someone who wanted to read Homer and who had no access to a translation would need to respect Homer's intentions to the extent at least of learning to read Homer's Greek. Even the most extreme proponents of the view that the author's intentions are something we can't hope to know are usually prepared to make at least this concession to the opposite view.

1.4   What do we mean by 'intention', however? Many different things. And we can find ourselves in unnecessary difficulties and victims of our own pedantry if we overlook the commonplace and unassumingly precise distinctions between different uses of the word that are conveyed by the common language.

'I didn't intend to say that' or 'I didn't mean to say that. It just slipped out.' Such a phrase normally presents no difficulties. Yet no one normally assumes that the speaker 'meant' or 'intended' nothing at all by the words he impulsively or absent-mindedly used.

What he intended to convey by them may be described simply by saying what he *meant in using them* or intended *by using them* to achieve. But a Congressman filibustering and still talking after fourteen hours may string together sentences which are clearly meaningless and yet the intention of his speech will be plain. He is both impeding legislation and communicating to his fellow Congressmen his wish to avail himself of his right to do so in this way. What he intends to achieve may be clear as well. But it may, on the other hand, be something he would prefer to conceal. His apparent intention may be to prevent legislation going through in what he takes to be the interest of his electors. But perhaps his real intention and what is foremost in his mind is his desire to pay off his debts by earning a bribe from the Mafia.

Intentions and dispositions indicated by the verbs to 'intend' and to 'mean' have, however, at least three things in common, for all the varied and subtle ways in which we use them. They are always assumed to be attributes of creatures endowed with consciousness: a computer is not usually credited with intentions, a child doing a sum usually is. They are unpremeditated: one may intend or mean to do something, one never intends or means to intend or mean to do it. They are never caused in the sense that they are observably explained, both necessarily and sufficiently, by a previous event. What someone does intentionally may be clearly predictable, like a generous man's forking out of a loan to an accomplished sponger who thinks he's an easy touch. It may also be explicable entirely in terms of antecedent events, in the unlikely eventuality of certain fatalistic or deterministic theories being true. Even the most extreme fatalist or determinist, however, is obliged to admit that the causation is only true in theory and that his explanation is in no way demonstrably true. Unless he is as devoted to his theory as the hero of Diderot's *Jacques le fataliste*, he is likely to distinguish, like other people, between deciding to walk and happening to fall downstairs and between accidental homicide and murder.[2]

An intentional act may be carried out instantaneously and forgotten immediately afterwards. This happens normally when one is very busy or driving a car. It may also take years or as long as Sir

Francis Chichester took to sail round the world. But however long the carrying out of an intention may take, an intention, as such, is, in its origin, spontaneous.

Among all the things we do and think which are covered by the words 'intend' and 'mean', there is one distinction, however, that is crucial and the fact that it is sometimes overlooked may have contributed to the theoretical confusion surrounding the words. My obviously fictitious Congressman performed his filibuster knowing that, if he did so, the bribe was as good as his. There was no doubt in his mind what would happen if he was successful in carrying out his intention just as there is no doubt in mine if I hurry to get money from the bank before it closes for the weekend. Contrast this with what happens to a detective searching hopefully for a clue or a doctor unable to diagnose a disease. Each has the intention of finding something and will know whether or not he has succeeded. But what he is looking for he doesn't yet know. He knows and he also doesn't yet know what it is he intends to achieve.

The intention of saying or writing something is the same, in this one respect, as the kind of intention shared by the doctor and the detective. In fact, we commonly speak of *finding* words to make ourselves understood or express our feelings. Usually we find the words we need as soon as we need them. But we have to *look for* the words we need when we are nervous, when we are speaking in a language which we don't speak well and when we are writhing, Flaubert-like, in the agonies of literary creation.

This is one of the reasons for which it makes perfectly good sense to claim that the intention of saying something is not always the same as awareness of what it is that one wants to say. The paradox that we somehow know and yet don't know what we want to find poses what seems to be a genuine problem in philosophy. It also explains why we usually accept without question the common distinction between intentions which are conscious (e.g. the intention of getting some money from the bank) and those which are not, like looking for the right words.

Yet 'unconscious' hardly seems the right description either of the striving to find the right words or to solve a problem. And if we think a little more about what we mean by the difference between the two kinds of intention, we can see that, among other things, it is a difference between the kind of intention that can be imagined or remembered and the kind of intention which can't.

I can remember walking to the bank to cash a cheque and imagine myself or someone else doing the same thing. I can also remember and imagine struggling to find the words I want to say. I cannot, however, imagine or remember struggling to find *particular words*. If I could imagine or remember this, it would only be because I had found them already (cf. Chapter 1, p. 28 above).

This may be one of the reasons for Wittgenstein's saying that 'Meaning is as little an experience as intending' (*Philosophical investigations*, p. 217a). There are intentions that can be imagined or remembered (and in this sense, experienced) but only intentions which have already been formed and require some time for their being successfully carried out. Looking for the words we need is never like this. A happy turn of phrase may occur to us when we are out for a walk. Solzhenitsyn, in a labour camp, composed a long narrative poem in his head, choosing a regular scansion and metre in order not to forget it, before he could get hold of a pen and paper to write it down. In the same way, a mathematician may find the answer to a problem and not commit it to paper or tell anyone for days. We can remember or imagine the desire and the determination to write down what we have thought; also the strain of the actual thinking and our surroundings at the time, perhaps the latter especially: the time of day, the sky and the trees outside. The thinking itself, however, is totally beyond recall.

1.5   If understanding what the writer or speaker meant were a matter of sharing his experience in imagination and, in this way, accurately guessing what was going on in his mind as he looked for and found the particular words he used, then those who claim we can't know what his intention was and what he himself meant to say would be right. Knowing what the original intention and meaning were is, however, altogether different.

Understanding, for one thing, presupposes necessarily that one's experience is different from that of the person one understands *as well as* sharing certain common features. It could never be a matter of becoming miraculously the person one understands, and this is something no speaker or writer could intend. If a drowning man calls for help, it is because he hopes that someone will throw him a lifebelt, not that those who hear him will undergo the illusion that they are drowning as well. Even the desperate cry: 'If you could only feel as I do!' is an appeal for no more than understanding. If it is possible to understand what someone is saying and to understand this, perfectly, it is because one is *not* that person.

The distinction is crucial and when put in those terms may be fairly obvious, but it is easy to see how, in theoretical discussions of what happens when we read, it is forgotten or denied. The struggle to find the words we need *is*, after all, something we can remember, if by struggle we mean the sense of discomfort, embarrassment and strain in certain (well-remembered) circumstances. We can remember talking foolishly in an acutely embarrassing situation or trying to make ourselves understood in a language we hardly know. We can remember groping not only for the right words but for what we actually wanted to say when writing. Remembering this ourselves, we can easily, moreover, imagine someone else having the same experience.

Then again, all expression (arguably) and most literary expression (certainly) refers to experience that can be remembered and imagined. The writer and reader imagine what is, in certain precise ways, the same landscape or the same costume or the same human features. They imagine themselves sharing the same intense emotions of grief and joy. (Think of Keats's Ruth 'amid the alien corn'.) This is one of the many things we assume when we say we understand a text.

Understanding may not depend on an *identity* of experience between writer and speaker or speaker and listener. It presupposes, none the less, some common element and constituent of experience, some common knowledge, for example, of what is meant by drowning.

If this were all that was required, however, and if one understood someone all the more perfectly to the extent that one's experience resembled his, communication would be both impossible and unnecessary. One would know already what someone else wanted to say. Yet, even in cases where closeness of experience and common understanding are profound, as with tribesmen hunting, *some* sign, imperceptible possibly to the uninitiated, may be needed at a crucial stage before the kill. Communication, even when we anticipate what someone is going to say, is always the communication of something new.

1.6 Paradoxically, it is our very skill in communicating with others that blinds us to the fact that it is a skill, analogous to the skill of the hunter or acrobat, in that it is unselfconscious; that is, unreproducible except in practice and therefore unimaginable and beyond recall. One need only think of the everyday virtuosity which enables us to observe, according to whatever situation we are in, not only the words but the style, rhythm and intonation that are appropriate to the situation: the different 'registers' we adopt when speaking to strangers or friends or when telephoning the fire brigade because the house is on fire or the bank manager because our account is overdrawn.

In the eighteenth century, literary criticism tended to regard all expression, even the writing of poetry and drama, in the way we normally and unthinkingly regard the finding of the words we need. A writer's thoughts, what he wanted to say, were one thing, it was commonly assumed, and, when he knew what this was, he found the most 'felicitous' expressions he could to convey them:

> True wit is nature to advantage dress'd,
> What oft was thought but ne'er so well express'd.
>
> (Pope, *Essay on Criticism*, ll. 296–7)

In many ways, this is an excellent description of what passed for 'wit' in the eighteenth century: the great universal commonplaces re-stated in a language which is confidently conventional.[3] In fact, it seems clear that the strength of the conventions, their clarity and their universal acceptance among the literate, made for the facility in their deployment which we ourselves associate with the unselfconscious expertise of everyday speech. The conventions, it was assumed, had their own kind of 'naturalness', that is, like all other conventions, their appropriateness to a particular kind of public and social occasion. To train oneself to be a poet meant acquiring certain recognised habits of expression and learning, to speak like a practised native speaker with no thought of the words and style themselves, other than as a means of drawing attention to what was there to be said:

> False eloquence, like the prismatic glass,
> Its gaudy colours spreads on ev'ry place;
> The face of nature we no more survey,
> All glares alike, without distinction gay:
> But true expression, like th' unchanging sun,
> Clears and improves whate'er it shines upon.
> It gilds all objects but it alters none.

Expression is the dress of thought, and still
Appears more decent as more suitable.

(ll. 311–19)

For Pope, there is no contradiction between regarding 'true expression' as 'the dress of thought' and as that which 'alters nothing'.

Today, few literary critics would accept this characteristically Augustan account of the way language works. Writers in the structuralist tradition as different as Professor Derrida and Professor Lyons (see pp. 20–2 above) have dismissed as 'metaphysical' the assumption that there is an identifiable thought, distinct from its expression. F. R. Leavis has spoken of the 'potency of the training' (*The common pursuit*, pp. 107–15) which tended to blind Dr Johnson to the 'poetic-creative use of words' in Johnson's discussion of all poetry and especially the poetry of Shakespeare. The writing of authentic poetry, it is now assumed, entails the discovery simultaneously of what one has to say and the way in which one has to say it and a poet is no longer praised for his accomplished conformity but for finding his own 'voice'. These changes in the way we think of language are, from certain points of view, an advantage – from that, for example, from which this book is written – though from the point of view of poetry, the advantages are far less certain. What may seem to us ignorance or naïvety in the way that Pope and Johnson thought of language proved, at the same time, in their own poetry and prose, to be the unselfconsciousness of any forceful utterance and of the exercise of any authentic skill.

1.7   There is another reason why we often fail to realise that the finding of words is a process which can be neither remembered nor imagined. After we have spoken or written something down, we become our own listeners or readers. This can sometimes astonish and disconcert us: when we re-read, say, a letter we forgot we ever wrote or when we hear a recording of our own voice; even when we hear our voice, as we speak, in a room whose acoustics bring out vocal qualities of which we are normally unaware. But hearing ourselves otherwise or reading what we have just written is so common an experience that we don't even think about it and don't distinguish for an instant between our thoughts before and after we have found the words we need.

It is a possibly unresolvable question whether 'expression' (*Ausdruck*) differs, in the way claimed by Husserl (in his *Logische*

Untersuchungen), from 'indication' (*Anzeichen*); whether, that is, we can know with absolute certainty what we mean when we are concerned simply with what we have to say, as distinct from what others may make of it. According to Derrida (*La voix et le phéno-mène*, pp. 15–44), there is no difference, and talking to oneself is merely talking to oneself as if one were another person. Moreover, the meaning we had when we spoke, since it can only be recaptured, if at all, through memory, is now as uncertain for us as for anyone else. This second argument is difficult to refute, though whether it disposes of Husserl's account of expression is another matter. The certain knowledge Husserl claims we have of what we mean is the certainty of immediate experience, not the certainty of memory or self-conscious reflection.

The philosophical argument doesn't therefore affect the question of whether we can imagine or remember finding the words we need; that is, the decision as to what, specifically, we wanted to say and how we wanted to say it. Reflection is thought about a decision that has been made, if not actually carried out, about a solution reached or words already found. This is why reflection itself, being a form of thinking, can only be reflected on in turn when it has reached a conclusion of some kind, provisional or definitive.

All immediate thinking (i.e. finding, discovering and deciding what or whether) is unselfcritical in the sense that we cannot reflect on it. If we do, it is simply because we have stopped looking or deciding while we reflect on the discoveries and decisions we have made. And because it is unselfcritical, we can delude ourselves in the process of thinking, in so far as the solution or decision we reach or the words we find are not of the kind we previously thought we would or subsequently believe we have.

This is why the kind of unconscious slip of the tongue described by Freud (see pp. 51–2 below) and the self-delusion that, according to Leavis, allows Snow to write in clichés are perfectly conceivable. Not that the *act* of self-delusion is something we can imagine or remember ourselves or anyone else committing.[4] We could never, by definition, know we were deceiving ourselves and hence never remember doing so, just as we could never knowingly make or remember making a mistake in arithmetic. What we can imagine or remember is our 'vague memory', as Leavis puts it, of the way we have seen or heard certain words or phrases used, our 'sense of power' as we use them ourselves and our general determination to impress; also our growing confidence as we go on writing or speaking in a (to us) recognisably impressive manner. We realise that we had forgotten that one cannot impress merely by wanting to impress or by using borrowed gestures. A growing inner discomfort, however, or the cruel observations of an honest friend may lead us to realise that this is in fact what we've done and that, as in a dream, we were merely deluding ourselves that we had something important and definite to say.

This is different from the 'unintended' wounding remark that just 'slipped out' and that one may realise one has made even before a Mr Knightley points this out. One had intended to be kind but a wild impulse – the sudden realisation that there was a good audience for a joke – led one to change one's mind. It is different again, obviously, from the behaviour of the filibustering Congressman (pp. 42-3 above) who is deceiving almost everybody but himself.

Less obvious but no less real is the difference between self-deception of this kind and the sublime hypocrisy, as Lawrence sees it, of a Nathaniel Hawthorne (see pp. 40-1 above). The compulsive imaginative writer may find in the act of writing the only possible release, the only means of affirming what he passionately feels and believes, when this is something he dare not admit, even to himself, in the language he speaks to his wife and fellow citizens. The incompatibility of intention here, however, is not in the act of writing itself, as in the case of cliché, but between what Hawthorne expressed in the language of romance and allegory and what he may have thought he had expressed after he had laid down his pen. I am not, of course, saying that this is true altogether of the real Hawthorne, only that it is conceivable.

1.8   This does not, of course, account for all the many ways in which a speaker or writer can be unaware of what he is saying. I have not, for instance, discussed the unawareness of the kind of audience one is addressing which can take the form of naïvety, pomposity or both or, as in the case of a visionary such as Blake or Balzac, a kind of *sancta simplicitas*. If the result of writing in this way is sometimes cliché, it is cliché of a different order and origin from that which is described by Leavis. How, though, can one talk of a single or consistent intention in a work which takes many years to write, many parts of which are subsequently changed and which incorporates extensive borrowings from the work of others?

An intention of course may take as long to carry out as the Count of Monte Cristo took to escape from his cell. It may also take many years to form, as in the case of writing a novel, and even though, from the point of view of what can be imagined or remembered, it takes literally no time at all for the words one needs to be found. The novelist reaching the point in his story he had long been planning to reach can only know when he gets there what actual form the story will take at this point. Changes he makes may or may not prove consistent with the original meaning and intention and this may or may not occur to the reader who subsequently compares the first draft with all the variants. It is quite possible, of course, for the alteration to correspond more perfectly to that intention than the very first draft. Alterations made after five years are in this respect no less reliable, necessarily, than those made after five minutes or five seconds. As for the incorporation of other writers' thoughts and words, this may, again, either strike one as an inconsistency, as when Balzac's David Séchard follows his proposal of marriage with a recitation to his betrothed of part of a treatise on printing (*Illusions perdues*, part 1), or as the perfect expression of what needs to be said:

What I say is no more according to Plato than according to me, since he and I see and understand it in the same way. The bees plunder the flowers wherever they find them, but the honey they make from them is theirs alone.   (Montaigne, *Essays*, 1, 26)

Perhaps the most perfect description of knowing what one means, even – or rather especially – in a work which conveys the experience, longings and observations of a lifetime, is Stendhal's reply to Balzac's criticism that *La chartreuse de Parme* suffered from certain defects of style and form:

I see only one rule: to be clear. If I am not clear, my *whole world* is anni-hilated. . . .   (*Correspondance*, 30 October 1840)

The form of *La chartreuse* is indeed magnificent, whatever Balzac may have thought and despite the abrupt ending for which Stendhal's publisher, who insisted on its being cut down at the last minute ('sabred', as Stendhal put it, to fit into two volumes), is alone to blame. It is magnificent because of that sustained knowledge of what he is doing of which Stendhal speaks when he talks of his need 'to be clear'. *La chartreuse* was, of course, dictated without interruption in only seven weeks, though this alone is not enough to account for its quasi-musical development of related themes and of strongly contrasted moods. Only the most confident mastery could explain this subtlety of organisation or his malicious and knowingly judged humour at the expense of his contemporary readers, who are implicitly contrasted with the bold young Frenchmen of the Revolutionary armies of forty years before.

The study of form has, notoriously, over the millennia, given rise to a pedantic and constricting conventionality, as well as contributing to the production of masterpieces which, like Racine's, more than justify the conventions they employ. Perhaps now that its despotism has been overthrown, we may come to think of it as something that corresponds, not necessarily to precedent but to consistency of intention, to a coherent 'world', in Stendhal's sense of the term, to a sustained moment of time in which a writer has known what he is doing and what he means; even if this has been over a period of many years and as a result of much agonised rewriting, in order to pursue more faithfully what he means and even if his mind has been on something more important for him than his own profundity and skill.

1.9   It is difficult in any discussion of what is meant by the word 'intention' to ignore the intentions discussed by Freud in his essay on 'Dostoevsky and parricide' (*Character and culture*), other observations by Freud on works of literature or Ernest Jones's famous study of *Hamlet*, as well as numerous other exercises in what has come to be known as 'Freudian analysis'. Freud is explicitly concerned with 'unconscious' motivation of various kinds and a psychic 'determinism' which is effective solely in so far as it operates beneath the level of conscious motivation. The neurotic patient, as we all know, is liberated from the compulsions and repressions by which his conscious life is dominated when, with the help of psychoanalysis, he is able to recognise them for what they are.

Nothing in Freud's account of neurosis or art contradicts, I believe, the view of intention I am defending and though nothing in his detailed analyses need necessarily be regarded as a matter of proven scientific fact, there is nothing either to cause us to reappraise our basic assumptions concerning the act of reading. On the contrary, I believe that Freud's own interpretations of painting and literature are those of a sensitive and cultured man and often a stimulus to imaginative understanding, even when one doesn't agree with a particular conclusion or emphasis.

My account of intention (in 1.8, above) is, I confess, influenced by Freud's account of 'speech disturbances' in the *Psychopathology of everyday life* and, in particular, of

those speech disturbances which can no longer be described as speech-blunders, for they do not injure the individual word, but affect the rhythm and execution of the entire speech, as, for example, the stammering and stuttering of embarrassment. But here, as in the former cases, it is the inner conflict that is betrayed to us through the disturbance in speech. I really do not believe that anyone will make mistakes in talking in an audience with His Majesty, in a serious love declaration, or in defending one's name and honour before a jury; in short, people make no mistakes where *they are all there*, as the saying goes. Even in criticizing an author's style we are allowed and accustomed to follow the principle of explanation, which we cannot miss in the origin of a single speech-blunder. A clear and unequivocal manner of writing shows us that here the author is in harmony with himself, but where we find a forced and involved expression, aiming at more than one target, as appropriately expressed, we can thereby recognize the participation of an unfinished and complicated thought, or we can hear through it the stifled voice of the author's self-criticism.   (pp. 77–8)

To clinch the point, Freud quotes from Boileau's *Art Poétique*:

> Ce qu'on conçoit bien s'énonce clairement
> Et les mots pour le dire arrivent aisément.
>
> (What is well conceived is clearly enunciated and the words in which to say it arrive easily.)

'Clarity' here, as in Stendhal's letter to Balzac, is defined not in Voltairean terms (see 1.6 above, note 3) as a perfect conformity between a verbal convention and its known and recognised referent but as a perfect consistency of intention and mastery of words.

1.10   There is one final possible objection to the assumption I have been defending so far which I should like to discuss. My understanding of what someone is saying may imply no reference whatever to his intentions, even to his 'unconscious' intentions in the Freudian sense of the word. It may be obvious from someone's accent that he comes from Wales and yet this, which one has quite correctly understood from the way he speaks, may in no way whatsoever be what he intends to convey, any more than he intends to disguise his accent. Only the Eliza Doolittles of this world habitually think of the way in which they form their vowels. Most people are like the American girl who liked my English accent and, when I told her I liked hers, said: 'I didn't know I had an accent.'

Again, someone may understand quite correctly from his reading of Stendhal that he had not read Hegel or of Philo that he had not read the Gospels.

'If she talks like that, it means she comes from Wales.' 'If he writes like that, it means he couldn't have read Hegel.' These are perfectly normal uses of the verb 'to mean'. The list of similar examples could be extended to include much that comes under the study of phonology and syntax as well as that of inscriptions and public records. Yet, it is perhaps obvious too that my two examples are examples of different kinds of evidence and meaning.

What we have in both instances, however, is something like what H. P. Grice calls 'natural' implications of the verb 'to mean' ('Meaning', in *The Philosophical Review*). Grice's own examples of 'natural' senses of the verb are the following:

(1) Those spots mean (meant) measles.

(2) Those spots didn't mean anything to me but to the doctor they meant measles.

(3) The recent budget means that we shall have a hard year.

In these examples, according to Grice, '*x means (meant) p* entails *p*'. Examples of non-natural senses are:

(1) Those three rings on the bell (of the bus) mean that 'the bus is full'.

(2) That remark, 'Smith couldn't get on without his trouble and strife', means that Smith found his wife indispensable.

Here *x means (meant) p* does not entail *p*. One may know why the conductor rang the bell but notice that he was mistaken in thinking the bus was full as there were still a few places on the top deck. One may understand the remark about Smith and his wife but happen to know also that he is perfectly capable of looking after himself. For Grice, 'non-natural' meanings are intended meanings, which are in turn defined as meanings that depend on someone's recognition of an intention. Someone's behaviour may be the consequence of this recognition but the recognition is necessary if the intention is to be fulfilled. In cases of 'non-natural' meaning, there is no question of behaviour *causing* a desired reaction. There is an obvious difference between erecting a road block to stop a car and waving it down.[5]

Unless I am misreading Grice, there is a fairly straightforward analogy between (a) 'These spots mean measles', (b) 'If she talks like that it means she comes from Wales' and (c) 'If he writes like that, it means he couldn't possibly have read Hegel.' However, the analogy is far from perfect. For (b) and (c) are both inferences from what is meant in Grice's 'non-natural' sense, that is, from what someone says intentionally, even though it is not an inference from what that person intends. (This is different again from the inferences from a writer's 'subject matter', as discussed by Hirsch – see pp. 109–10 below – as distinct from his actual intention.)

In the case of the Welsh accent, the assumption may amount to no more than that the speaker is talking in a way which to her is normal. She is not imitating or exaggerating a Welsh accent. This assumption amounts to very little as an account of her intention. But it is impossible to think of it as anything other than an assumption concerning intention and, like other such assumptions, it may be false or true.

The same can be said of all those studies of the grammar and phonology of particular utterances which are concerned with aspects of speech which are (at least in any ordinary sense of the word) un-intended: the choice of the phonemic structure of a language, its syntax, etc., which may have been consciously chosen at a certain stage by the child learning the language, but which it would be difficult to say that the native speaker *chooses* to employ every time he speaks or writes. The one question the linguistician needs to answer concerning his intention is whether he is speaking normally, that is, not, for example, distorting his normal pronunciation and syntax in order to sound like a foreigner. The one question concern-ing intention that the phonologist needs to ask, according to Benveniste, is whether a phoneme he hears is a constituent of mean-ing in a meaningful utterance in a natural language (see p. 17 above). The requirement is minimal but indispensable. Professor Chomsky, investigating language from a very different point of view from that of Benveniste, insists, similarly, that without refer-ence to the 'linguistic competence' of native speakers and their 'tacit knowledge' of and control over the linguistic forms they employ, 'there is no such subject as descriptive linguistics. There is nothing for its descriptive statements to be right or wrong about' ('Some controversial questions in phonological theory', p. 103).

The reference to intention in 'If he writes like that, it means he couldn't have read Hegel' is of a different kind. It is not just an inference from the fact that the writer is writing in a normal and unfacetious way. If the remark is intended seriously, it derives its validity solely from the assumption that one understands the writer's intentions well enough to know not only what he meant but what he couldn't possibly have meant as well. It calls, in other words, for a far more intimate understanding of the author's intentions than do the conclusions reached by the phonologist or grammarian. To say that Montesquieu couldn't have read Marx because he died long before Marx was born is, of course, an inference not from what Montesquieu wrote but from chronology. Such an inference may serve as a guide to Montesquieu's intentions: 'No, Miss Harris, I'm afraid he couldn't possibly be referring to Marx...', but in a negative sense alone.

As for Marxist analysis itself and in particular the kind of analysis that is concerned with 'false consciousness' and the contradictions in somebody's point of view, this clearly presupposes too a more or less complete grasp of what that person had in mind. The value of the Marxist approach to literature, like the Freudian, is that it suggests certain possibilities concerning the way people think and behave in certain well-defined family and social situations. Whether these are more than possibilities, however, can only be decided in the way that all attributions of intention are decided, irrespective of their philosophical provenance. And to claim that one's attributions are necessarily correct is both to affirm and to deny the freedom implicit in the notion of intention and 'non-natural' meaning. No way of reading, least of all the Freudian or Marxist, could dispense with the notion of intention itself.

2 *Which is why we can say certain things about what we read which are true but never deny the possibility that we may be wrong.*

2.1 Certain propositions are absolutely certain for no better reason than that they are tautologous. If a triangle, by definition, has three sides and I say that it has three, I can only be wrong if I go on to use the word in some eccentric or inconsistent way. Such statements are, in Kantian terminology, 'analytic' and also 'trivial', as distinct from 'synthetic' judgments in which, in a proposition of the form A is B, B is not contained in and thereby adds something new to the subject A. Empirical propositions and, according to Kant, certain non-empirical 'a priori' judgments are 'synthetic'. The problem to which Kant addresses himself is whether they can also be certain.

Most of what we say or assume about the utterances of other people is empirical and thereby 'synthetic', though discussions of genre may involve questions of purely formal definition and have the absolute certainty of analytic judgments. If a sonnet is a poem with fourteen lines, all of which rhyme with one another in some way, there can be no doubt whether we are talking about a sonnet or not. The human longing for certainty and infallibility is what has led many critics and scholars, over the centuries, to try and rewrite Aristotle's *Poetics* and produce a more complete and up-to-date taxonomy. Northrop Frye, perhaps the best-known contemporary practitioner of criticism of this kind, has, quite consistently, claimed that he is not concerned in the least with questions of 'value' or 'ethics' and that the critics' concern with genre precludes any reference to experience or historical fact.[6]

Whether empirical judgments of the kind which the study of literature usually calls for can be true or known for certain to be true is a far more difficult problem than any which is normally encountered in discussions of *genre* and it is possibly because of the difficulty that students of all degrees of seniority tend to despair of solving it and give in to the kind of debilitating scepticism which characterises literary studies and is in contrast to what Popper (*Objective knowledge*, pp. 99–101) calls 'dynamic scepticism', an attitude of 'hopeful critical inquiry', such as that which we find far more commonly among students of experimental science. This weak scepticism is not, however, peculiar to students of literature alone. Both G. E. Moore and Wittgenstein were conscious of the general mistrust of experience on the part of the average educated man and of the unreasonableness of the common prejudice against statements which derive their validity from experience alone. There is a common mistaken inference, Moore argues (*Philosophical papers*, pp. 233–5), that because a proposition like 'It is snowing heavily outside' is contingent (i.e. a proposition the contradictory of which is not self-contradictory) it is, for this reason alone, uncertain and only possibly true or that it refers to what, in some final analysis, is an illusory state of affairs.

The prejudice in question is of course peculiar to the educated who don't have to work with their hands, as Moore would probably have agreed. To contradict a proposition that follows, necessarily and tautologically, from another that one accepts is merely to contradict one's own words, whereas to doubt whether it is snowing, when one can see that it is, is to contradict the evidence of one's eyes. Perhaps if we lived as hunters or fishermen, we would have more respect for our senses.

Any statement made by anyone is open to question or dispute. But this is not in itself a reason for saying that it is not true or cannot be known to be true. In science or mathematics, the adducing of counter-examples is necessary to the process of correction and proof. In the study of literature, the unquestioning repetition of a judgment made by someone else is an obviously naïve form of incomprehension. This is why there is no such thing as an unassailable point of view in science, literature, politics or religion and why the question, 'How can you possibly defend what you're saying?' can only be answered in the form: 'I'll tell you when you tell me what objections you have in mind.'

'How do you know?' is a question that can amount to a serious objection: 'All right, you say you saw a lady in Elizabethan costume at the foot of your bed, but how do you know it was a ghost?' It can also be asked in a spirit of genuine amazement and disbelief: 'How do *you* know that?' or not in disbelief but in a sincere attempt to understand. Or it can be asked as a child asks it to tease his elders.

How readily and how reasonably we can answer the question, however, has little or nothing to do with the seriousness or suspiciousness with which it is asked. Apart from the fact that it depends on the ignorance of the questioner or the knowledge, patience and ingenuity that happen to go into the reply, it depends also on the number and kind of unexplained connections between the different parts of the questioned affirmation. A gifted and articulate critic asked to justify a particular reading would be able to add to what he had already said and offer a variety of alternative arguments and examples when asked to justify his claim. An answer to the question, 'How do we know the distance to the sun?' would lead to a similarly complex yet, for the expert, simple account of the connections between various phenomena and the measurements involved. Whereas if I were to say in a Law Court that I saw that particular car, whose driver I recognised, hit the cyclist and fail to stop and if I were asked how I knew that, I would be reduced to silence or forced back on an incompetent attempt to reproduce the relevant arguments from Moore or Wittgenstein or the classic attempts to solve

Descartes's puzzle as to how we ever know whether or not we're dreaming. Fortunately, it is very unlikely that any judge would allow the question.

The difficulty we have and that even the most subtle dialectician may have in saying how we know that something is true is not in itself a reason for thinking it may not be true after all. On the contrary, it can happen that those things of which we are as certain as we can be of anything – like the fact that we saw the car hit the cyclist – are the most difficult of all to justify when challenged.

This doesn't mean, though, that it's always correspondingly difficult to show or point out why one believes or how one knows such things to be true. There may be no other witnesses of the accident with the cyclist. The cyclist may not know what hit him and, in any case, the members of the jury weren't there. But there are occasions on which, referring to a present or permanent state of affairs, we can say: 'If you don't think it's inflammable, try putting a match to it.' Heuristic argument, of which this is the simplest form, has a kind of certainty impossible in an explanation of the unsuspected relations between phenomena. Unlike the latter, it asks for nothing to be taken on trust.

Now it is obvious that nearly all we say about what we understand from what we read calls for corroboration of this kind. 'A judgment is personal or it is nothing; you cannot take over someone else's' (Leavis, *Nor shall my sword*, p. 62). The literary critic justifying his interpretation may produce excellent reasons for believing what he does, but his explanation will still be in the nature of appeal: 'Surely, now, you can see what I mean!'

Yet it is obvious too that there is a world of difference between the interpretation of a passage from *Hamlet* and 'If you don't think it's inflammable, try putting a match to it', even if both are an appeal to experience and that the latter implies a degree if not a kind of certainty far greater than the former. One reason lies in the far greater variety of experience and knowledge that the former presupposes. Another is that simple observations of the latter kind can be taken and reported as matters of simple fact. Yet it would be self-defeating on the part of the critic who is calling for the recognition of what he hopes will turn out to be a common reading of the same passage to require that any single observation he presupposes, any link in the implicit chain of argument, should be taken on trust by his readers in this way.

In the natural sciences, though the language used is usually far more sophisticated, the immensely complex chain of reasoning is never open to questioning of the same kind or for the same reason. It is true that anyone can perform any experiment if he is able to or make any observation that has contributed to a branch of specialist scientific inquiry. But it is unlikely that any serious practising scientist would dream of reliving the history of science in this way. His business is, quite properly, with the making of history. The scientist knows, and the performing of relatively simple experiments will have confirmed this, that there is an immense amount of empirical knowledge that it is perfectly reasonable for him to take on trust. It is this confidence that makes it possible for Sir Karl Popper, whose ideas of certainty seem to derive principally from the natural sciences, to say that 'there is no absolute certainty, though certainty enough for most practical purposes' (*Objective knowledge*, pp. 78–80) and that knowledge is something that can 'progress' and 'grow'.

The study of literature is not something that can demonstrably 'progress' and 'grow' in this or any remotely comparable way, and the assertion that it can is often no more than thinly disguised academic salesmanship. This doesn't mean that the standards of literary study can't decline or be improved. There is a sense, presumably, in which the standards of scientific study can also decline or be improved, but this is not the same as saying that scientific *knowledge* can grow. How much it progresses and grows will depend after all on the behaviour of the natural world, on the extent to which it actually yields information, as much as on the knowledge and skill of the scientists.

Relative certainty of the kind that Sir Karl Popper attributes to scientific discovery (and which, unconvincingly, as far as I am concerned, he claims to be the only kind of certainty of which men are capable) is therefore something the student of literature is denied. For it to be possible, it would be necessary not only for him to perform the equivalent of a rigorously conducted experiment but for him to build on as well as correct and improve knowledge previously possessed by himself and other men. My point is not that the knowledge we can have of literature is, by its nature, less certain than the knowledge we have of science. It is simply that, unlike scientific knowledge, it has to be reappraised in order to be understood at all. The theoretical justification for the use of an electron microscope and the experiments that confirm the accuracy of its readings can be taken for granted when it has itself become an experimental tool. There is no such knowledge we can presuppose when we read a novel or poem.

If relative certainty of the kind the chemist, physicist, biochemist or astronomer can achieve is impossible for the student of literature, what kind of certainty then is possible for him at all? Can he be even partially certain of anything?

The seeming uncertainty of literary judgments when contrasted with other observations such as 'Fire burns', 'I saw the car hit the cyclist' or 'Water is a compound of hydrogen and oxygen' is due to something other than their complexity or the amount of knowledge they presuppose. And this seeming uncertainty is wholly different from the relative uncertainty (which is also relative certainty) of science. The grounds which justify the scientist in relative and justified confidence in the truth of what he says cannot possibly be reproduced by the student of literature. Any degree of certainty he achieves and any doubts it will be reasonable for him to entertain about what he says will have to be justified by wholly different criteria. One of the most obvious reasons is that the object of literary study, unlike that of the natural sciences is (in Grice's terms, see 1.10 above) 'non-natural' and not 'natural' meanings. Its object, in other words, is the subjective and intentional activity of other minds.

2.2   A mother knows when her baby screams in a certain way that the baby is in pain. We sometimes know what other people feel or want better than they happen to realise themselves. Grief or illness induce numbness, and the numbness itself, together with its cause, is sensed not by the sufferer but his friend.

How, if at all, was the mother proved right? Because she saw an open safety-pin stuck in the baby's bottom. And the friend? By the illness that a doctor later diagnoses or by the terrible ordeal of which the sufferer himself later speaks.

But the friend and the mother knew they were right, in any case. Their knowledge doesn't even need confirmation. The same is true of our understanding of ordinary pieces of information or news. Events may or may not subsequently prove that we had understood them correctly.

At the same time, our confidence that we understand correctly and that it is true that someone is feeling pain or means to say what we understand is a confidence which soon increases with experience, as in the case of the mother of the month-old baby who knows the difference between the crying that means hunger or wind and the crying that means pain. As Hilary Putnam has argued (*Meaning and the moral sciences*, pp. 97–117), it could not possibly derive from knowledge which we already possessed and from which our understanding of the howl or explanations derived. The theory that, as with scientific evidence, we need to know what truth-conditions need to be fulfilled if we are to know whether a statement about them is true is inapplicable to our understanding of language: 'one does not need to *know* that there is a correspondence between words and extra-linguistic entities to learn one's language. But there is such a correspondence none the less and it explains the *success* of what one is doing' (*Meaning and the moral sciences*, p. 111).

Because there is such a 'correspondence between words and extra-linguistic entities', i.e. because there is an actual turning to the left by the church, as well as verbal directions to this effect, our understanding of the words can be assumed to be correct and our repetition or summary of them a true statement by the criteria, for example, of Tarski's theory of truth definition.[7] The reliability of our understanding cannot itself be guaranteed; though, as a great many examples will normally suggest, this doesn't mean that our ability to understand is, necessarily, at all times, *unreliable*. A very crude version of the arguments of Moore and Wittgenstein (crude because Wittgenstein disagrees with Moore on many crucial points) is to say that a statement like 'It's snowing outside' or 'He told me there was a turning to the left' is certain unless some good reason for doubting it can be found.

What, of course, is a 'good reason'? Clearly, not any reason; and the merely hypothetical possibility that we may be wrong is not, for Moore, a good reason. A good reason can only be an alternative version of what was happening or what was said, like 'No, that's not snow, that's sleet', or 'You don't understand English, he said a turning to the right', which gives us two versions of the truth between which we must choose. Following Moore, then, we might say that our understanding of what we read may be certain and what we say about it true, in many particular instances. But we cannot deny that there may be real objections which so far have simply not occurred to us. Real objections have, after all, been found in the past to beliefs we had previously had no reason to doubt. It would

be absurd to deny that this could ever happen again and this is not
what either Wittgenstein or Moore is saying. There is a world of
difference, after all, between the real objection to what we believe to
be true and the merely hypothetical objection that a real objection
may be found.

2.3   Few men have been more aware of the difference than Samuel
Johnson (of whom it is said that, after a stroke, he composed some
Latin verses to see whether his reason was impaired) and for whom
'deliberateness' was clearly distinct from 'dogma'. What Johnson
says of the editor of Shakespeare in his own preface to Shakespeare
can be said of any critic or interpreter:

> That a conjectural critic should often be mistaken cannot be wonderful
> either to others or himself, if it be considered, that in his art there is no
> system, no principal and axiomatical truth that regulates subordinate positions.
> His chance of error is renewed at every attempt; an oblique view of the
> passage, a slight misapprehension of a phrase, a casual inattention to the
> parts connected, is sufficient to make him not only fail, but fail ridiculously;
> and when he succeeds best, he produces perhaps but one reading of many
> probable, and he that suggests another will always be able to dispute his
> claim.   (*Johnson on Shakespeare*, pp. 59–60)

And yet the fallibility of the critic of which Johnson speaks – with a
gloomy humility which is also a lively relish of the implication that
this is the common human lot – is what enables the critic to test and
confirm his readings, and if not finally, at least with relative certainty. The critic and the student of literature cannot hope to anticipate or answer all possible objections to their reading of a text. But
they can answer specific objections, especially when these are made
in the form of an alternative reading. They can admit they were
wrong, say where the proposed alternative fails or show that there is
no incompatibility between the two. They can do this by referring
to other parts of the text in question, by comparing the evidence for
the two alternative readings in dispute or by drawing attention to
the normal meaning of words. As a student of Dante, I was weaned
with difficulty from my cherished belief that the worms in the outer
confines of Hell were 'fastidious', in the sense of being choosy
about the particular blood they chose to suck:

> Elle regavan lor di sangue il volto,
>   che mischiato di lagrime a' lor piedi
>   da fastidiosi vermi era ricolto. . .

(These made their faces stream with blood, which mixed with
tears was gathered at their feet by loathsome worms)

(Inferno, III, 67–9)

It took a short lecture in etymology and a hunt through the best
available Latin and Italian dictionaries to convince me that my
exquisite Baudelairean worms were merely the creatures of my
ingenuity.

Johnson, when talking of the 'conjectural critic', had the editors
of texts principally in mind. But criticism and interpretation are
essential equally to the translation of texts. As a teacher of French,
I have always been grateful for bad translations of poetry or prose I
admire, because they give me a clear choice between the translator's
reading and my own. Mistranslation, of course, can have a profound
interest of its own and the approximate translation may be superior
to the original, as Pound claimed was the case with Gavin Douglas's
Aeneid. I do not think this can be said of Gide's translation of
Joseph Conrad's *Typhoon*, but Gide leaves us in no doubt as to how
he sees Captain McWhirr and it is up to us to decide whether this
Captain McWhirr is Conrad's:

Sa table aussi avait été chambardée: règles, crayons, encrier – tout ce qui
avait une place assignée et sûre – toutes ces choses à terre, comme si une main
malfaisante les eût arrachées une à une pour les lancer sur le plancher
mouillé.

L'ouragon s'était même introduit dans les aménagements de sa vie privée,
ce qui n'était jamais encore arrivé; et un sentiment de consternation envahit
McWhirr au plus profond de son phlegme. Et le pire restait à venir! Il était
content que l'incident fâcheux de l'entrepont ait été découvert à temps. Après
tout, si le navire devait disparaître, au moins il ne coulerait pas avec des gens
en train de s'entre-déchirer. Cela c'était profondément inadmissible. Et dans
sa protestation entrait une intention d'humanité aussi bien que le sentiment
des convenances.

(And his table had been cleared too; his rulers, his pencils, the inkstand – all
the things that had their safe appointed places – they were gone, as if a mischievous hand had plucked them out one by one and flung them on the wet
floor. The hurricane had broken in upon the orderly arrangements of his
privacy. This had never happened before, and the feeling of dismay reached
the very seat of his composure. And the worst was yet to come! He was glad
that the trouble in the 'tween-deck had been discovered in time. If the ship
had to go after all, then, at least, she wouldn't be going to the bottom with a
lot of people in her fighting tooth and claw. That would have been odious.
And in that feeling there was a humane intention and a vague sense of the
fitness of things.)

Gide's McWhirr is not, I would argue myself, like Conrad's,

vulnerable to shock and dismay. He sees his rulers, inkstand and pencils where they have fallen on the deck, unlike Conrad's McWhirr whose first startling thought is that they are 'gone' – no longer in 'their safe appointed places'. The sudden jolt to unthinking expectations is something that readers of Conrad will have come across before. A first-year undergraduate will have no difficulty in noticing the differences, especially in this context, between '*consternation*' and 'dismay', '*phlègme*' and 'composure', '*l'incident fâcheux*' and 'the trouble' and '*inadmissible*' and 'odious' – though, if he is unfamiliar with the kind of Anglophilism to which Gide enthusiastically surrenders, he may fail to notice the intention behind Gide's choice of words. For what Gide seems to be substituting for Conrad's far from superhuman but, in his own way, heroic merchant skipper is the glamorously inhuman British leader of men, a type of Englishman or Scotsman dear to the French imagination, especially in the period between the two world wars and of which Maurois's Colonel Bramble is another example, like the T. E. Lawrence of the legend – '*le Lawrence français*', as J.-F. Revel has called him in order to distinguish him from D. H. A far more accurate rendering of the English would be possible and one can therefore assume that Gide has chosen, knowingly, or otherwise, to re-create McWhirr in this way. If the portrait seems over-done and the upper lip almost too stiff for words, this is not incompatible with what we know of Gide's constant tendency to self-parody.

What is at issue here, as in any dispute over two or more readings of a text, is both the overall intention and effect of an entire work and the normal meaning of words. And this, whether it is found necessary or not to refer to the latter, will always be at issue in any conflict of interpretation, even in a discussion of poetry which departs as far as possible from normal usage and even when the disagreement is over the motivation of a character or the symbolic significance of a whole episode. The example from Gide's translation of Conrad may serve to illustrate, in fact, how much the overall effect of a novel may depend on a few words and how quickly it can be created and fixed in one's mind. Sometimes a dispute between readers can be resolved simply by pointing out a passage, a few sentences or even a few words that one of them has forgotten or read with wandering attention; though the problem in critical discussion is commonly to find how it is that two readings differ and for each of the readers to recall from which particular passage or passages their overall impressions principally derived. The resolution of differences demands that one should be able, at the very least, to agree on *where* one differs.

When one can agree on this, and when the disagreement centres on specific words and phrases, there is a likelihood that the disagreement will be settled by a close examination of the words in question and what precedes or follows them. Two readers may disagree over the meaning of one word. They are less likely to disagree over ten and less still over twenty or a hundred. They are also less likely to be mistaken about normal usage ten times or twenty than in a single instance and, if they end up by agreeing, they have good reasons to that extent for believing that their reading is correct.

An example of a disagreement of this kind is the dispute between F. W. Bateson and F. R. Leavis over the following lines from *The Dunciad*. This is Pope's portrait of the university graduate who goes in for politics and soon becomes a devotee of the goddess Dullness:

> From priest-craft happily set free
> Lo! ev'ry finished son returns to thee:
> First slave to words, then vassal to a name,
> Then dupe to party; child and man the same;
> Bounded by nature, narrow'd still by art,
> A trifling head and a contracted heart.
>
> (Book IV, ll. 499–504)

Bateson is unimpressed:

How is it that Pope, a master of language if ever there was one, has used his concrete terms with so little precision? In these lines, 'slave', 'vassal' and 'dupe' are virtually interchangeable. And so are 'bounded', 'narrow'd' and 'contracted'.   ('The function of criticism at the present time', p. 12)

Bateson's argument is directed both against Pope and against Leavis, who finds these lines superb. Leavis replies:

Words should be servants – the servants of thought and of the thinker; the badly educated child is made a 'slave to words' ... Such a child, grown to political years, naturally becomes 'vassal to a name'. The felicity of this expression takes us beyond cliché (the 'mastery of language' shown here is characteristic of Pope): the relation of personal subservience to a great patrician name (and a 'mere name', it is suggested) – a relation substituting for service of Principle – is with special point described contemptuously by the feudal term in an age in which feudalism is Gothick. And such an initiate into politics, expecting his reward for faithful service of Party, finds himself a 'dupe': he has been used, but can command no substantial recognition from

'Int'rest that waves on parti-coloured wings'. 'Vassal' and 'dupe' express quite different relations, and a moment's thought will show that they cannot be interchanged.

('The responsible critic or the function of criticism at any time', p. 171)

If it seems far more likely that Leavis is right than Bateson, this is because of what is implied by each of the two readings. If Bateson is right, then we must assume that not only 'slave' and 'vassal' are synonymous here but 'dupe' as well; that Pope was thinking only of the need to avoid repetition when he used them; that the subtly interrelated meanings of which Leavis speaks are merely the creation of a modern reader's ingenuity and their seeming appropriateness within the context of *The Dunciad* as a whole merely coincidental. All this is possible but not likely.

Appeals to common usage have the advantage that they lend themselves to probability tests of a fairly simple kind. The fact that they are not more often made and that literary criticism remains a field of seemingly endless and unresolvable conflict requires, then, some explanation. One explanation (mundane but, unfortunately, obvious) is that critics and academic students of literature are under far less pressure to resolve their differences than are natural scientists on whose discoveries the progress of technology and medicine depends. Genuine debate on differences of interpretation is, unfortunately, rare even in the columns of *The Times Literary Supplement*. A strikingly new approach is preferred, generally, to the detailed and circumstantial defence of an interpretation already made. Another explanation (for which no one is to blame) lies in the *difficulty*, usually, of knowing where interpretations differ, that is, of relating a general disagreement to a particular turn of phrase, or of knowing even *whether* they differ, in the sense of being mutually incompatible. Two readings of the same passage may be so dissimilar that the reader who doesn't look at the passage itself may assume that he is being told about two different writers. The commentary on *Le Cid*, published in the name of the French Academy soon after the play appeared, has little in common with that of a twentieth-century critic of Corneille such as Jean Schlumberger, for all the latter's anxiety to read *Le Cid* in a seventeenth-century frame of mind. Yet the two readings may involve no contradiction concerning the author's meaning and intentions and may differ only for the obvious reason that other things about a text can always be said.

No reading is ever conclusive in the sense of excluding any other

compatible reading. This is what I take it F. R. Leavis was saying
in his lecture on C. P. Snow:

You cannot point to the poem; it is 'there' only in the re-creative response of
individual minds to the black marks on the page. But – a necessary faith –
it is something in which minds can meet. The process in which this faith is
justified is given fairly enough in an account of the nature of criticism. A
judgment is personal or it is nothing; you cannot take over someone else's.
The implicit form of a judgment is: This is so, isn't it? The question is an
appeal for confirmation that the thing *is* so; implicitly that, though expecting,
characteristically, an answer in the form, 'yes, but –', the 'but' standing for
qualifications, reserves, corrections. Here we have a diagram of the collaborative–creative process in which the poem comes to be established as something
'out there', of common access in what is in some sense a public world.

(*Nor shall my sword*, p. 62)

However, this way of putting it can be misleading if it suggests
that anything one says about the poem not only lacks conclusiveness
but is necessarily inadequate as well, and that each judgment and
qualification represents an ever-closer approximation to an unattain-
able ideal of true judgment, something akin to Popper's notion of
the progress and logic of discovery in science.

Why literary criticism and the study of literature could never
grow or develop in this way has been suggested already (pp. 58–60
above); and also why the student of literature could never have the
same kind of relative certainty of the truth of what he is saying as
the natural scientist. There is no body of established knowledge
that the student of literature is able to take on trust in the way that
the natural scientist not only can but has to. His confidence lies in
his ability to make observations whose likely truth, compared with
other observations concerning meaning and intention, can sometimes
be demonstrated, and which can therefore justify his believing that
he is the possessor of a certain skill.

3 *But a true understanding of what is written or said does not
and could not possibly imply a complete sharing of the writer's
or speaker's experience; which is why a true understanding of
those whose experience differs from our own, including writers
from a distant past, is always possible.*

3.1 Some common experience is a necessary condition of communication between speaker and listener or writer and reader. We

need at least to know what stopping and going mean to understand the traffic signals. Children of eight are unlikely to understand the treatment of adult relationships in a novel by Sartre. Yet this common experience is never sufficient. Communication (see pp. 28 and 44 above) is always the communication of something new: the fact that we are told to stop here and not somewhere else: the fact that this could happen to a fellow human being, which had never occurred to us before. Psychologists and philosophers differ as to whether we are actually changed by what we learn and grow in awareness (or simply recognise what we have known from eternity) or respond to new stimuli in a way to which we are physiologically predisposed. This scarcely affects the issue here. Assuming that the disposition to respond is merely activated by what we hear or read, the activation either takes place or doesn't, and if it does, it takes place at a particular moment in time. Our impression that we are hearing or reading something we weren't prepared to hear or read is to this extent justified and not an illusion.

It follows from this that, as I have argued already, understanding what is written or said involves more than the sharing of an experience, and that the state of mind of the speaker or writer is necessarily different from that of the person addressed. This has been argued also, at length, by E. D. Hirsch (*The aims of interpretation*, pp. 17–74) who examines the practical and philosophical implications of this, once recognised, fairly obvious distinction.

One of its implications is that the speaker or writer may intend to say one thing only: perhaps to explain the way to the station; and yet any number of things might be said about his directions which are all true and yet express very different kinds of interest in what he was saying: the merely practical interest (which turning he meant), the phonological interest (in accent and pronunciation), the sociological interest (the convention of courtesy he used), etc. etc. Because there is an endless variety of possible valid statements about what he said, however, it doesn't follow (and no one normally pretends that it does) that he was saying an endless variety of things. This is, none the less, commonly argued by 'structuralist' critics when they discuss literary texts (see 3.5 below). It is also, irrationally, inferred from this that since the text conveys an endless variety of possible meanings, no one that we interpret can claim to be 'privileged' in the sense of being the true meaning, as distinct from others which are false.

This last crazy notion has a respectable version, as it happens, in the writings of W. V. O. Quine who, quite properly, in chapter 2 of *Word and object*, questions our ability to know what other people mean and intend and, in this and other works, attempts to construct a theory of language and a method of examination based on what he calls the 'indeterminacy of translation'. How do we ever know that we have translated, i.e. understood and explained to ourselves, what other people are saying correctly? Two anthropologists are studying a primitive people for whose language, which is unique, no dictionary exists. They notice that whenever rabbits appear and are hunted or cooked, the word 'gavagai' is used, and one anthropologist assumes it means rabbit, which it may. But how do we know they mean the whole rabbit and not an 'undetached rabbit part', as the second anthropologist thinks it may: that is, the part of the rabbit they regard as a special delicacy? Since we have to learn their intonation patterns and their grammar, how do we know that they are stating that a rabbit has been seen or exclaiming with delight at the prospect of a meal? Quine's point is that there is no means of resolving the discrepancy of interpretation for this or even for languages we assume we know, except by means of circular argument. ('He is referring to a rabbit because that's what "rabbit" means.') Reference to intention has always, within certain obvious limits, this crucial element of uncertainty.

How we cope with the possibility that we may be proved wrong when we say we understand someone or understand people in general is a matter of concern for anyone. It is very much my concern in this book. But how we cope depends on the grounds of our scepticism; that is, on why it is we think we may be wrong. Quine's distrust, as a philosopher, of any talk of 'intention' may derive, as Hilary Putnam has argued (*Meaning and the moral sciences*, pp. 44–45), from his failure to recognise that any explanation of someone else's verbal behaviour will be made in terms of his own interests as well as of those he attributes to the person he thinks he understands. Instead of two anthropologists from the same country arguing about what 'gavagai' means, imagine (says Putnam) one from the United States and another from Mars. Suppose the other culture has no words for whole rabbits but only words for rabbit-parts, which are of great interest, in any case, to Martians in everyday life. 'Then the Martians might well find the most "natural" translation of "gavagai" to be the Martian expression that *we* translate as "undetached rabbit-part". In short, "indeterminacy of translation" (and reference) is plausible *to the extent* that it follows from the interest-relativity of explanation' (*Meaning and the moral sciences*, p. 45). Professor Putnam's argument here, if I understand him correctly, has something in common with those of E. D. Hirsch, who talks of the 'double-perspective' implicit in our understanding of the words other people use, that is, a simultaneous taking into account of their point of view and our own (see Hirsch, *The aims of interpretation*, pp. 36–49).

3.2   Unless one respects the necessary distinction between talking and writing on the one hand and listening and reading on the other, many common and normal ways of talking about other people's meaning are bound to seem incomprehensible. The idea of 'unconscious' motivation, for example, would be untenable, if understanding someone meant neither more nor less than sharing that person's state of mind; whereas if we think of the obsessive patient, for example, telling himself one story and the psychiatrist understanding the story differently (and in a way which the patient may come to accept) we are not compelled to think of anything conceptually more difficult than the 'double-perspective' implicit in all understanding. There are, however, false and untenable ideas of psychoanalysis just as there are of the understanding of what people say.

One such idea is that the 'psychological' explanation of what is said in the language of fiction or fantasy is not only an interpretation but a reconstruction of the speaker's or writer's intentions in a form which is, necessarily, more reliable and true. That such an interpretation may be valid and probably true and yet in no way truer or more reliable than the text in question can be seen if we consider Empson's claim that in Wordsworth's *Prelude*, the mountains of the Lake District are a 'totem or father-substitute' (*Seven types of ambiguity*, p. 26). The plausibility of Empson's explanation can be seen if we consider the description in Book 1 (in the 1850 version) of Wordsworth's night-time row in a stolen skiff:

> She was an elfin pinnace; lustily
> I dipped my oars into the silent lake,
> And, as I rose upon the stroke, my boat
> Went heaving through the water like a swan;
> When, from behind that craggy steep till then
> The horizon's bound, a huge peak, black and huge,

As if with voluntary power instinct
Upreared its head. I struck and struck again,
And growing still in stature the grim shape
Towered up between me and the stars, and still,
For so it seemed, with purpose of its own
And measured motion like a living thing,
Strode after me. With trembling oars I turned,
And through the silent water stole my way
Back to the covert of the willow tree;
There in her mooring-place I left my bark, –
And through the meadows homeward went, in grave
And serious mood; but after I had seen
That spectacle, for many days, my brain
Worked with a dim and undetermined sense
Of unknown modes of being; o'er my thoughts
There hung a darkness, call it solitude
Or blank desertion. No familiar shapes
Remained, no pleasant images of trees,
Of sea or sky, no colours of green fields;
But huge and mighty forms, that do not live
Like living men, moved slowly through the mind
By day, and were a trouble to my dreams.

(ll. 373–400)

However, Wordsworth's own point of view, years after the event, is no less reflective and questioning than Professor Empson's. In fact, it is a great deal more so. It is possible that if the suggestion concerning Wordsworth's feelings towards his dead father had been put to Wordsworth and accepted in the way a patient accepts the explanation of his obsessions and in doing so is released from them, a subsequent version of the incident would have been much poorer, if it had been written at all. Certainly, the power of the poetry seems to derive (as Empson claims) from the power of the obsession. But the explanation, in any case, explains only a little. The

huge and mighty forms, that do not live
Like living men . . .

are associated not only with 'solitude/Or blank desertion' but with a 'grave/And serious mood' – filial mourning and respect perhaps but, for Wordsworth, something more than this and, explicitly,

a dim and undetermined sense
Of unknown modes of being . . .

To say that the inspiration of these lines is 'unconscious' is merely to point out what Wordsworth is himself admitting. His intense reliving of the incident and absorption in its peculiarities read like an evocation which is also an interrogation of experience. It has, in this respect, one of the characteristics of what many would regard as authentic poetry (see 4.7 below).

3.3   There is another aspect of writing, and especially of poetry, which it is difficult to account for if understanding is seen as simply a sharing and reliving of the writer's experience: namely, the writer's skill in the finding and deployment of words. It would be unlikely in the extreme that all the expressive effects of sound and the particular associations of words in the writing of a poet one admired were due to accident alone, even if the effectiveness is always partly accidental, a matter of the writer's having taken advantage of the opportunities for rhyme, alliteration, word-play and so on which the language simply happens to provide. (The only effects which we normally think of as *purely* accidental are seeming allusions to events or writings of which the writer couldn't possibly have known anything or connotations which defy the laws of etymology, such as my 'fastidious worms' which I though I had found in Dante.) Whether they are accidental may be a matter for speculation, as when one is discussing the many possible senses of 'buckle' in Hopkins's 'Windhover':

> Brute beauty and valour and art, or, air, pride, plume here
> Buckle!

But what is at issue here is whether the poet intended that effect and, as has been argued earlier on (see pp. 40-1 above), this is not a question of whether he was thinking about it before or after writing the words we read.

To take another example from Wordsworth, the poet may or may not have been thinking about the difference between the usual past tenses and the more archaic tense he actually uses, when he first thought of the opening lines of the poem:

> A slumber did my spirit seal . . .

One can easily imagine him seeing the felicity of the alliteration that makes 'slumber' and 'spirit' partly merge into one another when balanced against one another in this way and the spirit seem a prisoner beneath a 'sealed' entrance, profoundly, if unknowingly, lost to the world. One can easily imagine him, that is, seeing this *afterwards* and even being struck by the effect of the alliteration and rhyme in the lines that follow:

> A slumber did my spirit seal;
>   I had no human fears:
> She seemed a thing that could not feel
>   The touch of earthly years.

'Seemed' and 'feel' are easily assimilated into 'seal', it may have occurred to him, and the 'touch' of 'earthly years', though light, sounds in contrast distinct and hard as well as conveying the kind of 'feeling' that cannot be self-induced.

What is improbable in the extreme is that Wordsworth could have begun this poem by calculating, from his knowledge of the various expressive functions of rhyme and alliteration, that he would be able to exploit this particular one. It is improbable not only because of what he tells us in the *Preface to the Lyrical Ballads* about the importance of 'spontaneity', but because of the extreme unlikelihood of *anyone*'s being able to predict this highly unusual effect before finding the words that convey it. The unassuming artistry of the poem, in this respect, contrasts, in an obvious way, with the use of facile devices or '*recettes*': exclamations, apostrophes or the repeated drum-beat running through 'The Burial of Sir John Moore at Corunna'. It is their unusualness that makes it seem improbable that Wordsworth thought of the kind of sound-effect he wanted first of all and then found the words to fit. Even if he did, the finding of the words is something that took place as the result of a process which no one could possibly remember or imagine (see pp. 43–4 above). To recognise the effect as intentional and Wordsworth's mastery of language as real is consistent with a recognition of what is true of all communication and whatever the kind or degree of the writer's or speaker's skill.

3.4 The assumption that understanding is more or less perfect to the extent that it is a sharing of the speaker's or writer's experience is not only difficult to reconcile with our common assumptions about inspiration and motivation or skill in the use of language. It has been one of the most potent sources of confusion in our attitude to the writings of the past. In theology, especially, it has given rise to the belief, professed with varying degrees of sophistication, that the original intentions of the authors of the Scriptures are something we cannot hope to grasp and that their only true meaning is their meaning for us. This extremely difficult philosophical stance (which is all too often taken as a pretext for believing whatever one likes) has its origins in the critical study of the Bible in Germany and in German existentialist philosophy, notably in the work of Rudolf Bultmann and Martin Heidegger. The contribution of neither can be lightly discounted, and since the serious consideration they call for lies well beyond the scope or dimensions of this book, I find it necessary to repeat what I have said earlier on: that the presuppositions I am defending are, I believe, inescapable but by no means beyond question. The reader of Heidegger and Bultmann will find them subjected to a very powerful criticism indeed.

Since Bultmann's position owes much, avowedly, to that of his colleague, Heidegger, it is perhaps best to remind the reader of the profound implications for the latter of what is known as 'the hermeneutic circle', the idea that, in understanding anything, we understand the whole through understanding the parts and the parts through understanding the whole, most obviously when reading a complete sentence. The sentence itself is, of course, part of a larger all-embracing totality, constituted by all that we think that we know. That this totality changes as a result of individual growth and individual and historical change is obvious. But it is the totality which determines our understanding of particulars and which therefore prevents our understanding the words or experience of those with a different world-view from our own.

Bultmann's version of this theory is, to quote his own words, that

It will be clear that every interpreter brings with him certain presumptions, perhaps idealistic or psychological as presuppositions of his exegesis, in most cases unconsciously. But then the question arises, which conceptions are right and adequate? Which presuppositions are right and adequate?

(*Jesus Christ and mythology*, p. 48)

Nineteenth-century glosses on the New Testament '$\pi\nu\epsilon\tilde{\upsilon}\mu\alpha$', which we translate as 'spirit', reflect nineteenth-century idealism; those of the early twentieth century the modern preoccupation with psychology. There are no presuppositions, Bultmann argues, which are less inappropriate to a proper understanding of the language of the New Testament, unless possibly those of Heideggerian existentialism itself, which teaches us that understanding and experience are the same; though existentialism itself can do no more than make it clear that one can understand love, for example, only by loving. It can, in other words, prepare the believer for divine illumination through his reading of the Bible though it cannot tell him what that illumination will be. For the Bible is unique and unlike any other literature. In it 'a certain possibility of existence is shown to me not as something which I am free to choose or to refuse' (p. 53).

This personal understanding, in traditional terminology, is imparted by the Holy Ghost, who is not at my disposal. On the other hand, we can discover the adequate hermeneutical principle, the right way to ask the right question, only by objective critical reflection.   (p. 54)

Bultmann here returns, in a way, to the distinction between the kinds of interpretation appropriate to sacred and profane texts, which Schleiermacher, at the end of the eighteenth century, had denied and in doing so, inaugurated the critical study of the Bible. For Schleiermacher, the Bible was not unique in this way, only the revelation of which it spoke and of which other books could speak as well.

That Bultmann's position is one that subsequent theologians such as Wolfhart Pannenberg have found difficult to accept is not surprising. There is a real if remote similarity between the problem Bultmann raises, if not the solution he proposes, and that of 'indeterminacy of translation' raised by W. V. O. Quine (see 3.1 above). Pannenberg rejects Bultmann's distinction between 'personal understanding' and 'objective critical reflection' and between Bultmann's *Historie*, the bare recounting of the facts, and *Geschichte*, its existential significance for us (*Faith and reality*). Hilary Putnam sees all explanation as relative to the interests of those who explain and understand. As E. D. Hirsch has argued, the 'hermeneutic circle' can be broken in theory, as it is constantly broken in fact, through the listener's or reader's learning both what he expected to hear and what he didn't anticipate, and it is only in this sense that communication takes place at all.

The prerequisites of understanding, in other words, are not the same as understanding. What kind or degree of common experience and interest is necessary for communication to take place varies, almost certainly, from one instance to another and could never be measured or known in advance. All that we know is that we learn from others what we never knew before and sometimes in ways that seem miraculous, so small is the degree of shared experience in relation to the extent of what is said and understood. One has only to think of the response to devoted teaching of those born without sight or hearing.

3.5   Some years ago these questions were discussed in a much-publicised exchange between the late Raymond Picard and Roland Barthes, occasioned by the publication in 1963 of the latter's long essay called *Sur Racine*. The disagreement was one of interpretation. Picard found that, at almost every point, his reading of Racine was at variance with that of Barthes. It was also, however, a disagreement of principle, a dispute over how much a modern reader's understanding of Racine was bound to or could afford to be 'subjective'.

What is disappointing about the debate is that the conflict of interpretation took second place to the disagreement over principle, and Barthes, in the third round, made no attempt to defend his reading of particular passages of Racine which Picard found 'tasteless' and 'absurd', or to question Picard's few proposed alternatives. One may agree with him that Barthes's ingenuity runs away with him when he generalises from a particular observation and pronounces that there is not a 'tragedy where [the father] isn't present either virtually or in reality' (*Sur Racine*, p. 48), though here again it is up to Barthes to say why a father is present 'virtually' in a play like *Bérénice* when one is neither mentioned nor seen. It is less obvious that Barthes is wrong about the 'obsessive, unbridled and cynical sexuality' (Picard's own words) that he sees everywhere in Racine's plays (*Nouvelle critique ou nouvelle imposture*, p. 30) or that he is wrong, specifically, about the captive princess Aricie in *Phèdre*, who loves the chaste and noble Hippolyte.

According to Barthes, she wishes to 'burst open within him the secret of Hippolyte's virginity as one bursts open a shell' (p. 39). If she 'is interested by Hippolyte, it's specifically from a desire to pierce him, to make his language flow'. One may be disconcerted or enchanted by Barthes's poetic prose, the 'baroque' idiom which he believes may be the only 'serious' form of utterance left to criticism and which consists in offering to the imaginative reader a difficult (but not too difficult) code to decipher. But this is not to say that he is talking nonsense. Consider, after all, the way Aricie talks of her love for Hippolyte, whom, like Phèdre, she compares with Theseus:

> Non que, par les yeux seuls lâchement enchantée,
> J'aime en lui sa beauté, sa grâce tant vantée,
> Présents dont la nature a voulu l'honorer,
> Qu'il méprise lui-même, et qu'il semble ignorer.
> J'aime, je prise en lui de plus nobles richesses,

Les vertus de son père, et non point les faiblesses;
J'aime, je l'avouerai, cet orgueil généreux
Qui jamais n'a fléchi sous le joug amoureux.
Phèdre en vain s'honorait des soupirs de Thésée;
Pour moi, je suis plus fière, et fuis la gloire aisée
D'arracher un hommage à mille autres offert,
Et d'entrer dans un cœur de toutes parts ouvert.
Mais de faire fléchir un courage inflexible,
De porter la douleur dans une âme insensible,
D'enchaîner un captif de ses fers étonné,
Contre un joug qui lui plaît vainement mutiné;
C'est là ce que je veux, c'est là ce qui m'irrite.

(Phèdre, 11, i)

(Not that, by the eyes alone, weakly spellbound, I love in him his beauty, his so highly vaunted grace, those gifts with which Nature chose to honour him, that he despises himself and of which he seems unaware. I love, I prize in him more noble riches: the virtues of his father and not the weaknesses; I love, I shall confess, that generous pride, which has never given way beneath the yoke of love. Phèdre took pride for no reason in the sighs of Theseus; I am even prouder and will have nothing to do with the easy glory of exacting a homage for myself which is offered to a thousand others and of entering a heart open on every side. But to make an inflexible courage yield, to make an insensible soul know suffering, to bind a captive astonished by his chains, vainly rebelling against a yoke he loves; that is what I want, that is the thought that goads me on.)

Picard objects that none of Barthes's high-flown metaphors is in Racine, which is, of course, true; but the same could be said of his own more familiar twentieth-century figures of speech. (The idea that the language of commentary should approximate to that of the text resembles the idea that understanding is a virtual re-enactment of intention.)

In fact, Aricie contrasts the inconstant heart of Theseus with the 'generous pride' of his son and, adopting the language of gallantry, exalts the glory that would consist in 'enchaining a captive astonished by his shackles'. Her attitude is clear. She loves Hippolyte and, in order to justify herself, she observes that she has every reason to prefer to a philanderer, a proud hero who has never had the feebleness to fall in love. Surely, it's both an exaggeration and a lapse of taste to depict an Aricie lusting to rape Hippolyte.

(Nouvelle critique, pp. 31–2)

It would be a simple error on the part of Barthes if this had been what he literally meant. And there is no question of this at all. But it is an error too, and a real one, to claim that Aricie's fascination with the innocence of Hippolyte is expressed merely in order to

'justify herself'. At least, it is a claim for which there is no evidence
in the text. And though the language may be '*galant*' and correspondingly formal, this is scarcely incompatible with an effect of
intense under-statement. 'Le classicisme', according to Gide, 'c'est
l'art de la litote.' 'Her attitude is clear', in the sense that there is at
least one obvious explanation of a line like

> . . . porter la douleur dans une âme insensible

or

> C'est là ce que je veux, c'est là qui m'irrite.

But only one explanation? The generally unostentatious nature of
Racine's metaphors (the eighteenth-century critic Clément, struck
by their resemblance to those of vigorous everyday speech, contrasts
them, in this respect, with the language of poetry of his own day) is
such that they seem clear and simple when one reads them at first
and *before* one begins to think about them. This is why they may
astonish us but never bewilder or confuse. But what does '*porter la
douleur*' mean? Literally speaking, it means nothing, and in fact so
obviously that one has to allow one's mind to go free and follow the
associations of each word which, if one does, may leave one with
the impression of a devious assault and something like the effect of a
deft injection of venom at the very heart of '*l'âme insensible*'
(*Phèdre*, after all, is full of images of powerful and swift, yet covert
physical activity). The imagined crippling assault leads to the
thought, almost comic in its vividness, of an Hippolyte

> . . . de ses fers étonné,

the '*étonné*' conveying, as explicitly as possible, the extent to which
the imagined victim would be taken unawares. The question of
'taste' apart, it is by no means obvious nonsense to say that Aricie's
love, however heroic, is also a kind of lust. Picard says nothing of
the line which concludes the above passage, nor anything of the way
in which the movement of Racine's poetry can compel us, we may
find, to dwell (almost whispering) on the very last word:

> C'est là ce que je veux, c'est là ce qui m'irrite.

We can all, of course, look up what a seventeenth-century dictionary
puts after the verb '*irriter*'. But can we possibly say that all its
connotations are 'clear' to us – or what would amount to the same
thing – that Aricie is confessing to feelings she understands?

The reader may still prefer Picard's reading to that of Barthes or myself, which here closely resembles Barthes's, and for reasons which can be argued in terms of their relative plausibility. But this can scarcely mean, in Picard's terms, that

By relying, especially, on the certainties of language, on the implications of psychological coherence and on the imperatives of the structure of the genre, the modest and patient researcher succeeds in distinguishing evident truths which, somehow, determine zones of objectivity. (p. 69)

Nor can we say that

taking these as a starting point, he can – very prudently – hazard interpretations. (p. 69)

The researcher's 'prudence', if this is what he thought he was doing, would be pedantry and a sham, since it is impossible to think of any moment at which one could be reading Racine and not interpreting what one read. To quote Barthes once more:

What are called (if only this were ironically) the 'certainties of language' are only the certainties of the French language, the certainties of a dictionary. What is a pity (or a pleasure) is that an idiom is never anything other than the material of another language, *which doesn't contradict the first* and which is itself full of uncertainties ... Each epoch may believe that it possesses the canonical sense of a work, but one need only extend one's conception of history a little in order to transform this singular into a plural meaning and the closed into an open work of literature. The very definition of the work changes: it is no longer a historical fact, it becomes an anthropological one, since no history can exhaust it. (pp. 18 and 50)

It is difficult to argue against the view that there is no one meaning we can assign to a text as a whole or to any part of it; that is, nothing we can say about it which invalidates everything else we might say. Where the argument collapses and where, without realising it perhaps, Barthes begins to sound like Professor Picard, is in those pages where he goes on to talk of the 'objectivity' which a new 'science of literature' will eventually achieve, based not on particular interpretations of text – this will continue to be the task of 'literary criticism' – but on the polyvalence and symbolic openness that makes a play like *Phèdre* not a 'historical' but an 'anthropological' phenomenon.

The error lies in thinking that a work of literature is *unique* in being open to a virtually infinite number of interpretations and evaluations, whereas this is, on reflection, true of *any* human utterance. An eighteenth-century critic is likely to understand *Phèdre* in a different way from a reader living today. But this does not mean that he will understand the play in a way which is incompatible with our own and which presents us with a conflict of interpretations. He may or may not. But, in so far as either is possible, he is no different from a contemporary of our own. Moreover, and this is where Barthes's postulated 'science' is an impossibility, it can only be by 'understanding' and (if one talks about it) by engaging in literary criticism, that one can be aware of the work of literature at all. Its ideal infinite polyvalence and openness is bound to remain a beautiful phantom of the mind, the 'anthropologist's' report, in reality, merely another history of the criticism of Racine.

We can truly understand *Phèdre* but in our own way, necessarily; there is no other; though in a way – to employ a very common metaphor, which is more than a metaphor, for we are talking of a phenomenon we don't understand – which keeps the past, even the remote past, alive.

3.6 The fact that we communicate, as Chomsky has written (*Reflections on language*, pp. 137–227), is, in many ways, still 'mysterious', whether we talk of communication through the written word or through speech or gesture. What the science of psycholinguistics confesses, for example, that it is unable to comprehend is how we are able to guess so much of what we don't actually even hear; how it is that so many of the words in a message that, in a laboratory, are deliberately obliterated are correctly guessed and interpreted under carefully controlled experimental conditions; how well men can understand one another even when the radio or telephonic reception is poor. A necessary element in communication when it is present, though not an indispensable one (communication is possible without it) is rhythm and intonation, the significant *movement* of anything written or said. A message spoken in a staccato rhythm with long inexplicable pauses between syllables and in an expressionless voice, however loudly and distinctly, will be understood less easily, over a faulty transmission, than a message spoken with a 'natural', i.e. recognisable, intonation and rhythm. And the significant movement of what is written or said is often what first may catch and hold our attention. This is what T. S. Eliot may have had in mind when he wrote:

What is surprising about the poetry of Dante is that it is, in one sense, extremely easy to read. It is a test (a positive test, I do not assert that it is always

valid negatively), that genuine poetry can communicate before it is understood. The impression can be verified on fuller knowledge; I have found
with Dante and with several other poets in languages in which I was un-
skilled, that about such impressions there was nothing fanciful. They were
not due, that is, to *mis*understanding the passage, or to reading into it something not there, or to accidental sentimental evocations out of my own past.

(*Selected essays*, p. 238)

The distinction between 'communicating' and being 'understood'
need not be taken too rigidly (there is no need to speculate here
whether Eliot himself would have wanted it to be so taken). The
communicating is itself a way of being understood, even though at
this early stage of understanding, it may be impossible to explain to
oneself or others or to paraphrase what one has seen or heard. To
speculate whether the meaning of individual words or phrases or
their intonation and rhythm are the first to 'come across' is again
pointless here. They may well appear to us as simultaneous and
inseparable, though when we are reading poetry, the intonation and
rhythm seem to communicate themselves at a very early stage of
comprehension. This can be true not only of some of the poetry of
our own time but of that of a remote past, even that of an age whose
pronunciation we may doubt whether we could reproduce or, if we
could go back in time, understand. Perhaps the pronunciation was
not as different as all that. In any case, as Eliot says – and the observation seems to me of the utmost importance from the point of view
of the history of language – Dante is, 'in one sense, extremely easy
to read'. So too is Villon. Compare the following lines with a version
written in the early 1960s by Robert Lowell.

> Et les autres sont devenus,
> Dieu mercy! grans seigneurs et maistres;
> Les autres mendient tous nus
> Et pain ne voient qu'aux fenestres.

(*Le Testament*, ll. 233–6)

> Some men have risen – are grave
> merchants, lords divines;
> Some only see bread, when
> it's out of reach in windows.

How does one read this aloud? Which words is one supposed to
stress? Where is one supposed to pause? The fifteenth-century
French reads far more easily than the twentieth-century English.
And Lowell's version scarcely gains in coherence by his omission of
any equivalent of Villon's ironical '*Dieu mercy!*'

In successful poetry, the particular choice and order of words and the strong punctuation marked by line endings and rhymes or alliteration and assonance work as a kind of stage direction. Reading the poetry, either silently or aloud, is a matter of re-enactment not of the intention but of a rôle, that of a poetic persona. (The character of the persona may or may not approximate to that of the poet, but that is another matter.) Compare, for instance, the two very different versions of Petrarch's *Una candida cerva* by Ronsard and Sir Thomas Wyatt:

Le vintième d'Avril, couché sur l'herbelette,
Je vy, ce me sembloit, en dormant un chevreuil,
Qui ça, puis là, marchoit où le menoit son veuil,
Foulant les belles fleurs de mainte gambelette.

(Le Second Livre des Amours, iv)

Who so list to hount, I know where is an hynde,
But as for me, helas, I may no more:
The vain travaill hath weried me so sore,
I ame of them that farthest commeth behinde.

It is a difference, for the reader, between becoming the courtier whose weariness is the weariness of passion (it is difficult *not* to convey through the voice the plodding regularity of the fourth line of Wyatt's sonnet) and becoming the aesthete dwelling with sensuous ecstasy ('*F*oulant les belles *f*leurs') on each detail of an exquisite spectacle. How often can one read the poetry of one's own contemporaries as easily or have so many reasons for confidence that one has understood them?

What of the *value*, however, of what we read today? Surely, the interest and importance for the modern reader of Villon and Wyatt are bound to be different from what it was for the poets themselves and their original readers. No doubt. But the idea that they are necessarily different and bear no relation to their original value has no more justification than the belief that we are unable to form any idea at all of their original intention and meaning.

4 *We cannot possibly understand what is written or said unless we understand its interest and importance for the writer or speaker; which affects inevitably its interest and importance for us. Evaluation, in this sense, and interpretation are the same.*

4.1   Not even a modern Catholic theologian whose professed viewpoint is Thomist, it will be objected, will read Dante in the same spirit and value him for the same reason as Dante's own contemporaries. His views of Hell and Purgatory are unlikely to be the same. Does this mean that his judgment is more or less correct than if he had lived six centuries earlier? Or that there is one correct evaluation of the *Divine Comedy* for our own time and civilisation and a different one for the distant past or future? When, in that case, may we expect the future to begin, as far as criticism of Dante is concerned?

'Value judgments', one is repeatedly told – that is, one's own preferences – are no concern of the serious student of literature. The value judgments of others – that is, the phenomenon of public taste – may be of interest from the point of view of the sociology of literature. But the study of value here, it is often claimed, should itself be 'value-free'. Value judgment may be unavoidable and tolerated as such, but as a cynical friend of mine once put it, tolerated only among consenting adults in private.

There are two aspects of understanding what has been written or said which are, none the less, unavoidable and which are normally taken for granted. It is necessary first of all that we should understand the interest and importance for the speaker or writer of what is said or written; and this is not something that *accompanies* his intention, it is intrinsic to both his intention and meaning. In fact, the intention behind and the meaning of identical utterances vary according to the nature of their interest and importance for the writer and speaker. The same phrase doesn't mean the same thing when it is said in earnest as when it is said for fun. 'Help, I'm drowning!' doesn't mean the same when a silly schoolboy is larking about in a pool as when he finds himself in serious difficulties. The conversion of Gide's Anthime Dubois in *Les caves du Vatican* means something very different for the reader who is taken in by Gide's mock solemnity and for the reader conscious of the tongue in the cheek. The Lord's Prayer means something very different again for the wholehearted believer and for the casual observer of religious custom or for the non-believing actor playing the part of a believer in a film. However grim, momentous or trivial the example, there is no imaginable instance in which, without misunderstanding, to that extent, what he had said, one could fail to understand the kind and degree of seriousness with which someone speaks or writes.

This is one obvious aspect of understanding. The other is the assessment, for want of a better word, that we make of the interest and importance for the other person of what he says in terms of our own ideas or sense of what is interesting and important. We make such an assessment every time we take in what we hear or read. If we didn't, we would become the person we understand and cease to be ourselves: an inconceivable event to which, none the less, certain common views of the nature of understanding seem to lead. There are, of course, experiences and feelings which are shared when communication takes place, though the fact of communication taking place at all precludes their being shared completely. The most bitter grief and the most heartfelt sympathy are by definition distinct from one another, and though the former may be possible only through a sharing in imagination of the grief, the imagined grief and the reality can never be the same. The grief of bereavement, after all, has a different cause from distress at another's loss.

In cases where there is little or no sympathy for the person who speaks with genuine seriousness, the difference between saying and understanding is obvious. Yet the understanding, if it is correct, still entails a recognition of the importance of what is being said for the speaker or writer. Hitler's speeches, it is usually now assumed, were spoken in earnest. Not to recognise this would have been seriously to underestimate them. Yet the recognition is never assumed to imply a conversion to Nazi doctrine. Nor is the psychiatrist who comments on a patient's obsession usually thought of as sharing it, or the mild humanist thought to be prone to the religious fanaticism he deplores.

In any case one may imagine, none the less, the recognition of the kind and degree of seriousness of what is written or said is bound at the same time to be a recognition of the kind and degree of seriousness it has for ourselves. And the latter will vary enormously according to one's mood, one's circumstances, one's particular interests at the time, one's state of mental alertness and the passage of time. The pang of sympathy at a beloved friend's grief will almost certainly grow less intense over the years, and yet one will not, when one remembers how he looked and what he said, be any less inclined to believe that the grief was genuine. Yet it may be a piece of sentimental play-acting to pretend ten years later that one feels as distressed as one felt at the time. The Jewish historian may make a deliberate effort to share the state of mind of a Nazi Jew-baiter in order better to understand it, and may succeed for a time if he becomes sufficiently engrossed in the exercise to forget for a time his own murdered relatives. Whether he is fascinated or appalled, he may still, none the less, continue to recognise the genuineness of the vindictive passions in the documents he reads.

The distinction I am making is, I hope, on reflection, obvious, but there are many occasions when it is forgotten or overlooked. And I believe that this is one of the main reasons why so much confusion and controversy have arisen over whether we can or ought to make 'value judgments' at all. For it is easy to agree that one aspect of our response to what is written or said is subjective in the sense that there is no necessary reason why it should be shared by anyone else as a matter of either fact or principle. And it is impossible to imagine any occasion on which one took in what someone was saying without responding to it subjectively, without some degree of sympathy or antipathy, interest or boredom and without some sense of how much or how little it affected one's own concerns. Jones may be passionately sincere when he talks of the abuses of social security or the increasing power of the Trades Unions. And I may only long to be out of earshot. But my judging the intensity of his indignation and my longing to escape are not two successive experiences taking place in successive moments in time. If it so happens that I don't want to go away at once, this will be because I feel more sympathetic at first or at least more patient or tolerant. In the same way, one can become irritated or bored, after twenty lines or so, by a poem whose intense seriousness one continues to recognise, for all one's impatience.

Yet if it is true that, in this sense, there is no distinction between these two aspects of judgment – what one might call perhaps its 'subjective' and 'objective' aspects – there is another sense in which they are clearly not the same. If they were the same, the psychiatrist's diagnosis of his patient would vary with his own feelings of boredom and distaste, sympathy and interest, as would the Jewish historian's assessment of the state of mind of his Nazi. It is, in fact, impossible to conceive how, if they were the same, the state of mind of the person who understands and of the person who is understood could be seen or thought of as different; that is, how understanding could take place at all, or even the illusion of understanding. For the degree and kind of interest in what is written or said would be exactly the same for both only if their experience were, in every possible way, indistinguishable.

An analogy might be made between these two aspects of understanding and what we know to be true of ordinary perception and imagination. We know that the pale disc racing through the clouds is the moon, and yet we know too that the moon can be seen and thought of in many different ways, all of which are perfectly consistent with one another. It is impossible not to think of the moon or to see it in one or more of these ways if one is thinking about it at all, impossible not to think of it as seen from somewhere – from its surface, for example, or from far away. And yet we know too that the moon is not *only* what we see. Seeing an object is never, in any case, seeing simply what the camera sees. If we know that it's the moon and not the illuminated clock on the town hall, we *see* the moon. We see through and beyond the mere visual image. In fact, there is never a 'mere visual image'. When we're driving near the coast, what we took for a grey wall may suddenly turn out to be not a wall but the sea. There is a little shock of readjustment and we literally *see* something different. I'm here repeating what I believe to be a commonplace of psychology.

It is an intrinsic assumption of understanding and judgment, just as it is an intrinsic assumption of perception and imagination, that the object is distinct from and independent of our particular way or ways of being aware of it. This is why judgment is really a good word to use of a process which is, by its nature, only partially subjective, even in cases where one turns out to have been wrong. To talk of 'judging' a poem or judging what someone says is not wholly dissimilar from our judging distances or a carpenter's judging the right angle for the chisel with his eye. There is an analogy too, though this may sound preposterous at first, with divine judgment, in that our judgment of what is written or said is made *sub specie aeternitatis*. This does not mean that our judgments are infallible or that they are not open to correction or qualification. But it does mean that they are implicitly taken to refer to a fact which, if it is true, will always be true. If it is true that Jones is speaking with genuine contempt when he makes jokes about immigrants and is not being merely facetious, then this will always have been true, irrespective of what different people may think at various times of racialism or facetiousness.

Again, if it is true that Molière's eulogy of Louis XIV at the end of *Tartuffe* (in the speech of the *Exempt*) is an expression of admiration for what a great king can do, then this is as true today as when it was written.[8] Actors and producers are, of course, reluctant today to play it 'straight'. It sounds almost outrageously obsequious. And playing the speech for laughs, and making the *Exempt* look and sound like a French Osric, is sometimes justified on the grounds that what we make of the speech now can have no possible bearing on what Molière himself may have meant. Yet it is improbable in the extreme that Molière did not write the speech to express wonder, gratitude and admiration. Not only because Louis had saved Molière and the play from the Tartuffes in the Church, the Parlement and the Court who had campaigned to prevent it from being staged; but because the play, like *Dom Juan*, needs a miraculous ending. Only what is almost a miracle can bring a resourceful hypocrite down and save the innocent and gullible. And it is difficult not to see the intervention of the king as providential in precisely this way. Only the king is able to override the legal processes of which a Tartuffe is a natural master. Actors and producers who make the *Exempt* seem like a clown and the king a mere *deus ex machina* run the risk of making the ending of Molière's moral thriller seem merely farcical. Molière, of course, had his own reasons for admiring Louis XIV and we (especially with our knowledge of his reign after Molière's death) may have our reasons for deploring what Louis came to represent. But this should not make it impossible for us to feel something akin to Molière's veneration, as well as recognising it for what it is. For in the play the king's intervention and his superb detective work in seeing through Tartuffe's stratagems seem only barely possible. Tartuffe, we are made to realise, could so nearly have got away with it. The king represents an ideal but scarcely-to-be-hoped-for possibility. Interestingly enough (though this is presumably a matter of etiquette also) he is not even mentioned by name. If the interpretation I am suggesting of the ending is right, then there are good reasons also for seeing it as yet another expression of Molière's stoic wisdom. For what Molière is calling on us, through the *Exempt*'s speech, to admire is *only* an ideal possibility.

Two readers may, of course, agree quite readily with this interpretation of Molière's intentions and yet differ considerably, as a
matter of 'taste', in enjoying the ending of the play immensely, on
the one hand, or, on the other, finding it still excessively courtly and
unreal. The same reader may respond to it far more joyfully on one
occasion than on another and yet without changing his mind about
what, for Molière, was crucial. Taste, as judgment in its subjective
aspect is commonly called, is notoriously variable. And yet, since it
is indistinguishable in experience from objective judgment and inconceivable without it, its variability has limits, restrictions imposed,
in the nature of things, by objective judgment itself. It is impossible,
for example, to react as if it were intentionally facetious to a work
whose seriousness one acknowledges, though one may find it tedious
in the extreme or comic in ways of which the author seems unaware.
F. R. Leavis's exasperation with the poetry of *Paradise Lost* is at the
same time a positive tribute:

His strength is of the kind that we indicate when, distinguishing between
intelligence and character, we lay the stress on the latter; it is a strength,
that is, involving sad disabilities. He has 'character', moral grandeur, moral
force; but he is, for the purposes of his undertaking, disastrously single-minded
and simple-minded. He exhibits everywhere a dominating sense of righteous-
ness and a complete incapacity to question or explore its significance and
conditions.   (*Revaluation*, p. 58)

The restraint imposed by judgment on taste is not a matter of
deliberate fair-mindedness or consistency. It is inevitable and often
unconscious, as is the part played by taste in determining judgment
and prompting us to see in what we hear or read things we had
never (in the full sense of the word) *appreciated* before. The notion
of taste and the word itself have come into disrepute since the study
of literature became an academic activity. And yet we couldn't live
without it. Taste, moreover, has the advantage over conscious
judgment that though it has no pretensions to truth, it is by nature
honest, an expression of what we really feel, which may or may
not be in a state of anxiety to buy tickets for the latest production of
Pelléas et Mélisande. The volatile nature of taste, when it's not
ruined by a sense of what one ought to enjoy, may lead one in the
direction of true judgment, in so far as taste, if it is healthy, is never
the slave to fashion, intellectual or otherwise. A genuine enjoyment
of Dickens and Mark Twain, for example, in the days when they
were not respectable among students of literature, led a number of

academic critics to realise the falsity of the conventional highbrow view.

4.2 It may be argued, none the less, that a very wide difference of opinion and predilection may be found between those who agree on the importance and interest for the writer or speaker of what is written or said but who differ on practically everything else. A sane and liberal-minded psychiatrist may listen to the speech of a psychopathic politician and agree with the politician's fanatical admirers in the crowd that he is talking in deadly earnest. Yet their judgment of the performance will be very different indeed. Dr Johnson, when talking of the excesses of 'wit' among what he (somewhat disparagingly) called the 'metaphysical' school of poets, took as one of his examples the way they 'yoke together by violence the most heterogeneous ideas' (*Lives of the poets*, vol. 1, p. 11). The same characteristics are commonly singled out for praise today among the admirers of Marvell and Donne. What, if anything, determines who is right?

Before trying to answer this question, one needs to remind oneself that, even if such a state of affairs were desirable, it would be impossible, in the nature of things, for there to be universal and constant unanimity in matters of judgment and taste. And this is not only because some people are more perceptive and some much older or much younger than others; it is because the intensity of one's enjoyment, admiration and interest varies according to one's physical condition and the time of day, and may vary even more according to what one already knows. In the days when I used to see a lot of Russian films, I could never enjoy the much-lauded epics of Eisenstein nearly so much after I had seen those of Pudovkin or Donskoi's *Childhood of Maxim Gorki*. It is not surprising, Leavis writes of Coleridge and Scott, that they 'should have found *Tom Jones* exhilarating...Standards are formed in comparison and what opportunities had they for that?' (*The great tradition*, p. 3). One may disagree about Eisenstein or Fielding but Leavis's general point is, I imagine, born out of common experience. So too is the fact that the intensity of one's enjoyment, admiration and interest varies according to the point of view one is defending in an argument about a novel or a film. One sometimes finds oneself defending something one had never particularly admired, and defending it wholeheartedly, because of what seems like a dismissal that overlooks certain virtues and strengths.

As for what determines who is right, it may be necessary to refer back to what has been already argued concerning our understanding in general of what has been written or said. For if 'taste' and 'objective judgment' are never separate and distinct experiences, they are also indistinguishable in experience from understanding. To understand what someone is saying is not a matter of understanding merely the words in isolation and the grammatical connections between them. It means also understanding the interest and importance for the writer or speaker of what is written or said, distinguishing between the cry for help made in jest and the same cry – that is, the same words – uttered in genuine fear.

We have already seen that the experience and the act of uttering words and the experience and act of understanding them are, necessarily, *dissimilar*; and that understanding of what is written or said may be demonstrated in a virtually unlimited number of ways. When structuralist critics talk of 'open texts' and of the limitless variety of interpretations to which they are open, they are merely attributing to certain texts a universal characteristic of communication.

It would be nonsensical to infer from the fact that there are many ways of showing that one has understood, that therefore correct understanding is never possible or that there can never be good reason for believing it to occur; and equally wrong to argue from the volatility and extreme variety of people's unfeigned responses that no judgment can ever be more than an expression of personal preference or dislike. It is obvious that there are innumerable ways of misjudging and misunderstanding, but then the number of ways in which someone may understand and judge correctly are virtually unlimited too. Deciding who is right is not therefore a matter of selecting from the variety of possible judgments one that is more true than any that have yet been or might ever be made. To say that the 'last word' on any subject has been uttered is either untrue or a rashly worded expression of enthusiasm. The rightness of a judgment depends on the understanding it presupposes of the intention of what has been written or said, and hence the interest and importance for the writer or speaker; and there is *no one way* in which this can be conveyed.

4.3   It may even be true, as hedonists claim, that ultimate preferences are beyond dispute, in ethics as in matters of taste, and that though one cannot pretend not to prefer some people's preferences to others, to 'judge' them is beyond all human capacity, in that one can only speak for oneself in this respect and for those who share one's own preference or aversion. Perhaps this is the point of the warning in the Sermon on the Mount that we should not judge lest we be judged in turn; or what Lawrence meant when he said that 'Anger is just but judgment is never just' (*Studies in classic American literature*, p. 27). Whether one is drawn to this view of ethics or not, however, does not affect the question of who is right when two people who agree on what is being said react to it in totally different ways. It is perfectly conceivable that both may be right in believing that they understand the spirit and letter, and even though their judgments *seem* incompatible, as could be the case see pp. 89–90 above) with Dr Johnson and a modern admirer of Donne. In fact, the judgments could be described as truly incompatible only if the two readers or listeners understood what was being said in mutually contradictory ways; if the liberal psychiatrist, for example, and the fanatic listening to the psychopathic orator disagreed as to whether he happened to be advocating the persecution of one part of society by another; or again, if they agreed on this but understood by persecution very different things; if the fanatic, for example, shared the frequent inability of the violent even to imagine the suffering of others and enjoyed, in this respect, a child-like innocence. To say that ultimate preferences are beyond dispute may not be as good philosophy as to say that values differ because people's capacity for understanding differs and hence even the way they use the same words. But this again does not affect the issue of whether two widely differing judgments of what has been written or said may or may not both be indicative of correct understanding. There is no reason to infer from the fact that they differ that one at least is necessarily mistaken.

4.4 One of the advantages of thinking of judgment in this way is that, if judgment really is like this, then there is no need for anyone to worry because he cannot feel what he thinks he is supposed to be feeling when he reads a certain novel or poem or goes to a play to which someone he admires has responded with greater or less warmth and intensity. One can enjoy and appreciate the point of outrageous and irreverent judgments of artists one is supposed to admire and, freed from the constraints of convention, enjoy that growing confidence in one's feelings without which they can never grow truly keen and discriminating. Perhaps the greatest damage inflicted on the feelings and consequently the minds of the educated by the so-called 'teaching' of literature is the terror of instinctive feeling it has inspired.[9]

Another reason for hoping that this view of judgment will come to be accepted consciously, as well as implicitly, is that it may remove some of the confusion surrounding the question of criticism and its relation to religious belief and political commitment. There is a fairly extensive body of writing devoted to the former, dating from the period between the wars when T. S. Eliot, 'classicist in literature' and an 'Anglo-Catholic in religion', was the dominant figure in poetry and criticism; and to the latter since the revival in the last twenty years of Marxism.

I have no wish to suggest that the debates I refer to have been due to one simple misunderstanding and have proved sterile to the extent that no one has spotted the mistake. The notions of 'understanding', 'belief' and 'commitment' are certainly not always simple or self-explanatory. Some of the misunderstanding, at least, however, has derived from the tendency I have discussed (perhaps by now *ad nauseam*) to mistake perfect or complete understanding with the complete sharing of an experience, amounting to self-identification with the person one understands. Some misunderstanding also is due to the false distinction commonly made between interpretations of meaning and judgments of value, the latter of which, it is often assumed, are subjective in the sense of being neither false nor true.

Eliot himself seems to share or, at least, not to have questioned these two assumptions in his scrupulously argued and confessedly unsatisfactory note on poetry and belief in his essay on Dante:

If you deny the theory that full poetic appreciation is possible without belief in what the poet believed, you deny the existence of 'poetry' as well as 'criticism'; and if you push this denial to its conclusion, you will be forced to admit that there is very little poetry that you can appreciate, and that your appreciation of it will be a function of your philosophy or theology or something else. If, on the other hand, I push *my* theory to the extreme, I find myself in as great a difficulty. I am quite aware of the ambiguity of the word 'understand'. In one sense, it means to understand without believing, for unless you can understand a view of life (let us say) without believing in it, the word 'understand' loses all meaning, and the act of choice between one view and another is reduced to caprice. But if you yourself are convinced of a certain view of life, then you irresistibly and inevitably believe that if anyone else comes to 'understand' it fully, his understanding *must* terminate in belief. It is possible, and sometimes necessary, to argue that full understanding must identify itself with full belief. A good deal, it thus turns out, hangs on the meaning, if any, of this short word *full*. (*Selected essays*, pp. 269–70)

Eliot is talking simultaneously here of 'a certain view of life' and the poetry (in this instance, the poetry of Dante) which expresses it. He is talking therefore, though he doesn't say so, of two different senses of the word 'understand'. A view of life can be remembered, imagined and reflected on in various ways: by thinking of a landscape, say, or a supernatural vision or a formula such as the Marxist dialectic. The meaning and the importance of the picture or the abstract figures is felt to lie in the details on which the mind fixes, and to transcend these at the same time. The view of life can therefore be communicated and shared, conversions made or contemplated (as one thinks about what it must be like to be a Christian or a Marxist) and understood, partially or completely, in this sense.

The communicating through words of that view of life is another matter. The person to whom it is communicated cannot share the experience of communicating it if only because writing and talking are not (at least not wholly) available to reflection or memory as experience. To understand even the words with which one wholeheartedly agrees and which refer to one's own most intimate experience – to understand completely, in this other sense of the word – is to do something more than share a view of life.

It involves, moreover, irrespective of whether what is said is congenial to the person who understands, an appreciation of its interest and importance for the writer or speaker. In this sense it is possible for the modern agnostic to judge 'objectively' (in the sense defined earlier) aspects of the work of Dante in precisely the same way as the hypothetical fourteenth-century reader who admired his politics, theology and art. If it is a matter of judging such matters as the extent of Dante's own seriousness, or the moral distinctions implied by the portrayal of Francesca da Rimini as compared with the Simoniac Popes, there is no reason at all why the judgments should not coincide. If it is a matter of sharing Dante's admiration for a particular theologian, such as Siger of Brabant, the modern reader will possibly miss implications and emotional overtones which, for certain contemporaries of Dante's, would be unmistakable. It does not follow, of course, that the pious contemporary would have shared Dante's or Siger's beliefs more readily than a reader of our own times, for Dante's admiration for Siger may well have been unorthodox. The task of refuting his doctrine had been given to Aquinas and he was murdered after having 'syllogised' what Dante himself refers to as 'unpopular truths' (*Paradiso*, x, 136–8).

Does the modern catholic, none the less, understand Dante all the better for being a catholic, and the contemporary of Dante's even better still through believing what he believed, as a result of living when he did? Of the modern catholic, it may well be true, though it is by no means true necessarily or for any obvious reason. Take the believer who not only shares certain of Dante's specific beliefs and pieties but who responds to Dante's Italian and art. There may well be occasions when, as a result of fatigue, distracting personal worries or seasickness, he finds his attention wandering and puts the *Paradiso* down, while his atheistic companion picks it up and reads with sustained wonder and respect. The former's wandering attention no more implies renunciation of faith or a new interpretation of Dante's intentions than the latter's serious enjoyment is evidence of conversion into the Christian faith. One's appreciation and understanding of a belief or a view of life one doesn't share may well at times be keener than those of the true believer.[10]

What Eliot calls 'full poetic appreciation' could only mean understanding of the poet's intention in the senses I have already indicated. It could not mean virtually becoming Dante, and if it meant mistaking one's own beliefs for Dante's, then it would be 'appreciation' of something other than poetry. It is therefore difficult to see why conscious commitment to or unquestioning acceptance of a view of the world and one's place in it should be a prerequisite of understanding of any writing which expresses it, or why a modern atheist should not respond to and understand *The Divine Comedy*.

The atheist who has understood *The Divine Comedy* or the Bible in this way is someone who knows what it must be like to be a Christian, even though he is unable to regard the truths they proclaim as true in what for him is anything other than a possible, as distinct from the actual world. And yet our sense and notions of the actual world depend also on what we think might be true. The historian, the journalist, the astronomer and the detective see or fail to see possible implications of the evidence by which they are confronted, and are more or less successful according to whether they are more or less endowed, in this sense, with imagination. Hence

the precise and crucial difference made by what is read and understood to our notions of reality itself. Hence too the importance to
almost any government or church of what the public is allowed to
read, and the tendency of any organised society to transmit from
one generation to the next an oral or written canon of legend or
what is known in the West as the 'classics of literature'. The notion
of literary 'criticism' which Eliot chooses to defend derives from the
belief that people should be allowed to decide for themselves what
literature is good for them to read, and that the only authority to
which they should submit in this respect is that of what they accept
as reason. It is a difficult belief, as Eliot points out, to defend. But it
does not (and could not possibly) amount to a belief in the complete
irrelevance for the critic of questions of value or belief. As Eliot
rightly concludes: 'It would appear that "literary appreciation" is
an abstraction and pure poetry a phantom'. To argue that one text
is more worth reading than another is to imply that certain things
are of greater interest and value than others. The atheist who admires
The Divine Comedy (unless, like Stendhal, he admires Dante as a
fore-runner of the modern critical spirit and religious scepticism)[11]
is likely to find himself admiring Dante's Christianity.

The difference, none the less, between being a Christian and
admiring Dante's Christianity is real. At least, it is the assumption
that it is real that justifies liberal objections to censorship and belief
in the critical spirit. The Biblical scholar, however devout and convinced of the truth of Revelation, is, like the agnostic critic of Dante,
concerned with exegesis alone, as long as his subject is the meaning
and intention of the Biblical text. Should he seek as well to argue
the historical truth of the Gospels, he would be talking about something other than the text. He would be talking about not only what
the evangelists believed but what he himself, for various reasons,
believes to be true about the world.[12]

4.5 Understanding, we are sometimes told, however (see 3.4
above), is not a prerequisite but a consequence of faith. Religious
men exhort us to believe so that we may understand and Marxists to
engage actively in the life of our time so that we may grasp, through
'praxis' if not faith, what we would otherwise be unable even to
conceive. This is also what we are told by Heidegger and Bultmann
(see 3.4 above).

Taken in its purest possible form, however, this doctrine could never amount to any more than saying that a certain kind of experience or knowledge is a prerequisite of understanding; and this has never been in dispute. The kind and degree of common experience or knowledge necessary for understanding to be possible vary considerably from one situation to another: from that of trained hunters communicating by signs to that of readers of a notice saying 'Danger, keep out'. The kind of experience or knowledge acquired through faith or the intervention of the Holy Spirit is very different from that acquired through knowledge of dangerous things in enclosed spaces, at least different from the point of view of theology. In the context of an argument such as this, it is the same. So too is the experience or knowledge of the world gained through 'praxis'.

The converse view – that we are changed by what we read and hear – is equally difficult to dismiss. The question is whether there are any constant and invariable features of what people read and hear *in particular instances* which change them in predictable ways, or whether changes in behaviour and disposition are the result of all the influences that come to bear on them combining in unpredictable ways.

The latter view is, in both theory and practice, the easier view and also the one most favoured in Western democracies. It follows, after all, that if certain writings or utterances exercise an intrinsically beneficial influence and certain others one which is intrinsically harmful, it is detrimental to the interests of society and the individual that the latter should ever be heard or read; though, in this case, *quis custodiet ipsos custodes?* There is an obvious similarity between the views of those who uphold a canon of literature on ethical grounds and those who favour, for ethical reasons, some form of censorship.

The ethics and aesthetics of Kant are sometimes taken as the most helpful starting point for those who wish to justify either of the latter points of view, though Kant, with his profound conviction that freedom was inalienable and behaviour moral only in so far as it was free, can be appealed to also on libertarian grounds. For Kant, neither moral choice nor aesthetic judgment are matters of merely personal preference or even social conformity, but a disinterested acknowledgment of what is best for humanity. The best in ethics is that which can, without contradiction, conform to a 'universal law'. In aesthetics, it is what corresponds to an ideal order in nature; and even if this order is unreal it is one inevitably (for Kant) which human beings desire. In the contemplation of the beautiful object, human powers are at their most harmonious and alive. The tonic effect of such contemplation is simultaneously emotional and intellectual. If Kant's ethics and aesthetics still command respect (both the conclusions and their elaborate and systematic defence) it is perhaps because no more obviously sound basis for a rational justification of personal preferences has been found.

Among the modern theorists of literature whose approach to the problems of aesthetic judgment has been avowedly Kantian are René Wellek (*Theory of literature*) and E. D. Hirsch (*The aims of interpretation*, ch. 6). And the latter finds in Kant's *Analytic of the beautiful* what he calls 'the only possible grounds for asserting the inseparability of literary description and value judgment' (p. 101). To summarise, very inadequately, Hirsch's summary of Kant: the common predisposition which is a prerequisite of any common knowledge of objects of any kind whatever is a prerequisite also of any common awareness of the same works of art. There is no way in which we can meaningfully talk of the same picture or poem being seen or read by different people unless we assume that, in certain precise senses, it is being seen or read in the same way. The nature, moreover, of this predisposition, or 'inner ratio', 'can be discovered in no other way than by feeling' (Kant, section 21). 'Feeling' (a term which Hirsch prefers to the more vague and abstract 'value') is, then, a kind of cognition and, as such, either false or correct. The weakness of this argument, for Hirsch, is that the correct feelings and predisposition are assumed by Kant to be those in which the object appears as beautiful as it possibly can appear and in which there is the most harmonious possible quickening of mental powers. As an alternative to this criterion of correctness, Hirsch proposes fidelity to the artist's or writer's intention.

This is not perhaps the relatively minor departure from Kant that Hirsch presents it as being, and he, in fact, argues the case for the 'objectivity' of value in the same essay, without recourse to Kant:

For example, the degree to which some element in a poem receives emphasis in our experience of it will be partly determinant of its structure for us, partly determinant of what it *is* in our cognition of it. At the same time, the imposition of emphasis implies a judgment about relative importance – importance to us as well as to the poem since the poem for us is our cognition of it.

(p. 103)

A more banal version of the same argument is the one I have already used, namely: that understanding of what someone has said is inevitably understanding of how seriously, facetiously, literally or ironically he or she was speaking and entails 'evaluation' at least to this extent. Moreover, since complete indifference to what is written or said is possible only through complete inattention and since attention implies some degree of interest, the nature of one's own interest is bound to be affected by that which one (rightly or wrongly) assumes to be intended in the words one thinks one understands.

To that extent, we are affected by what we read or hear, and the clearer the meaning and more powerful the import, the more profound its effect on individuals or, where a large audience is involved, on society as a whole. The nature of this effect may or may not be something which experimental psychology is able to establish. This is obvious from the inconclusiveness of the public debates on such matters as the effects of pornographic writing. To deny that there can be any common predictable effect is, however, to ignore what is entailed in the understanding of words. Even more implausible, of course, is the view that 'although art and literature can do a great deal of good, they can never do any harm' (Mishan, *Making the world safe for pornography*, p. 132).

4.6   By 'seriously', of course, I do not mean 'solemnly':

'It warn't the grounding – that didn't keep us back but a little. We blowed out a cylinder-head.'
   'Good gracious! anybody hurt?'
   'No'm. Killed a nigger.'
   'Well, it's lucky; because sometimes people do get hurt.'

(*Huckleberry Finn*, ch. 32)

Nor do I mean 'ethically'. The term is not being stretched when one says that Hitler's threats and promises were uttered seriously; in a way too which he would himself perhaps have regarded as ethically justifiable but which the reader or listener who found them ethically intolerable could still, without hesitation or contradiction, describe as seriously intended.

One may, of course, recognise the seriousness of what is being said without being changed in any way by it, without succumbing, for example, to Hitler's magnetic appeal. And one may be roused by the expression of feelings which merely repel other people or leave them cold. Ian Robinson, in *The survival of English*, objects to the interpretation at the time of writing of the English Obscene Publica-

tions Act which put the onus of proof that a publication is likely to
'deprave or corrupt' on the prosecution and suggested that 'deprave'
and 'corrupt' should not be seen as referring to subsequent behaviour but to the immediate effect of any work on trial. Witnesses,
he argues (pp. 163–70), should speak as literary critics and answer,
where necessary, the question, 'Has it corrupted you?' with '"Yes
...Look how it works *here* and *here*. This is depraved isn't it?"'
His account of the farce of calling 'expert witnesses' is one of the
many admirable things in his book, but to 'corrupt' and to 'be
depraved' are not the same thing. The one means to produce a
powerful but undesirable effect, which is what the two brave witnesses who confessed they found the novel *Last exit to Brooklyn*
corrupting were assumed to be saying; the other may refer to what
merely repels, an effect which is unpleasant but not necessarily undesirable. Honest witnesses and jurymen who happen to be immune
from a book's power to corrupt may, when compelled to read it, be
disgusted to the point of near-indifference.

What then is the kind and degree of seriousness in what is written
compared with the predisposition to respond seriously, if we are
talking of the actual effect on individuals and society of the written
word? Those who deny that the written word can do harm and
who dispute the claims for any canon of literary or sacred texts often
point out this obvious disparity between intention and effect where
large numbers of readers are concerned. Yet among the circumstances which explain people's predisposition to respond, the spoken
and written word is itself highly relevant, and where attitudes are
rooted in habit and convention, the signals of seriousness are more
swiftly detected than where men and women agree merely to leave
each other alone. A holiday crowd at London Airport is a less
promising audience for a preacher than his own congregation sitting
expectantly in their pews. Hitler's speeches were made at what was,
for him, the right historical moment and drew on prejudices which
had been made respectable by habit and constant repetition. The
fear of those who oppose the unrestrained depiction and exhibition
of pornography and violence is that these will themselves enhance
the susceptibility of large numbers of people to pornography and
violence.

There is a sense in which any canon of literary or sacred texts
creates itself, for good or evil, from various points of view. The ten
poets and orators of the original Greek canon were not commissioned

by the school-teachers who gave them 'classical' status; nor were the evangelists by St Jerome. Yet the establishment of a canon by priests or pedagogues implies commitment to a particular view of the world or ethics, however narrow or comprehensive and flexible; and the feelings, beliefs and behaviour of a society are bound to be determined proportionately to the authority it enjoys. This is why the kind of literary criticism which is concerned with the question of the classical status of various pieces of writing (the criticism of Arnold and of Leavis, notably) is quite consistently preoccupied as well with the question of the general good of society as a whole.

Leavis himself points out also (see pp. 159–60 below) how dependent the individual writer will always be on the expectations and attitudes of the public for which he writes and how 'great' creative writing presupposes necessarily the existence of a public which is, in some real sense, 'educated'. Stendhal in 1836 attributed his failure to write comedy for the stage to the existence, after the French Revolution, of a public divided by the mutual hostilities and fears of one class towards another and distracted by the cares of politics and business. The society for which Molière had written had not only been more highly educated but 'had been brought to the point at which its members were able *to feel at ease together and therefore laugh at the same things* [au même point de *détente pour le rire*]' (*Mélanges de littérature*, vol. III, p. 431). His own contemporaries had lost, in other words, what R. G. Collingwood has described as that ability to 'collaborate' with an artist and not merely 'overhear' him, which is indispensable to the continued production of any art (*The principles of art*, pp. 323–4).

The ability to write or speak seriously, in other words (for there is no reason to think that art is any different from any other kind of utterance in this respect), presupposes an initial relationship between writer or speaker and his audience, an expectation, at least, on the part of the writer or speaker, that he will be taken seriously in a certain way. Seriousness is, in this respect, no different from humour and, as the example from Mark Twain may indicate, humour (here, pretty grim humour, obviously) and seriousness are often indistinguishable. The conditions which render humour and seriousness possible are, in other words, the same as those which make language itself possible. Like language, humour and seriousness presuppose some common understanding and, as a result of this, the communication of something unexpected and new.

4·7   The impression that something unexpected and new has been
said may, however, have nothing to do, in reality, with whether we
happen to be reading or hearing it for the first time. What we read
and hear is often so swiftly understood that we register it, as it were,
absent-mindedly, while the shock of the unexpected may occur to us
even when we re-read something we have read many times before.
The latter impression is one to which the utmost importance has
been attached by thinking people in the past. Eliot seems to be
referring to it when he talks (pp. 80–1 above) of poetry which
'communicates' before it is 'understood' and l'Abbé Bouhours, in
the seventeenth century, described it as the *je ne sais quoi*, a phrase
which, unfortunately, has become trivialised beyond redemption.
The *je ne sais quoi* can easily be associated with what we call simply
the *beauty* of a piece of writing.

In recent years, 'beauty' has had a thin time, in academic circles
at any rate, and many would today agree with I. A. Richards's dis-
missive account (*The principles of literary criticism*, ch. 2) of what
he describes as 'the phantom aesthetic state'. The study of aesthetics,
he claims, is merely a misconceived endeavour to understand what
should properly be understood as the realm of 'value'. Richards's
own psychological theory of value has, as it happens, commanded
no more irresistible assent than the aesthetic theories he condemned
(see for example Empson, *The structure of complex words*, pp. 414–
429) and it is worth pointing out that the *impression* that beauty
exists, none the less, and has to be accounted for in some way, recurs
obstinately; and though it may be a delusion, is also a historical fact.
If one is incapable of giving any account at all of the impression, one
may be deprived of the means not only of explaining one's own
experience but of disputing other people's attempts, mistaken
though they may be, to do the same thing and to see beauty as a
quality inhering in objects or as the object of a special kind of awareness.

The sense of something that has communicated itself to us,
though we cannot adequately say what, is if not the only at least one
of the most distinctive attributes of what is usually meant by
'beauty'. In Croce's systematic account of the impression, for
example, the primary form of knowledge is itself aesthetic, and to
feel beauty is to perceive intuitively some aspect of reality, even if
the knowledge thus gained is 'pre-conceptual'. The logic of Croce's
system has often been disputed and even ridiculed, and is today out

of fashion, nowhere more than in Italy itself. I have no wish to defend the system myself or even to attempt to summarise it. But in its simplest form, what Croce is saying is, none the less, unexceptionable and a matter of common experience.

The impression that something has been communicated to us but that what this is we cannot yet say is common enough. So too is the certainty that one cannot say or predict all the possible true things that might be said about even a simple and very short lyric poem. On reflection, of course, as has been argued above (see pp. 79–80), this certainty can be justified by the fact that this can be said not only of poetry but of any human utterance. However, the non-trivial sense in which we cannot fully account for what has been said is the sense in which we cannot explain its effect on us as we read or hear it, other possible interpretations apart. The common language tells us, appropriately enough, that we have been *moved* or, to use the deliberately non-technical language of Bouhours's contemporary Boileau, 'ravished' and 'transported' (*Réflexions critiques*, x). Moved or transported where, however? Ravished by what human-seeming power? If poetry can change us by the mere fact of its communicating itself to us, this doesn't mean that we can always explain the change or the difference it has made.

What seems to us a satisfactory explanation, and may well be so for our immediate purposes, is often, of course, an explanation which suggests some new unsuspected connection between phenomena and a whole new perspective and not one which leaves all possible questions answered (see pp. 57–8 above). Leavis's reading of Blake's 'Sick Rose', which he contrasts with Shelley's 'Music when soft voices die', might be one such example:

> Its intensity is not one of emotional insistence; there is none of the Shelleyan 'I feel, I suffer, I yearn'; there is no atmosphere of feeling and no I.
>
> (*The living principle*, p. 90)

or his account of Wordsworth's 'characteristic mode of preoccupation' which

> was that of a mind intent always upon ultimate sanctions, and upon the living connexions between man and the extra-human universe.
>
> (*Revaluation*, p. 165)

'Explanation' here of a quality that has struck one as inexplicable, for all the strength and distinctness of that quality, is not likely to

make the poetry seem less inexplicable or less beautiful. The explanations themselves need to be explained. What is the 'I'? What are
those 'living connexions' of which Leavis speaks? The criticism
does not become a substitute for the poetry or its conceptual equivalent, and the modern reader is not, after reading the criticism,
necessarily in a better position to understand the poetry than the
contemporaries of Blake or Wordsworth. 'It has taken two generations to catch up with him', Nietzsche wrote of Stendhal (*Beyond
good and evil*, VIII), and Stendhal himself talked of being read, if
not in his own lifetime, in 1880 or 1935. Great writers, like
Stendhal or Blake, are often in advance of their time. What seemed
outrageous or incomprehensible to the majority of their own small
circles of readers when their work first appeared now intrigues and
appeals to a vast public. This is not to say, however, that modern
criticism has solved the problem of what it is that makes Blake's
poetry seem disturbingly strange, or the atmosphere of *La chartreuse
de Parme* magical. Modern criticism has often purported to do so,
as when Martin Turnell tells us that Fabrice del Dongo's tree, which
he tends and goes out of his way to visit on a clandestine visit to his
childhood home, 'is a phallic symbol', his fear that his brother may
have cut it down, 'a fear of castration', and the Freudian symbols
'a complete explanation of the character's motives' (*The novel in
France*, pp. 209–10). If this were a 'complete explanation' (see
pp. 70–2 above), this episode in *La chartreuse* would now tell us
no more than we are told by Turnell.

4.8   The insistence that something one has read is beautiful and
the confessed inability to say why is often the best possible evidence
that the reader has understood what he or she is reading and is, if
nothing else, aware of a problem to be solved. Whether we are
talking of problems or mysteries scarcely affects the issue here. Even
if there is no such thing as a mystery, as distinct from a problem,
we can all agree that problems exist. So-called teachers of literature
are, none the less, often intolerant of that inability to explain. The
word 'beautiful' is often, reprovingly, underlined.

    There is often impatience too with the student's confession that an
episode in a novel or play or a character seems 'real' or 'convincing'.
A whole school of Shakespeare criticism has devoted its energies to
arguing that Shakespeare was not a great creator of characters but a
master of language, and that to insist on the one was to deny the

other: a view that has been adopted, though from a different stand-point, by Roland Barthes in S/Z with regard to Balzac.

It is, of course, true that talk of 'beauty' or 'living characters' has, in the past, served as a substitute for thought, and been inspired not by a sense of the inexplicable but by the all too common need to insist and bluster. The worst as well as the best and most helpful kinds of critical exchange have been conducted in such terms and, very probably, always will be. At its best, however, the assertion that a character or incident in a book is 'real' resembles the claim that a piece of writing is 'beautiful' in that it is a kind of endorsement by the reader of what is written which, at the same time, is not an attempt to explain it away; and the corresponding impression, even when not put into a few simple words by the reader, may well be evidence of perfect understanding.

Yet this impression may have nothing to do with the amount of attention devoted by a writer to matters of detail. Readers of Constant's *Adolphe*, in which physical characteristics are not mentioned at all, may not be able to draw or provide material for an 'Identikit' portrait of the hero and heroine, but have a strong enough sense of their physical reality, none the less, to be disconcerted by an illustration which fails to correspond to what they have imagined. This may happen too when one comes across an illustration of a character in Balzac, even if the artist has been faithful to Balzac's own typically detailed and specific visual instructions.

This is not to deny the importance in certain writers of specific visual effects. In Flaubert, pre-eminently, what is seen by the reader is seen nearly always in a certain perspective and from a certain point of view. The image, as when we see Emma Bovary through her husband's or Léon's adoring eyes, tells us something about the person who sees as well as the object of vision. Yet Middleton Murry was almost certainly right to expose what he called 'the pictorial heresy' (*The problem of style*, pp. 78–83), the belief (held by Rémy de Gourmont, for example) that writing could and should aspire to the conditions of painting. Murry quotes from the Queen's description of Hamlet:

> Anon as patient as the female dove
> When that her golden couplets are disclosed
> His silence will sit drooping

(v, i, 308)

and comments on the 'concrete image... evoked to give definition to the silent thought': 'The image is made to rise not before the vision but the imagination'. Even Flaubert's precise and often elaborate 'visual' effects amount to no more than a controlled and sustained suggestiveness and one in which 'visual' effects combine with the suggestions of other senses.

F. R. Leavis too has written at length of the illusion that imagery is ever *merely* 'visual' (*New bearings in English poetry*, pp. 14–16, and *The common pursuit*, pp. 15–18) and quoting from Keats's *Ode to Autumn*:

> And sometimes like a gleaner thou dost keep
> Steady thy laden head across a brook

he comments:

As we pass across the line-division from 'keep' to 'steady' we are made to enact, anagogically, the upright steadying carriage of the gleaner as she steps from one stone to the next. And such an enactment seems to me properly brought under the head of 'image'.   (*The common pursuit*, p. 17)

In the *Ode to Autumn*, in particular, the personified season, while vividly evoked in human terms, defies reduction to any graphic illustration.

It is, moreover, a matter of common experience that the illusion of reality (which is never a matter of developing a mental photograph or assembling a mental jigsaw puzzle) can be obtained from the worst as well as from the best kind of writing, the writing which communicates, as in Flaubert or Keats, the most precise and sensitive visual awareness and the writing which is visually uninformative or, on close examination, visually incoherent. Poems and stories which seem to us, when we read them carefully, nonsensical as an account of what anyone could see, or cluttered with useless information, enjoy, none the less, a large admiring public. We ourselves, though we now see where they are meretricious, may have ourselves derived from them the illusion of reality. We may do so again, if we pick them up for relaxation when tired or running a heavy cold.

This is because our entertaining the illusion of reality (which, as such, is an illusion of visual reality as well) is possible only through uncritical reading, to which a heavy cold or fatigue may be particularly conducive. Our ability to become absorbed in what we read is not merely a willing suspension of disbelief. It is a positive act of faith in the writer and endorsement of all he says.

The mistake of literary critics and of those concerned to promote the academic study of literature in the past has been to assume that this uncritical absorption in illusions is possible only when one reads qualitatively inferior work or when one misreads work of distinction. The critic and psychologist D. W. Harding is one of the few to have noted that this state of mind is characteristic of *any* absorption in fiction or drama on the stage or screen. Since the 1930s, for example, critics of literature and society have often spoken of cheap fiction and bad commercial films as offering 'wish-fulfilment', of providing the poor and wretched with an escape into a glamorous world in which they 'identify' with the privileged. As a metaphorical description of what happens, this may be true, but, even in the cinema or in front of the television at home,

we don't seriously believe that the spectators are sitting there in the same psychological condition as opium smokers in a dream, supposing themselves actually to be in some world of fantasy. (They can pass each other sandwiches or stand up to let someone else get to a seat, all in the real world, though they watch the screen.) It seems to be a case where a vivid metaphor has been taken literally without realization of the extent of pathological disorientation that the supposed psychological process would imply.

('Psychological processes in the reading of fiction', p. 143)

What Professor Harding suggests is that the satisfaction is more in the nature of that derived from recognising a particular desire; one's personal recognition receiving support and hence strength and clarity from the realisation that the desire is publicly sanctioned, that is, recognised by the author and other readers:

What is sometimes called wish-fulfilment in novels and plays can, therefore, more plausibly be described as wish-formulation or the definition of desires. The cultural levels at which it works may vary widely; the process is the same. It is the social act of affirming with the author a set of values. They may centre round marble bathrooms, mink coats and big cars, or they may be embodied in the social milieu and *personae* of novels by Jane Austen or Henry James...We may lament the values implied in some popular forms of fiction and drama, but we cannot condemn them on the grounds of the psychological processes they employ. The finer kinds of literature require the same psychological processes, though putting them to the service of other values.   ('Psychological processes', p. 144)

It is in this sense that any reading of imaginative literature is bound to be uncritical if it is to take place at all. To be critical is to reflect on what one has read, to recognise the quality of one's enjoyment or dislike and the difference, if any, that what one has read has made to one's sense of possibilities. Such reflection can only take place, however, if the reader has first of all been lost in what he reads, absorbed and unreflecting, in the way any novelist or dramatist intends that he should be.[13] To be incapable of such absorption, to find the novel or poem 'unconvincing' or 'dead' or 'artificial' or 'unreal', is to be incapable of putting one's faith in the writer and of undergoing the spell of his words.

That inability to lose oneself in the text may, of course, be justified. The writer may be unworthy of trust. He may himself be, in Leavis's words, only 'superficially interested in the words on the page' (see pp. 151–3 below), intending and hoping to impress but with little else to convey. Here, although the reader's reaction is spontaneous, it may be a sure (and conceivably a trained) instinct which leaves him staring blankly at the page. On the other hand, though the writer's inspiration may be real and powerful, it may be of a kind which the reader recognises sufficiently well to find repulsive or dangerous. The late E. K. Bennett of Caius College, Cambridge, once started reading *Mr Tasker's gods* by T. F. Powys on a railway journey. Bennett was an exceptionally kindly man, and after a chapter or two, he threw it out of the carriage window.

What is interesting, if one wishes to understand the enormous popularity of fiction and screen drama which a minority of *cognoscenti* despise, is the question of the initial predisposition on the part of the reader or spectator to enjoy or despise. 'Commercialised' fiction and screen drama tend to follow predictable sequences of suspense, glamour, relief and so on. They offer more scope for the academic student of genres, in this respect, than the more 'serious' art of modern times. The devotee of inferior art usually has a well-tested notion of what to expect and of what particular kind of day-dream-like satisfaction he or she will be able to find. Often the very paucity or conventionality and perfunctoriness of the information provided by the text can ease the process of assisted daydreaming, when a more disconcerting and unconventional story would spoil the anticipated fun. The devotees are usually quite honest about this and talk of liking a good 'thriller' or a good 'weepy'. In the nineteenth century, the distinction between 'serious' and 'commercial' writing was less obvious than it is today. Balzac, Dickens and even George Eliot catered for the desire to project one's own self-pity, one's sense of immense injustice recognised all too late, the theme of the typical self-pitying fantasy, on to an imagined victim: Smike, Goriot or Maggie Tulliver.

The satisfaction afforded by what Harding calls 'wish-formulation' can clearly be profound, whatever the nature of the wishes,
though this does not, in any way, invalidate his distinction between
this kind of dreamlike state and authentic hallucination.[14] What
Harding is describing from the point of view of a professional
psychologist is what I have myself been describing as the change
that can be made in a person by his recognition of what is of interest
and importance to the writer. This 'change' need be described as
nothing more than the sense of some new possibility, the realisation
that this or that not only is conceivable but can be seen as important
as well.

The sense of conviction and reality is not merely one of the forms
that a sympathetic reading of imaginative literature can take. It is
the only form, however or whether it is actually conveyed in words.
It may or may not be also something one would readily describe as
a sense of beauty as well. Solzhenitsyn's *Cancer ward* is not, in any
obvious sense, 'beautiful', though the much-discussed paradox that
the ugly and atrocious can be redeemed through art may be justified
here by the reader who finds the author's viewpoint not only bear-
able but ultimately reassuring as well, evidence of the ability of a
humane and unassumingly representative human sensibility to
survive.

Experiencing the sense of reality and conviction is, in any case,
equivalent, if only remotely equivalent, to seeing the point of a joke.
And it is interesting that we should often attribute beauty not only
to novels and poems but to jokes as well. A comic situation can be
'beautifully' funny. 'Seeing' the joke, like responding to the poem,
is a sympathetic endorsement of the intention of its perpetrator, an
endorsement which we may or may not wish to acknowledge to
others or to ourselves. The improper story sometimes rouses within
us interests and desires we would prefer to disown. To explain a
joke is notoriously difficult, but we don't normally assume that the
inability to do so is evidence of not having understood it at all. To
explain why one has found a novel or a poem 'beautiful' and
'convincing' may be difficult to explain as well. Fortunately, only
the more unreflecting self-styled 'teachers' of literature will regard
such a failure as evidence of incomprehension.

THOUGHTS ON HOW WE READ

5 *The student of literature is a student of history.*

5.1 From an academic point of view, the reflections I have set out so far can best be summarised in the single phrase: *The student of literature is a student of history.* 'History' and 'literature' are not synonymous terms. Most of what constitutes history has, clearly, nothing whatever to do with literature: the history of conquest and government, of technology and science. Yet literature belongs, in every aspect, to history, whether we think of the work of literature as a representation of life as seen from a particular historical view-point; as itself a historical document and the product of historical forces; or of its diffusion and influence as a historical fact, a profound influence on feeling and belief, comparable to the influence of myth and legend.

The point, when made in this way, may seem so obvious as not to need making at all. And further reflection on the way in which the terms are normally employed merely bears out that, in saying this, one is saying nothing unusual. We talk, for example, of the 'history' of astronomy and the historian may talk of the 'literature' of the subject or the literature on it, distinguishing in doing so between what people have thought and written and the actual development of knowledge and skills. The former is part of the latter but the two are clearly distinct. The distinction corresponds to that which E. D. Hirsch has drawn (*Validity in interpretation*, ch. 2) between the 'intention' of what is written and its 'subject-matter'. The historian of astronomy, according to Hirsch's view, will realise that its development has been due in part to astronomers under-standing what their predecessors were saying better than their predecessors had understood this themselves, and developing impli-cations of what they had written of which the latter had been un-aware and which it would be a mistake to infer from what they had intended. The same is true of the history of any developing discipline, whether scientific or purely philosophical. There is a sense, accord-ing to Hirsch (pp. 57–61), in which Kant was able to say quite legitimately that he understood certain things in Plato better than Plato himself. The philosopher or scientist need not concern himself with the distinction between implications of what a predecessor intended and implications of what they were saying which were, none the less, real in the sense in which those of Plato's argument were real for Kant. Their concern is with the philosophical or scientific issues. They are, in a precise sense, making and living history. For the historian himself, on the other hand, the distinction is crucial and to attribute to a scientist or philosopher of the past thoughts he never entertained or discoveries he never made is to misrepresent the past and misrepresent even the process of ongoing thought and discovery.

5.2   Poetry, drama and fiction no less than science and philosophy belong to the history of what has been thought and believed. One reason we may have for wanting to remind ourselves that they do not belong to a phantom world outside time, or to an inferior type of historical evidence, is that this is precisely what is so often argued and assumed even by some of their most insistent admirers. How often a particular reading of a poem is justified without hesitation on the grounds of 'external evidence' or by arguments drawn from a knowledge of its historical background. In the once-standard *Grands écrivains de la France* edition of La Fontaine it is assumed, for example, that a mere court poet could not possibly have intended an invidious and disrespectful comparison between the Dauphin and the King in *Les compagnons d'Ulysse* (Book XII, Fable 1 of the *Fables*), even if this is what the punctuation and syntax of the first published versions suggest. The punctuation is emended by the editor accordingly.[15] The view that the comparison is, indeed, invidious and the whole poem an elaborately polite and sardonic criticism of the Dauphin and what he represents is not, usually, entertained, because it runs counter to our ideas of seventeenth-century servility. Yet it is possible to see the poem not only as a far more subtle and powerful achievement when read in this way (and incidentally better written on the level of elementary French) but as a more fascinating historical document. With its revised punctuation and gloss, it appears both conventional and needlessly digressive.

The point is not that 'external evidence' for a reading is never valid or admissible. This would clearly amount to a nonsense. All 'evidence' we adduce to justify an interpretation is, in one sense, 'external'. We need to know the poet's language before we read his poem and knowing this language entails a great deal more than knowing the meanings given in the dictionary. The difference between the reading of La Fontaine I happen to favour and that given in Régnier's edition is between the view that La Fontaine's writings on power and responsibility were those of an unusual writer, with a mind of his own (as well as enormous skill in conveying what was in it), and the view that he was, in both thought and expression, little more than an ordinary courtier.

The word 'evidence' tends to be over-used, anyway. After we read a poem, we are not, at least at first, like detectives or chemists trying to make sense of various disparate forms of data. Our reading derives from what we (unreflectingly) assume to be the poet's meaning and allusions. It is only when we argue about our reading with someone else that talk of evidence, 'internal' and 'external', makes some kind of sense. In this connection, my view that La Fontaine is uncomplimentary towards the Dauphin is based partly on evidence from within the poem – the poem, as a whole, seems to bear this out – and partly on 'external' evidence too. La Fontaine is comparing either two of the Dauphin's own military campaigns (see note 15) or his own inglorious campaign of 1690 with Louis XIV's brilliant crossing of the Rhine of 1672. 'External' evidence or corroboration might also include the fact that not all court literature approved by the king was merely obsequious. Boileau's first *Epitre*, read before the king on the occasion of his introduction to the court, is, for all its eulogious deference, a clearly worded objection to the government's neglect of the peasantry and preoccupation with military expansion abroad.

Usually, as in this instance, the disagreement between those who go on so-called 'internal' and those who prefer 'external' evidence is between those who find in a poem a meaning and implications which are, in some way, unique as well as clear and strong and those who see it as merely conventional. Either view may be justified. It depends on the poem in question. But

A critic must be able to *feel* the impact of a work of art in all its complexity and its force. To do so, he must be a man of force and complexity himself, which few critics are. A man with a paltry, impudent nature will never write anything but paltry, impudent criticism.   (D. H. Lawrence, *Phoenix*, p. 539)

A conventional reader is unlikely to notice the unconventional thoughts and feelings that characterise authentic literature, though he may see them when they are pointed out and a good critic may therefore have his uses.

5.3   The usefulness of authentic literature to the student of history lies in the qualities that make it authentic. When we talk of literature as a term of approbation, we are thinking of the communicative power of the work we have in mind, whatever form this may take. The outstanding poem or novel says more and says it more distinctly than other kinds of writing: not in the sense, obviously, that it gives more information, but in that which Leslie Stephen had in mind when he wrote of the 'historical revelation' presented by the *Divine Comedy*:

> The historical revelation is the more complete because Dante was not a commonplace or average person, but a man of unique force both mental and moral.   (*English literature and society in the eighteenth century*, p. 6)

There are many questions the historian will want to ask concerning Dante's Florence to which Dante gives no answer at all. The study of literature is never a substitute for that of other kinds of history, despite the lazy view once assumed that it is precisely this. But questions about an age and a civilisation, as distinct from particular human activities, are questions to which the writers of the past who were men 'of unique force' are specially qualified to answer or to raise. And the reason lies in their ability to transcend the inadequacies which mark much if not most of what we write and say on questions of more than immediate concern:

> As a student of the present instant, I apply myself to the task of sounding public opinion on the important issues of the day. I ask questions, I note and compare the answers. What do I do then but have the rather awkwardly expressed ideas which my communicants have formulated as to what they believe they believe, or what they are willing to reveal ... In this respect, the student of the present is scarcely any better off than the historian of the past.
>
> (Marc Bloch, *The historian's craft*, p. 51)

'Poetry matters because of the kind of poet who knows what he feels and what he is interested in' (F. R. Leavis, see p. 151 below). Such poets are, at any time, rare. This is why, paradoxically, it is the exceptional individual who may be, historically, 'representative' in one crucial sense of the term.

This view of 'representativeness' coincides at various points with those of Lucien Goldmann, as developed in his *Dieu caché* and *Pour une sociologie du roman*; though it has the advantage of not depending, as Goldmann's theories depend, on vast and possibly inaccessible information if the claim that a writer is representative is to be verified. For Goldmann (as for Leavis and Leslie Stephen), only the 'great' work of literature is truly representative and its representativeness is not apparent in its 'content', that is, in the way in which it 'mirrors' reality and gives voice to the aspirations and concerns of its original readers (*Pour une sociologie du roman*, pp. 337–63). This is a characteristic of much mediocre or inferior writing at any time. The great work of literature, Racine's *Phèdre* or Malraux's *La condition humaine*, is characterised by the extraordinary 'coherence' and power with which it gives shape to a historically determined view of the world held by a particular social group: the group of seventeenth-century Jansenists to which Racine, despite his defection to the theatre, owed his origins and to which he returned after *Phèdre*; the revolutionary masses and intelligentsia of the period between the two world wars.

Goldmann's long discussion of Malraux in *Pour une sociologie du roman* ends on an avowedly tentative note. *La condition humaine*, for Goldmann, expresses and clarifies the dilemma of the Marxist revolutionary of this period, torn between the need for individual initiative and heroism and the need for submission to a grand revolutionary strategy. In the case of Malraux's fictitious reliving of the insurrection of Shanghai, it is a question of whether the local communists should seize power on their own or accept the temporary supremacy of Chiang Kai-Shek and the Kuomintang, as favoured by Moscow and the higher echelons of the party proper. The conflict and choice are not merely tactical, however. Malraux's genius, for Goldmann, lies in his realisation of how this determines every feature of the individual life (the marriage of the two revolutionaries, Kyo and May, for example, whose story is 'one of the most beautiful and pure' love stories of the twentieth century) and not merely of life but also of death. Kyo's death is given meaning and in a sense redeemed by its place in the revolutionary struggle as a whole. For Goldmann, Malraux enjoyed a positive advantage in writing his novel in not belonging himself to the communist party or accepting the official communist view of history. Yet its remarkable coherence and power are not, he explains, enough to justify the claim of its representativeness. What exactly, he asks, is the relationship between the 'structures of the intellectual life' which this and Malraux's other writings reveal and define and 'the structures of the economic, social and political life of France and Western Europe between the two wars' (*Pour une sociologie du roman*, p. 276)?

Goldmann himself, regrettably, never lived long enough to press the question further or suggest more than hypothetical answers. Even if one feels that his enquiry is one that it is possible to pursue, one needs to ask therefore in what it would have had to consist. One question, inevitably, would be whether the structures of economic and political life and those of the work of fiction are, in any sense, isomorphic, reducible to and explicable in terms of one another; whether the distinction Goldmann draws, moreover, between 'content' and 'structure' is one that he or anyone else is able consistently to maintain. In *Le Dieu caché*, where the relevant historical information is so much less in quality as well as less complex than in the later examination of Malraux, Goldmann draws a series of fascinating parallels between the situation of the seventeenth-century Jansenists (families of jurists and *parlementaires* from whom effective power was being taken by the King on whom they continued to depend) and that of the tragic heroes and heroines of Racine, victims of injustice imploring the intervention of an absent god. The plight of the latter is, however, in no obvious sense a matter of 'structure' rather than 'content' and in the case of the least convincing of the parallels, the scene in which Junie addresses Britannicus knowing that Nero is almost certainly listening (*Britannicus*, II, vi), the suggestion that *Nero* is the 'hidden god' does little to substantiate the view that Racine's plays are remarkable for 'coherence' (see *Le Dieu caché*, p. 365).

The view of representativeness I am defending here is far less dependent than Goldmann's on such vast imponderables, and on such complex issues of definition, though it is in no way incompatible with Goldmann's approach. The view is simply that, in answer to Marc Bloch's question: 'Whom do you believe?', the answer has to be: 'Someone capable of not only telling but knowing the truth, if only the truth concerning his own, that is at least one person's, feelings, thoughts and beliefs'.

5.4   Some of the objections, none the less, to a history which is exclusively concerned with outstanding individuals are obviously justified. The fate of a people is only partially affected by that of its conquerors and rulers. The outstanding poet or philosopher gives us some idea of what was felt, thought and believed in his time but no one would ever dream of claiming that the only feelings, thoughts and beliefs were the ones he shared, though this was often assumed until recent times. More recently, in fact, the vast increase in the scope of historical enquiry has given rise to serious doubts as to whether we can really know anything at all about the past. If we can, even now, know so little about how people lived, is the little we know properly speaking knowledge? So we are constantly asked; and what is 'history' anyway?

To the student of literature, modern historical scepticism resembles the scepticism concerning the possibility of our knowing the intention of a poet or novelist, which was discussed earlier in this chapter. It has also done much to strengthen that scepticism. How, we are asked, can we avoid seeing in the lives of men and women of the past or in the poem or novel a reflection of our own interests and values which may show us what these are, but which obscures the object of enquiry? How do we escape from the prison of subjectivity?

An answer to this objection was suggested on pages 73–80 above and it is corroborated in what has been written on historiography by R. G. Collingwood and Marc Bloch. For Collingwood 'an act of thought is not a mere sensation or feeling. It is knowledge and knowledge is something more than immediate consciousness' (*The idea of history*, p. 287). In Part v, he develops and defends the notion that if the historian re-enacts the past, he does this in a precise sense, by thinking and knowing what was thought and known in the past, but in his own way and from his own point of view. In his discussion of Dilthey, in Part iv, he takes issue with the view that knowledge of past lives is possible only through an inward experience (*Erlebnis*) of those lives:

This conception of the historian as living in his object, or rather making his object live in him, is a great advance on anything achieved by any of Dilthey's German contemporaries. But a problem still remains, because life for Dilthey means immediate experience, as distinct from reflection or knowledge; and it is not enough for the historian to *be* Julius Caesar or Napoleon, since that does not constitute a knowledge of Julius Caesar or Napoleon any more than the obvious fact that he *is* himself constitutes a knowledge of himself.   (p. 172)

Collingwood's own conclusions lack, possibly, the force of self-evident truth. To appreciate the problems of the past is one thing, and his reminder that historians usually confuse the problems of the past with their own is salutary. However, to say that their solution can be re-lived or re-enacted is perhaps to forget that this is possible only if we know nothing of the solution.[16] This does not detract, however, from the value of his insistence that knowledge of other people's intentions (however one defines 'knowledge') is not necessarily more or less perfect according to whether we feel as they do or share the same experiences and the same ideas of what is important and interesting.

Marc Bloch, in *The historian's craft*, points out how judgment of the past is in no way inconsistent with understanding, if by judgment we mean an understanding of intentions. The historian is not a 'sort of judge in Hades, charged with meting out praise or blame to dead heroes' (p. 139). But, imagine a general on the battlefield:

If the forces are approximately equal on either side, and he loses, it is perfectly legitimate to say that he has manœuvred poorly. If such mishaps were habitual with him, we should not deviate from the most scrupulous judgment of fact by observing that he was, doubtless, not a very good strategist... There is something else. Has our general, perchance, led his troops to defeat intentionally? We should not hesitate to charge him with treason: because in plain language that is the proper word for it. It would be a pedantic refinement for history to reject the aid of the simple and direct vocabulary of common usage. Next, we must still try to understand how contemporary ethics regarded such an act. Treason can be a sort of conformity, as with the *condottieri* of bygone Italy.   (pp. 142–3)

This judgment is independent of what we happen to think of the *condottieri* ourselves, in so far as it is objective, though it clearly affects what we may think of them as well.

The inescapable fact that we judge the past by our own standards and in terms of our own interests in no way precludes us therefore from understanding the actions of people in the past or their own very different interests and standards. It precludes this only if it makes us over-hasty in our attempts to understand and blinds us to the ways in which interests and standards differ. This is as true of what we learn of Renaissance Italy as of what we learn, from the Gospels and other sources, of the life and beliefs of Judaea and Galilee.

Our interests and our idea of what is important dictate what we look for in the past, though not, except in the degree to which we lack curiosity or imagination, what we find. This is why one objection to the student of literature's kind of interest in the past is invalid: the objection that such an interest focuses on literary texts and the lives and careers of men of letters and ignores what can be discovered concerning the condition of society as a whole. *Any* interest in history, it may be retorted, is selective, in so far as the historian has any interest in what he is studying at all, and all histories, even the most ambitious and comprehensive, record a minute fraction of what actually occurred. As the anonymous reviewer in *The Human World* (1971, 5) put it, Martin Ballard's idea of 'objective assessment' in this respect, is merely an illusion:

By any objective assessment . . . the claims of neither Titus Oates nor Tiberius Gracchus to immortality could seriously be put forward against those of, say, Pobedonostsev or Ito Hirobuni. Yet professors of history would be permitted to profess ignorance of the Russian and Japanese statesmen without a blush of shame.   (*New movements in the study and teaching of history*, p. 3)

Not even the most literary of literary students could ignore the relevance of the Civil War to Marvell's 'Horatian Ode' or of the history of trades unionism to *Hard times*, and there is no recorded event in the past which can, in principle, be declared irrelevant to a particular interest, not even the career of Ito Hirobuni. Relevance, however, is the crucial consideration, and when the student of literature ignores this (ignores, for instance, the true history of trades unions and takes Dickens's strikers as generally representative) his particular focus may rightly be called myopic.

5.5   There is one final objection that I wish to consider to the pre-suppositions I have described as inescapable. It is not the only possible objection still left. I can only answer the objections that have occurred to me or that I have come across in reading and conversation. It is, however, a major objection and involves a philosophical issue which has so far not been discussed.

The objection can be summarised, more or less, as follows. There is, properly speaking, no object of knowledge in the sense of something which can be shown to exist before it is spoken or written about. Nor (and this amounts to the same thing) are there thoughts to which I merely give expression and which are there, already formed, before the formulation takes place. There is only what I say and write, a certain *text*, which stands in an explicit or implicit relationship to other texts, to which the intentional activity of the writer or speaker (for in the terminology of structuralism and the age of the tape-recorder, a text can be spoken) is merely incidental and can be dismissed as irrelevant. We neither create history *ex nihilo* nor reassemble the actions and thoughts of the past. We are neither solipsistic artists nor children playing with jigsaw puzzles.

Certainly, if we talk of what is materially accessible for investigation and discussion, this view is difficult to dispute. Materially, there is only what has been recorded in various ways, or rather, the recording itself: *what* has been recorded is, after all, not materially demonstrable and, as such, one may agree with Derrida (see pp. 20–1 above), it belongs from the point of view of the investigator to what is, literally, a 'metaphysical' realm.

Not even Derrida, however, believes that 'metaphysical' assumptions and especially assumptions concerning meaning and significance are avoidable. They can, at the best, he maintains, be constantly recognised as such through an act of recognition which is at the same time one of acceptance and repudiation. (Derrida's devotion to this unending and unendable process of *différance*, as it happens, bears a certain family resemblance to André Gide's cultivation, in the early years of the century, of an attitude of sceptical openness or *disponibilité* and both Derrida and Gide acknowledge a debt to Nietzsche.)

The language that we sometimes think we 'use' has an organising power and a complexity far greater than we can even begin to imagine. This is argued also by Michel Foucault who, while differing from Derrida in many respects, argues that we delude ourselves if we believe that we are ever masters of words. The study of history enables us to glimpse a succession of different 'orders': logical, practical, ethical, scientific and, in each case, linguistic. These are marvellously coherent within and among themselves and form, at any one time, a single 'episteme', a set of preoccupations which enable us to think of the world as coherent and ordered in all its aspects, but which imposes, at the same time, drastic limitations on the power of any individual to see beyond them. 'A certain Chinese encyclopaedia', he quotes Borges as saying, divides the animal kingdom into the following categories: '(a) belonging to the emperor, (b) embalmed, (c) tame, (d) sucking pigs, (e) sirens, (f) fabulous, (g) stray-dogs, (h) drawn with a very fine camel-hair brush, (i) *et cetera*, . . . (m) having just broken the water-pitcher, (n) that a long way off look like flies' (*The archaeology of knowledge*, p. xv). We may laugh at this, but we will laugh 'uneasily'. Our own taxonomies and our own idea of a taxonomy may appear equally absurd in their confidence, when contemplated from the viewpoint of another order.

How, then, do we escape from the mental prison-house that this view of history implies? In the conclusion to *The archaeology of knowledge*, Foucault answers the objection that he, the historian, is attributing to himself a freedom he denies to others:

For you give yourself the whole field of a free space that you even refuse to qualify. But are you forgetting the care with which you enclosed the discourse of others within systems of rules ... ? You make revolution very easy for yourself, but very difficult for others. It might be better if you had a clearer awareness of the conditions in which you speak, and a greater confidence in the real action of men and of their possibilities. (p. 208)

Foucault answers this by denying that the limitations are limitations that he or anyone else has imposed. He does not claim immunity from the conditions he, in any case, sees as inescapable. The order of discourse can be changed but not – or at least not 'exclusively' or 'instantaneously' – through the intervention of 'the subject', i.e. an individual. The objection that it can is surely inspired, he retorts, by a certain fear, the fear that makes someone talk in terms of 'consciousness' when he is told of a 'practice, its conditions, its rules, and its historical transformations' (pp. 209–10). Why such a fear? The answer can only be 'political'.

Foucault's idea of what can lead to a genuine revolution in the order of knowledge and discourse is itself, of course, political; and though he leaves it to others to draw the political implications, it is not difficult to see how his own notions of such a revolution coincide at certain points with those of the explicitly Marxist philosopher, Louis Althusser, whose re-reading of Marx in the perspective of modern structuralism is according to Piaget (*Le structuralisme*, pp. 105–8) among the most successful adaptations of the methods and assumptions of one discipline to another. For Althusser, a society without 'ideology' is inconceivable; that is, a society without the illusions of objective truth which have characterised all societies of which we know anything at all (*Pour Marx*, pp. 238–43). For 'ideology', it is tempting to read, in Foucault's sense of the words, 'episteme' or 'order of discourse and knowledge'. A revolutionary change in discourse is, of course, possible and Althusser, like Foucault, borrows gratefully Bachelard's term, an 'epistemological break' with the past. It is possible, however, and has proved possible in the case of Marx, only through work on the ideological assumptions of the past – there is no privileged access to a true state of affairs beyond them – and by an acceptance, through conscious practical intervention in the world of phenomena one is examining, of one's own 'historicity' (pp. 186–97). The examination of this world should itself be thought of as a political act and, as such, a transformation, *as well as* an examination of this world.

This brief, though I hope not unrecognisable, sketch of three of the most influential writers on human affairs today may give some idea of the formidable authority which anyone who objects to the notions of 'reading', 'history' and 'literature' I have been defending may feel entitled to call upon. In the present climate of intellectual opinion, especially in France and the United States, these notions can easily be dismissed as the superstitions of a reactionary who has failed to keep up not only with Derrida, Foucault and Althusser but also with Nietzsche, Marx and Freud.

The simplest answer to the latter objection is to say that much in the arguments I have just outlined is unexceptionable. The 'historicity' of the thinking, speaking, writing subject is undeniable. We do read and understand from a historically specific point of view, and the nature of our reading and understanding is, inevitably, determined in part by that point of view. This is the point of E. D. Hirsch's insistence on the distinction between the 'meaning' of a text and its 'significance' for us. It is true also, presumably, that to think purposefully and in an original or revolutionary way means, inevitably, sharing, if only to comprehend them, certain assumptions of the past, in the way Marx, initially shared those of Ricardo and Hegel.

There is a difference, however, between progress in the human sciences and progress in the natural sciences, which both Foucault and Althusser tend to minimise. The difference lies in, among other things, the kind of knowledge assumed: the knowledge of natural phenomena, to which knowledge of what people mean when they talk about it is incidental (see pp. 109–10 above), and the knowledge which is nothing more nor less than the knowledge of what people mean.

The objection I am discussing in this section is, precisely, that this latter kind of knowledge is impossible or, at least, so uncertain as to lead to self-delusion if one persuades oneself that one is capable of possessing it. And this objection would be valid if it followed from the fact that reading is so subjective and so much conditioned by the historical perspective of the reader that it precludes knowledge of the kind that can be expressed in statements that are true. It would be valid also if, because the words one uses determine (wholly or in part) the thoughts one expresses, the critic and historian were therefore inevitably falsifiers of other people's meanings and cast in the rôle of *traduttore traditore*.

It does not, of course, follow that the subjectivity and historicity of the reader preclude him from knowledge of the intentions of writers in the present or the past. As was argued in section 5.3 of this chapter, it is precisely because of this historicity and subjectivity that communication is possible through space and time and a realm of 'inter-subjectivity'. Nor, even if it is true that 'thought' is inconceivable without some form of 'linguistic expression', does it follow that we cannot know or say what other people mean.

In order to argue this, however, it is necessary to admit the full force of one of the contentions in the philosophical debate to which I referred at the beginning of this section. This is the view that words owe their communicative power to something other than individual or mutual agreement or choice (the view discussed in Plato's *Cratylus* and by Lewis Carroll's Alice in her conversation with Humpty Dumpty) and that there is therefore a necessary interrelationship between particular concepts and particular terms. This view has been maintained, with varying degrees of inflexibility, by philosophers at various times and by anthrolopogists and linguisticians, among them Emile Benveniste in his essay 'Catégories de pensée et catégories de langue' (*Problèmes de linguistique générale*). It amounts, in its most extreme and consistent form, to a denial of the possibility of conveying ideas which do not conform to the conceptual framework of the language one uses. As such, it is consistent with the notions of thought, knowledge and individual initiative developed by Foucault, and Derrida's polemic against what he calls the 'metaphysics of intuition and presence': against the view, in other words, that language can be seen as compliant to individual intention and meaning. A modest but devastating disagreement with this view is developed by E. D. Hirsch in his essay 'Stylistics and synonymity' (*The aims of interpretation*). It is modest in so far as it seeks only to show that synonymity is sometimes possible, and devastating in that, even if this can be shown to be occasionally true, it means that the interrelationship of words and concepts may be neither absolute nor necessary.

Hirsch's argument is one that I happen to find convincing, but the view of reading I have been developing here doesn't depend on it. In fact, it would be a poor defence of the inescapability of an assumption to say that it depended on one set of contestants being right in a matter of genuine philosophical controversy. Hirsch himself never pretends, in any case, that the issue is anything other than philosophical or that his conclusions amount to a dismissal of the problem. I prefer to assume then that what Hirsch calls the 'conventionalist' view may be right, and that thought is genuinely and invariably at the mercy of the language in which it is expressed. The critic and historian will then indeed, for all their scruples, be expressing their own thoughts and not those of the men and women whose words they read.

This is different, however, from saying that they are expressing no thoughts at all. This is not what the conventionalists want us to believe. The thoughts, moreover, may be thoughts about real events. Again this is not normally denied. So the fact that the thoughts that the critic or historian utter are not identical with their thoughts when they were reading or with the thoughts of the men and women on whose views they are commenting doesn't mean that there is no reference of the first set of thoughts to the second or the third, or that the relation between these three mental occurrences is accidental or impossible to assess with any degree of certainty or precision. This too in no way follows from conventionalist premises, and conventionalists, who are often scrupulous scholars, would be unlikely to pretend that it did. A simple example might be used to illustrate the point and to summarise the preceding arguments.

A mother and father are reading a letter from a grown-up daughter saying she will be home on Thursday. They disagree as to whether she means this week or next. But her birthday is this Friday and at the beginning of her letter, she said she would be at home for that. Not all meanings are as easy to determine as the meaning of 'Thursday' in this context. But the example may serve as a simple paradigm of all interpretation of texts or spoken utterances, whether one takes a conventionalist or the opposite view.

What the parents are thinking of when they say 'Thursday' is (again on either view) different for each of them. The father is wondering whether he should go to a football match he wants to see that night if this is to be his daughter's first evening at home. The mother is planning the shopping and meals. What they are each thinking is again different from their daughter's thoughts who (her parents are strict and old-fashioned Catholics) intends to break the news to them of her engagement to a boy named Cohen. Yet there is no possible doubt or disagreement (the initial confusion having been resolved) as to what 'Thursday' means or which Thursday is meant. What the daughter means when she says 'Thursday' is something concerning which statements can be made which are either false or true. This will be the case, moreover, not only for the parents, who are the people directly addressed, but for anyone else who reads the letter, neighbours, relatives or the nice young Catholic boy next door who has a nasty shock coming next Thursday as well. In the same way, the historian or critic, who may or may not belong to the audience the writer of the text is addressing (who will be reading a poem addressed to mankind in general or a letter from an ambassador to his Minister at home) will think and express his own thoughts as he reads the text and still be right or wrong about the author's intentions.

He will be right or wrong also (to take an example as different as possible from that of the daughter's letter) about James Joyce's intention in a passage from *Finnegans wake*. Joyce's meaning may be difficult to determine and there are many passages in which it may be doubted whether the term 'meaning' is appropriate at all. It it not, however, beyond the powers of critical insight to make some accurate comments on Joyce's intention in writing in this way; and on the difference, for example, between Joyce's manifest interest in language in this late work with its constant ambiguities and puns ('nat language', as Joyce puts it, 'in any sinse of the world') and in the earlier more obviously prosaic *Dubliners*. It is also quite possible to be wrong about this intention: to argue, for instance, that the verbal complexity serves as a camouflage for the uninitiated and a decipherable code for those who share Joyce's own cabbalistic lore. Jonathan Culler is almost certainly right to say that the 'unread-ability' of *Finnegans wake*, 'the violent ambivalence of the work, is not an obstacle to be overcome by judicious translation into an inter-pretative language but rather the mark of a thematic project which determines the practice of writing' (*Structuralist poetics*, p. 106). Not even the most devoted structuralist or post-structuralist could read *Finnegans wake*, however (and it is to this initial claim which I made at the beginning of this chapter that I wish now to return), without making some such assumption concerning Joyce's 'project' or, to put it in Saussurean terms, without distinguishing between 'langue' and 'parole'.

PART III

Chapter 4

THE UTOPIANISM OF
ROLAND BARTHES

(1)

The appeal of 'structuralist' and 'semiological' ideas is perhaps nowhere better conveyed than in the concluding essay of *Mythologies*, written in 1956. The study of linguistic signs, Barthes writes, 'demystifies'. What is 'signified' by language – that illusory 'real world' which the conventionally minded think of as independent of language and as something which language merely serves to reflect – will turn out, after all, to be merely a function of language, a constituent of the linguistic sign itself. The illusory solidity and naturalness of what is merely an artefact will be seen for what it is and its mystifying powers eliminated. The French mystique of wine, for instance, and of literary culture, of logical 'clarity' and of the great universal passions and human needs which literature identifies and celebrates, will be seen in a true perspective: that is, as no more 'natural' than the laws of commercial exchange.

And yet a real world exists. The study of language is not a denial of reality but one of the means to a more realistic view of the world. It is one of the collaborative tasks – another being the promotion of authentic political and social progress – leading to a 'reconciliation of the real and of men, of description and explanation, of the object itself and of the object of knowledge' (*Mythologies*, p. 247). Saussure points the way forward. Semiology,

cette vaste science de signes que Saussure a postulé . . . n'est pas encore constituée. Pourtant, depuis Saussure même et parfois indépendamment de lui, toute une partie de la recherche contemporaine revient sans cesse au problème de la signification.

(that vast science of signs that Saussure postulated . . . is not yet constituted, though, ever since Saussure and sometimes independently, much of contemporary research has been returning incessantly to the problem of signification.)

(*Mythologies*, pp. 185–6)

Not only contemporary research. Barthes could have added (as his allusions elsewhere to the influences on his work justify one in suggesting) the Marx who diagnosed what he saw as the 'false consciousness' of bourgeois and other 'ideologies': those hypo-statisations of temporary class interests into would-be universal attributes of mankind; or the Sartre whose hero in *La nausée* listens to men swapping stories in a café and concludes that

a man is always a teller of stories, he lives surrounded by his own stories and those of other people, he sees everything that happens to him in terms of these stories and he tries to live his life as if he were recounting it.

Roquentin, in *La nausée*, finds joy and even the prospect of salvation from the world of time and change in the determination to be just that – neither more nor less than a teller of tales, the writer of a book.[1] Marx, and the later Sartre, see the ending of 'false consciousness' as possible only through revolutionary endeavour leading to the final elimination of human exploitation and the possession and control by all men and women of the products of their labour. Barthes himself provides, in the name of 'semiology', an academic version of contemporary eschatology. 'For now', he seems to be saying, 'we see through a glass darkly; but then face to face: now I see in part, but then I shall know even as also I am known.'

The prestige of structuralism owes much to the fascination which Barthes has exercised for twenty years on a public both inside and outside the universities and which has given academic criticism the same general appeal as avant-garde poetry, fiction and philosophy. The structuralism of Barthes and of Claude Lévi-Strauss is the obvious successor to the existentialism of Sartre. The appointment of Lévi-Strauss in 1959 and Barthes in 1977 to chairs at the Collège de France was, as is traditionally the case, the official recognition of a new orthodoxy and a reputation already made. Yet Saussure himself, had he lived to see it, while no doubt gratified by the creation of a new chair of Semiology, would perhaps have been uneasy that Barthes should be its first professor. There are at least three possible alternatives confronting anyone who considers the problem posed at the end of *Mythologies*: to continue on the path hopefully indicated here and in the 'Eléments de sémiologie' of 1964; to accept the 'mystification' of language as inevitable; or to see the problem as radically misconceived. From his many candid admissions in recent years, it would appear that Barthes may now be inclined to accept the second of these alternatives, even possibly the third; and that he has now, in any case, abandoned the first.

(II)

According to Stephen Heath, Barthes read Saussure's *Cours de linguistique générale* in the summer of 1956 (Heath, *Le vertige du déplacement*, p. 57) just before writing the concluding essay of *Mythologies*, and after the short articles which make up the rest of this book had first appeared in various left-wing newspapers and reviews. These have been rightly praised for their perceptiveness, subtlety and wit. Together they constitute an ingenious *Dictionnaire des idées reçues* of the early 1950s, far richer than Flaubert's *sottisier* of the century before. And they now have, for all their acerbity, and more than any novel of the time, a strong period flavour for anyone who lived in France at that time. But they are a contribution to a 'science of signs' only in the most general (and least scientific) sense of the term. Clichés of thought and feeling are shown to be such by reference to the intention that, presumably, dictates their use. We are shown, in other words, what people *really meant* when they told us that the child Minou Drouet had 'natural' poetic genius; or that France was 'afflicted by an over-production of. . .economists, philosophers and other dreamers' who had 'lost all contact with the real world' (Pierre Poujade); or that General de Castries ordered a steak with chipped potatoes after the armistice ending French rule in Indo-China. The mystique of *le bifteck et frites* ('the alimentary sign of Frenchness') is, of course, lost in translation.

How, though, does one escape from mystification and cliché? *Can* one escape? This certainly is a problem with which Barthes has never ceased to wrestle, and to which the 'science of signs', for a number of years, seemed to offer an eventual solution. The victim of mystification may or may not confess that he has failed to see the full implications of the words and images that had held him under this spell. The patriotic Frenchman, for example, may readily agree with Barthes's account of the biological and moral connotations of the terminology associated with the favourite national dish, and claim that General de Castries's *frites* made not only a good meal but an excellent gesture as well, in the best military French tradition; whereas the police inspector who used elaborate literary prose in the course of his testimony against Gaston Dominici may not have

wanted to admit to others or himself that he was less concerned
with the truth than with playing to the public gallery.[2] Mystification
takes place where there is an incompatibility between what the
speaker or listener says or understands and what he thinks he says
or understands (see pp. 47–9) above). Where there is no such incompatibility, one must conclude either that there is no mystification
at all or that it is due to something else: ignorance, for example, of
all the possible implications of what one says or believes that one
understands.

An example of the latter, for Barthes, is the use of tautology: '*Le
théâtre, c'est le théâtre*', '*Racine, c'est Racine*', '*Un sou, c'est un
sou.*' In tautology

On peut voir ... l'une de ces conduites magiques dont Sartre s'est occupé
dans son *Esquisse d'une théorie des émotions*: on se réfugie dans la tautologie
comme dans la peur, ou la colère, ou la tristesse, quand on est à court
d'explication.

(One can see ... one of those magical modes of conduct with which Sartre is
concerned in his *Sketch for a theory of the emotions*: one takes refuge in
tautology as in fear, or anger or sadness when one is short of an explanation.)

(*Mythologies*, p. 240)

Yet literary criticism too, he confesses in an article of 1963, is ultimately tautological:

La 'preuve' d'une critique n'est pas d'ordre 'aléthique' (elle ne relève pas de
la vérité), car le discours critique – comme d'ailleurs le discours logique – n'est
jamais que tautologique: il consiste finalement à dire avec retard, mais en se
plaçant tout entier dans ce retard, qui par là même n'est pas insignifiant:
Racine, c'est Racine, Proust, c'est Proust; la 'preuve' critique, si elle existe,
dépend d'une aptitude, non à *découvrir* l'œuvre interrogée, mais au contraire
à la *couvrir* le plus complètement possible par son propre langage.

(The 'proof' of a criticism is never that of an 'alethic' order (it is not dependent on truth), for critical discourse – like logical discourse, for that matter –
is only ever tautological: it amounts ultimately to saying, with some delay, but
by placing itself entirely in this delay, which is thereby by no means insignifi-
cant: Racine is Racine, Proust is Proust; critical 'proof', if it exists, depends
on an aptitude not for *discovering* the work in question, but, on the contrary,
for *covering* it as completely as possible by means of its own language.)

(*Essais critiques*, p. 256)

One could spend some time profitably discussing the logic of this
argument or, rather, the way in which Barthes uses words: his fondness for the legislative 'all' or 'never', for example, his ostensible

precision (critical discourse, we are told on the previous page, 'inte-
grates' the language of the text in question in a way 'exactly'
resembling integration in the mathematical sense of the term) and
his gift for recasting or at least seeming to recast concepts by an
ingenious exploitation of etymologies and play on words.[3] The
definition of criticism is, to say the least, equivocal. Is the 'delay'
here an escape from tautology or not? The answer is presumably
both yes and no, that is some kind of 'neither' or 'both' sustained
by some implied dialectical tension. What emerges from the essay,
none the less, is a view of criticism which is unremarkable in its
claims. The criticism of the 1960s is not, we are told, better in-
formed or necessarily more perceptive than that of a century or three
centuries before. The criterion of its success is fidelity to a text and,
at the same time, its capacity for using a language which embodies
the interests of the critic and his readers.

This unambitious and unexceptionable view is in contrast, however, with the claims elaborated for semiology in the essay already
referred to in *Mythologies*, in the long article of 1966, 'L'analyse
structurale des récits', and in *Système de la mode* (1967); or for a
'scientific' 'anthropology' of the reading of literary texts in *Critique
et vérité* (1966). These writings belong to the period later referred
to in the quasi-autobiographical *Roland Barthes par Roland Barthes*
(1975):

A l'origine de l'œuvre, l'opacité des rapports sociaux, la fausse Nature; la
première secousse est donc de démystifier (*Mythologies*); puis la démystification
s'immobilisant dans une répétition, c'est elle qu'il faut déplacer: la *science*
sémiologique (postulée alors) tente d'ébranler, de vivifier, d'armer le geste, la
pose mythologique, en lui donnant une méthode; cette science à son tour
s'embarasse de tout un imaginaire: au vœu d'une science sémiologique succède
la science (souvent fort triste) des sémiologues.

(At the origin of his work, the opacity of social relationships, the false Nature;
the first attempt to shake himself free is therefore an exercise in demystification (*Mythologies*); then demystification itself becoming immobilised through
repetition, it is this which has to be displaced: semiological *science* (then
postulated) seeks to undermine, to vivify, to arm the gesture, the mythological
pose by giving it a method; though this science in its turn becomes confused
with a whole realm of the imaginary: the hopes of a semiological science give
way to the (often dismal) science of the semiologists themselves.)

(p. 75)

'Eléments de sémiologie' is a detailed exposition of the method
and terminology developed in Saussure's *Cours de linguistique*

générale and of subsequent qualifications and developments as these would appear to a student of the subject in 1964 shortly before the publication of the writings in which Emile Benveniste, from the point of view of linguistics, and Jacques Derrida from that of philosophy questioned certain of Saussure's fundamental tenets (see pp. 16 and 20 above).[4] The examples used to illustrate Saussure's terms, for instance the two orders of the 'syntagmatic' (the actual sequence of linguistic units) and the 'paradigmatic' (the category to which each unit belongs); or of *'langue'* (language conceived as virtual and available) and *'parole'* (language in use); of metaphor and metonymy; and of the triad of the sign which is at the same time 'signifier' and 'signified', as distinct from 'referent', are all taken from the cinema, from psychoanalysis and the culinary arts rather than from literature. The student of literature for whom the book is primarily intended is thus left in the suspense of which Barthes is master. Examples are also taken, as in the densely analytical *Système de la mode* (an application of semiology), from the world of fashion and fashion magazines.

That costume, irrespective of sex, age, class or climate, constitutes a kind of language is obvious as soon as it is pointed out. There is probably no more ingenious and plausible interpretation of 'vestimentary codes', to use Barthes's own term, than Thorstein Veblen's account, in *The theory of the leisure class* of 1899, of various forms of barbaric display in China, Africa and the drawing-rooms of nineteenth-century London and New York. The question, of course, is *what* kind of language or code; and in answering this, Barthes himself, it has to be said, only creates confusion. The notion that costume is susceptible to the same forms of analysis and description as the sound system of a language or its semantics is, on the face of it, so preposterous that one is bound to ask how the notion could ever seem plausible. The idea that 'symbolic rites, the forms of politeness, military signals, etc. etc.' are comparable to (that is, presumably, isomorphic with) the written and spoken language originates in Saussure (*Corps de linguistique générale*, p. 25); and according to Barthes, the specific notion of a semantics of costume in Trubetzkoy's *Principes de phonologie* (p. 19). There may, of course, also be a deep satisfaction to be gained from reducing all sets of conventions, including, by anticipation, those of literature itself, to the same level of significance and revealing in each the same degree of complexity. Without using the word, it is clear that Barthes regards the world of fashion, as revealed by *Le Jardin des Modes* and by *Elle*, as no less barbaric than it had appeared earlier to Veblen. Its elevation to a subject worthy of academic study might be taken as implying a corresponding devaluation of all the other cultural artefacts which have traditionally featured in programmes of liberal education.

Whatever the motivation and appeal of the exercise, however, one can see now that it was possible to pursue it to such lengths only because of the respectability, during the 1950s and 60s, of a certain view of linguistics, which Barthes was later to abandon and which is discussed at length on pages 12–19 above: a certain view of linguistics and a certain view of science. Fundamental, it is commonly assumed, to any systematic enquiry is the definition of terms, the recognition of hypotheses and working assumptions. Yet this, it turns out, is for Barthes not so much a means as an end:

> Quant au classement linguistique, sans doute mieux approprié au vêtement écrit, il fait malheureusement défaut; la lexicologie n'a proposé que des groupements idéologiques (champs notionnels), et la sémantique proprement dite n'a pu encore établir les listes structurales de lexèmes.

> (As for the linguistic classification most appropriate to the item of clothing as written, it is unfortunately not yet to be found; lexicology has offered only ideological groupings (notional fields) and semantics, properly speaking, has not yet been able to establish the structural lists of lexemes.)
>
> (*Système de la mode*, p. 113)

The system of classification we are offered is therefore alphabetical, with the justification that a more 'natural' or 'rational' set of categories could be justified only on 'partial, in fact ideological grounds'.

The absence of an appropriate classification is revealing; clearly, the Saussurean vision of a 'vast science of signs not yet constituted' still lies at the heart of Barthes's thinking and writing in *Système de la mode*. Revealing too is the notion of a system of classification that would not be 'partial' or 'ideological': that would not, in other words, derive from anything so unreliable as a mere human belief. Science thus conceived resembles far more the all-embracing positivism of Comte (whose postulated benefits included also a future reorganisation of society) than experimental science as normally understood today. A system of classification which is merely provisional, and which the practising scientist commonly regards as such, is altogether different from one which has not yet even been formed.

The point is made, in effect, though Barthes's work is not mentioned, in the essay of 1969, 'Sémiologie de la langue', in which Benveniste questions the programme of study elaborated by Saussure:

How can linguistics delimit and define itself except by delimiting and defining its own object, which is language? But can it then fulfil its two other tasks, which we are told are the first it has to execute, the description and the history of languages?   (*Problèmes de linguistique générale II*, p. 46)

Benveniste also, in the same essay, distinguishes between languages and codes of different kinds and points out the unique distinguishing features of any natural spoken language. In no other system of signs, he argues, is there any equivalent of the two 'levels' on which the spoken language operates, simultaneously and necessarily. In no other system is there an equivalent of the organisation on one level of a finite number of phonemes into morphemes or lexemes and thereby into sentences which, on their own level of significance, have a virtually infinite variety and scope of reference.

The distinction between the two levels, that of the 'semiotic' and the 'semantic', is the one previously made in the major essay of 1964 on 'Les niveaux de l'analyse linguistique', which is also concerned with the terminology and assumptions appropriate to each. Since Benveniste's account goes to the heart of the issue, I hope I will be forgiven if I quote his actual words once again:

The phonemes, morphemes, words (lexemes) can be counted; they are finite in number. Sentences are not.

The phonemes, morphemes, words (lexemes) have a certain distribution on their respective levels and a certain function on a higher level. Sentences have neither distribution nor function.

An inventory of the different uses of a word might never end; an inventory of the different uses of a sentence couldn't even begin.

The sentence, which is a matter of indefinite creation and limitless variety, is the very life of a functioning language. We can conclude then that, with the sentence, we leave the domain of language as a system of signs and enter another world, that of language as an instrument of communication, whose expression is discourse.   (*Problèmes de linguistique générale*, pp. 129–30)

To attempt to describe and analyse one of these domains in the language appropriate to the other is to attempt the impossible. On the 'categorematic' level (from the Greek *katēgorēma*, 'predicate') there is no equivalent of the 'concrete phonemes' which can be 'isolated, combined, enumerated':

Is there even such a thing as a categoreme? The predicate is a fundamental property of the sentence, it is not one of the units of a sentence. There are not many different kinds of predication. And nothing would be changed in this account of things if for the word 'categoreme' the word 'phraseme' was used instead.   (*Problèmes de linguistique générale*, p. 129)

What is said here of the would-be 'phraseme' could be said also, presumably, of the 'gustemes' of Lévi-Strauss and the 'vestemes' of *Système de la mode*.[5]

The distinctions drawn in Benveniste's essay are so unambiguous that it is extraordinary to see the same essay referred to by Barthes in justification of the view that

what is most reasonable is to postulate a homological relationship between the sentence and discourse as a whole in so far as the same formal organisation most probably governs all semiotic systems, whatever their substance and dimensions.   (p. 11)

This is said in the essay, 'Analyse structurale des récits', of 1966 (reproduced in *Poétique du récit*, 1977), and it is this essay which carries Barthes furthest in the direction of a systematic semiological account of literature.[6] The fact that it is a James Bond story, *Goldfinger*, which receives the appropriate attention rather than a novel by Flaubert or Stendhal, lends it what may seem like the same ominous or exhilarating purificatory detachment as *Système de la mode*.

Commercial fiction, of course, like folk-tales or children's stories, obeys the dictates of genre far more readily than those works which (since Flaubert and Stendhal and increasingly as the notion of a distinctive 'highbrow' literature has developed) have owed their success to their power to disconcert. The reader of *Goldfinger* expects James Bond to be in constant danger of death, but is confident that he will escape by inches; that he will succumb gloriously to temptation and emerge with his virility and *sang-froid* unimpaired. It is scarcely surprising therefore if the organisation of the narrative should fall into the categories neatly provided by Barthes: the episodes in the swimming-pool and at Fort Knox having no 'sequential' relation to one another but being related on the level of action to the extent that the characters are the same, 'one can recognise here the epic (a collection of multiple fables)' ('Analyse structurale des récits', p. 32). What is absurd (though it may also seem attractive) is to see this arrangement of levels as corresponding to some other necessity than that of convention and the expectations of a particular public. This is not to deny the psychological or social interest of these conventions and expectations (which Barthes ignores). The absurdity lies in the view that a narrative, however conventional, could correspond to the same *kind* of necessity as the phonemes that make up a sentence.

It is, in fact, a disservice to Barthes to dwell at any length on his attempts at systematic analysis during this period. Unfortunately, though he has never pursued them any further and has expressed some distaste for them since (see p. 137 above), he has never formally repudiated them, and they continue to be reprinted. This is true both of the experiments in semiology and of the projected 'anthropology' of different readings of literature which in *Sur Racine* and *Critique et vérité* are proposed as a ('scientific') alternative to literary criticism. Here too it is the demon of legislation and reform by which Barthes is carried away, and both books are enlivened by suggestions of work to be done,[7] complaints of the still unaccountably backward state of literary scholarship and visions of a future synthesis of learning. His reputation as a stimulating supervisor of research is obviously well deserved.

'Objectivity' and an authentically 'scientific' view of literature, Barthes contends, can be achieved on two levels: on the first by a return to the forgotten arts of rhetoric and by the integration of these within the programme of semiology (*Critique et vérité*, pp. 61–3); on the second, the 'anthropological' level, by a study of all the meanings which have been found in the same work of literature over the years or centuries or, in other words, the 'myths' to which it has given rise (*Critique et vérité*, pp. 49–56): 'one can propose to call *science of literature* (or *écriture*) that general discourse whose object is not such and such a meaning but the very plurality of the meanings of a work, and *literary criticism* that other discourse which assumes openly, at its own risk, the intention of giving a particular meaning to the work' (p. 56). From the point of view of this 'science', all interpretations of meaning and significance are valid, even Professor Jasinski's claim that Andromaque is the actress Du Parc and 'therefore' Pyrrhus is Racine (*Sur Racine*, p. 164). 'Of all the studies I have quoted', Barthes writes, having mentioned most of the living critics of Racine, 'I dispute none. I can even say that, for their different qualities, I admire them all' (pp. 166–7).

That 'proposed' study of the different interpretations of Racine is not something, needless to say, that Barthes has undertaken himself, or rather not something on which he has wasted his time. Unless conducted from a candidly critical point of view, as in Mario Fubini's long out of date but still illuminating *Racine e la critica*, it is difficult to see how it could be anything other than the dreariest kind of academic history, and how even then it could escape from the danger of bias and misrepresentation by the fallible historian. As for the notion that semiology will yield 'analyses which are *certain*' (*Critique et vérité*, p. 62), and all the more certain for their implying no reference at all to the author's intention (pp. 59–63), the hope, for reasons which have been suggested by Derrida and Benveniste, and subsequently Barthes himself, is without foundation.

(III)

The abandonment of such a hope is recorded laconically in an autobiographical note a few years later:

au vœu d'une science sémiologique succède la science (souvent fort triste) des sémiologues; il faut donc s'en couper, introduire, dans cet imaginaire raisonnable, le grain du désir, la revendication du corps; c'est alors le Texte, la théorie du Texte.

(the hopes of a semiological science give way to the (often dismal) science of the semiologists themselves; so he must break free from it, introduce into this all too reasonable realm of the imaginary, the grain of desire, the claims of the body: so now the Text, the theory of the Text.)

(*Roland Barthes par Roland Barthes*, p. 75)

The theory of the 'text', as elaborated in *S/Z* of 1970 and *Le plaisir du texte* of 1973, derives partly from Derrida's critique of Saussure and his theory of *écriture* (put crudely, the notion that 'writing' and 'speech' are very different manifestations of language, the former patently independent of the controls and answerability of the speaker), partly too from the synthesis of linguistics and psychoanalysis elaborated by Jacques Lacan. Lacan's thought is too diffuse and subtle to be characterised much more precisely than this; but, like the phenomenology of Sartre, it seeks to identify the 'physical' with the 'psychic', the image and sign with the manifestations of need and desire. The following passage from Barthes is very Lacanean indeed:

L'endroit le plus érotique du corps n'est-il pas *là où le vêtement bâille*? Dans la perversion (qui est le le régime du plaisir textuel) il n'y a pas de 'zones érogènes' (expression au reste assez casse-pieds); c'est l'intermittence, comme l'a bien dit la psychanalyse, qui est érotique: celle de la peau qui scintille entre deux pièces (le pantalon et le tricot), entre deux bords (la chemise entrouverte, le gant et la manche); c'est ce scintillement même qui séduit, ou encore: la mise en scène d'une apparition–disparition.

(The most erotic part of the body is, surely, where the *clothes leave a gap*. In perversion (which is the régime of textual pleasure) there are no 'erogenous zones' (which is a boring officious expression, in any case); it is the intermittence, as psychoanalysis has shown, which is erotic: the skin glimmering between two garments (the trousers and the sweater), between two edges (the half-open shirt, the glove and the sleeve); it is this glimmering itself which seduces, or rather: the staging, as it were, of an act of appearance–disappearance.)

(*Plaisir du texte*, p. 19)

There is possibly a reminiscence here of the game of 'Gone! here!' ('Now you see it, now you don't!') which, for both Freud and Lacan, constitutes the infant's initiation into 'the concrete discourse of the environment' and which is played by deliberately picking up and dropping his rattle.[8] It is, in any case, here the primary apprehension of language (in phenomenological terms, its essence) with which Barthes is preoccupied. The pleasure or enjoyment (an inadequate translation of *jouissance*) which criticism, at best, merely acknowledges or betrays, is defined as indispensable to any future 'materialistic' theory of the text (*Plaisir du texte*, p. 97). Were not Epicurus, Diderot, Sade and Fourier, after all, each in his own way, avowed eudemonists (p. 101)? 'Science', though, is now seen as a crude grasping at reality. 'We are perhaps scientific through lack of subtlety' (p. 96). And the question of 'pleasure' is raised to 'render more difficult a return of the text to morality, to truth: to the morality of truth' (p. 102). Needless to say, a coherent or systematic exposition of the theory is as yet impossible, and perhaps also ultimately impossible; just as the text which is the occasion of pleasure or *jouissance* is as much absent as present, inaccessible to interpretation. To say anything of value about either is thus a matter of communicating what one has to say through the medium of aphorisms (Barthes, like Derrida, is an admirer of Nietzsche), powerful and daring plunges, as it were, beneath the surface of everyday language into the depths in which subject and object are glimpsed briefly as one and the same.

In *Le plaisir du texte* Barthes's contempt for the notion of 'truth' and 'the morality of truth' is taken a stage further than in *S/Z* of three years earlier. In this analysis of Balzac's *Sarrasine*, the stated intention is to 'maltreat' (*malmener*) the text (p. 21); to shatter it, through analysis, into its various constituent 'codes'. Yet the actual comments on the story are disconcertingly respectful, and contain, in note form, perceptive but philosophically unremarkable comments on Balzac's symbolism and psychology. The two principal 'codes' in fact – the 'proaïretic' (from the Greek *proairetikós*: deliberately choosing, concerned with purpose) and the 'hermeneutic', the attention paid to problems raised in the story and their various solutions – amount to no more than two of the common and probably inescapable conventions of narrative. The proaïretic code is the code of 'actions and behaviour', though we are reminded that it is the narration not the 'characters' in the story who determine what this should be (p. 25), 'for the proaïretic sequence is only ever the effect of an artifice of reading'. Its foundation is 'empirical rather than logical' (p. 26). The notion that there is an alternative to an 'artifice' of reading, and that the 'logical' and 'empirical' reading of a text are mutually exclusive terms seems like one of the many survivals in *S/Z* of the 'scientific' aspirations of the earlier writing. With the appearance of *Le plaisir du texte* and, two years later, *Roland Barthes par Roland Barthes*, it became increasingly clear that his 'Saussurean' phase was at an end.

(iv)

What the account of Barthes I have offered so far fails to explain, I realise, is how an intellectual writer so prone to intellectual error for many years, and so contemptuous after this of the 'morality of truth', should have continued to exercise such an enormous appeal to students of literature and ideas. To say that, among Barthes's many inconsistent pronouncements, a number are remarkably illuminating (from any point of view probably, and from that from which this book is written certainly) may sound more like an evasion on my part than an explanation. It is the power and charm of his prose (his *écriture*, a word he encourages us to dwell on) which the student of intellectual fashion is likely to acknowledge and try at least to understand. This is lost in translation, partly because of its lightness and uninsistent suggestiveness, which are those of French writing at its best. Like Gide and Valéry, both of whom he admires,[9] he can write in a sophisticated contemporary idiom prose whose movement and implicit attitude to the reader recall the great prose writers of the seventeenth century.[10] It is also because of something which is peculiar to his writing and which the translator can only recapture by chance:

Son discours est plein de mots qu'il coupe, si l'on peut dire, à la racine. Pourtant, dans l'étymologie, ce n'est pas la vérité ou l'origine du mot qui lui plaît, c'est plutôt *l'effet de surimpression* qu'elle autorise: le mot est vu comme un palimpseste: il me semble alors que j'ai des idées *à même la langue* – ce qui est tout simplement: écrire (je parle ici d'une pratique, non d'une valeur).

(His discourse is full of words that he cuts off at their root, so to speak. However, in etymology, it isn't the truth or origin of a word that pleases him, it's rather *the effect of over-impression* it allows: the word is seen as a palimpsest: I seem, when this happens, to have ideas *on the level of language itself* – which means, simply: writing (I speak of a practice, not a value).)

(*Roland Barthes par Roland Barthes*, p. 88)

The true writer, he has observed on a number of occasions, resembles Plato's Cratylus, who argued that words and their referents were necessarily, not freely related. Barthes can justify his fondness for verbal play and the exploitation of homonyms and etymologies on the grounds that the writer ceases, at least ostensibly, to be in control of what he writes, that is, to be the person who *chooses* his words – the authority of the conscious subject is undermined; on the grounds too that the tyranny of forms and fixed meanings is undermined as well. Among the writers most often quoted by Barthes in recent years is the late Georges Bataille, for whom the subversion of language, including his own, by a process of deliberate self-contradiction and self-mockery, appears to have been its principal justification.

To refuse to take oneself seriously is of course attractive. '*L'esprit du sérieux*' was for Sartre one of the most conspicuous examples of 'bad faith', and the Devil, according to Chesterton, fell by the laws of gravity. Barthes's own frequent candid helplessness, like his aim of being carried away not by dogmatic passion but by the fortuitous associations of language, is probably what appeals more than anything to admirers of his prose. It is also what enables him to write particularly well on one of the French works he most admires, Flaubert's *Bouvard et Pécuchet*. In some of his most interesting passages of criticism (by any standards) he compares the irony of Balzac, in *Sarrasine* and elsewhere, with its wholly unironical attitude towards itself[11] and its own positive standards, with the 'multivalence', something quite different from irony, that we find in Flaubert's later prose. To exorcise one kind of cliché, one 'stereotype', it is not enough merely to impose another:

Le seul pouvoir de l'écrivain sur le vertige stéréotypique (ce vertige est aussi celui de la bêtise, de la 'vulgarité'), c'est d'y entrer sans guillemets, en opérant un texte, non une parodie. C'est ce qu'a fait Flaubert dans *Bouvard et Pécuchet*: les deux copistes sont des copieurs de codes (ils sont, si l'on veut, *bêtes*), mais comme eux-mêmes sont affrontés à la bêtise de classe qui les entoure, le texte qui les met en scène ouvre une circularité où personne (pas même l'auteur) n'a barre sur personne; et telle est bien la fonction de l'écriture: rendre dérisoire, annuler le pouvoir (l'intimidation) d'un langage sur un autre, dissoudre, à peine constitué, tout métalangage.

(The only power of the writer over the vertigo of the stereotype (which is also that of 'stupidity', of 'vulgarity') is to enter into it without the benefit of quotation marks, by means of a text and not a parody. This is what Flaubert has done in *Bouvard et Pécuchet*: the two copyists are copiers of codes (they are, if you like, *stupid*), but as they are themselves affronted by the class stupidity which surrounds them, the text which presents them opens up a circularity in which no one (not even the author) has any advantage over any-one else: and this is, of course, the function of writing itself (*écriture*): to render derisory, annul the power (the intimidation) of one language over another, to dissolve, as soon as it is constituted, any metalanguage.)

(*S/Z*, pp. 104–5)

Bouvard and Pécuchet themselves, Barthes might have added, surrender to the temptation to which Flaubert himself surrenders repeatedly in his letters and *almost*, one might say, in his last novel: 'to see people's stupidity and be no longer able to tolerate it' (ch. 8). The critic's account here is almost completely satisfying (see, how-ever, pp. 171–5 below).

One seems bound to come back to religious language to account for the appeal of Barthes and the direction of his later writing. In a sense, it is a profound humility of which he seeks to define the pos-sible conditions, and which *Bouvard et Pécuchet* exemplifies. There is also in the notion of the 'text' and of that absorption of the reader in the object of attention (that dissolving of the unreal, merely 'ideological', dissociation of subject and object) something remini-scent of the Hindu, Buddhist and Christian disciplines of self-transcendence through contemplation. The spiritual exercises of St Ignatius of Loyola receive an extensive and sympathetic com-mentary in *Sade, Fourier, Loyola* (1971), while in *L'empire des signes* (1970), he is avowedly fascinated by the ordering in Japan of the rituals of everyday life in such a way as to promote a form of awareness free from the self-assertion and merely unintelligent materialism of France and the Western world.

What Barthes recognises (usually) is the difficulty of such release from the demands of the so-called 'real world' and the rarity and unusualness of the circumstances that allow it: the extraordinary achievement, for example, of *Bouvard et Pécuchet*. Even a privileged state of awareness such as that of being painfully in love leads to the realisation that folly is not an experience necessarily of depersonalisation, as literature has led us to believe during the hundred years since Rimbaud: 'For me, the loving subject, it's the very opposite: it is becoming a subject, not being able to prevent myself from being one which drives me mad.' This is said in what may be his most remarkable achievement and can be read as a long sustained prose poem, *Fragments d'un discours amoureux* (p. 142).

Yet the intelligent acknowledgment of the difficulties of self-transcendence, the identification of subject and object, is not enough to make Barthes a reliable spiritual guide, and he would almost certainly be the last person to claim this as his own ambition or rôle. It is as a confessional writer that he has most to say to his contemporaries. (One of his finest essays, as yet uncollected, 'Ecrivains, intellectuels, professeurs' of 1971, assigns the rôle of analyst to the students and that of patient to the professor himself.) And what he confesses principally is an immense nostalgia for the impossible world he himself calls Utopia. In his first book, which made him famous, *Le degré zéro de l'écriture* of 1953, he concludes his brief review of the literary history of France by anticipating a literature (or rather *écriture*) which will be free from the institutional and stylistic conventions which are those of the society against which the writer (*qua* writer) rebels:

Chaque écrivain qui naît ouvre en lui le procès de la Littérature; mais s'il la condamne, il lui accorde toujours un sursis que la Littérature emploie à la reconquérir.

(Each writer who is born puts Literature on trial; but if he condemns it, he grants it, none the less, a reprieve of which Literature takes advantage to conquer him anew.)

(p. 64)

'None the less', contemporary literature (that is, by implication, the contemporary literature worthy of the name):

se sentant sans cesse coupable de sa propre solitude...n'en est pas moins une imagination avide d'un bonheur des mots, elle se hâte vers un langage rêvé dont la fraîcheur, par une sorte d'anticipation idéale, figurerait la perfection d'un nouveau monde adamique où le language ne serait plus aliéné.

(constantly conscious of guilt for its own solitude...is an imagination, none the less, hungry for a certain joy in words, hastening towards a language glimpsed in a dream, whose freshness, by a sort of ideal anticipation, would convey the perfection of a new Adamic world, in which language would no more be subject to alienation.)

(pp. 64–5)

Such a consummation depends not on literature itself but on the achievement of a classless society.[12] In *Sade, Fourier, Loyola* it is again a certain highly organised Utopianism that Barthes reconstitutes; finding, in Fourier's pluralist world especially,[13] that respect for all 'differences' in which Barthes now sees the only hope of social progress.

In the present, Utopia is, as its name implies, to be found nowhere – that is, in the 'Text' (with a capital T):

Le Texte, par exemple, est une utopie; sa fonction – sémantique – est de faire signifier la littérature, l'art, le langage présents, en tant qu'on les déclare *impossibles*; naguère, on expliquait la littérature par son passé; aujourd'hui par son utopie: le sens est fondé en valeur: l'utopie permet cette nouvelle sémantique.

(The Text, for instance, is a Utopia: its – semantic – function is to make the literature, art and language which are present signify in so far as one declares them impossible; once literature used to be explained by its past; today by its Utopia: meaning is founded in value; the Utopia allows this new semantics.)

(*Roland Barthes par Roland Barthes*, pp. 80–1)

A clue to Barthes's meaning here is to be found in one of his few diatribes against those from whom he differs, the members of the Société des Amis du Texte,

casse-pieds de toutes sortes, qui décrètent la forclusion du texte et de son plaisir, soit par conformisme culturel, soit par rationalisme intransigeant (suspectant une 'mystique' de la littérature), soit par moralisme politique.

(interfering bores of every kind, who decree the foreclosure of the text and its pleasure, either through cultural conformism, or intransigent rationalism (suspecting a 'mystique' of literature) or political moralism.)

(*Plaisir du texte*, pp. 26–7)

The 'foreclosure' of the text is the insistence on one reading and one reading only of a poem, a novel or a play, the failure to see the multivalence of significance and value that any spoken utterance or piece of writing can afford. The 'Utopia' or (literally) *nowhere* of the text lies in its irreducibility to any one meaning or value. Barthes's wonder at the thought of this (on reflection) obvious characteristic of the spoken and written word (see pp. 68 and 79 above) recalls once again that of Sartre's Roquentin more than thirty years before at the thought of a book, *any* book, which he would write and which would 'not exist, would be above existence' (*La nausée*, p. 250) (in the language of phenomenology, of course, that of which one is immediately aware can be contemplated and defined, without the question arising whether or not it 'exists'). However, where Sartre moved from the quasi-religious devotion to literature, which he has confessed he shared with his hero Roquentin, to a more Marxist view of literature and history, Barthes has condemned what he calls the 'naïveté' of his own commitment in *Le degré zéro de l'écriture* (see *Roland Barthes par Roland Barthes*, p. 81) to a world of social uniformity. He has also, increasingly, spoken of political commitment as an abuse of the Freudian super-ego, the voice of 'le père politique'. Progress now, he claims, can be seen in what has already begun to emerge.

une philosophie pluraliste... hostile à la massification, tendue vers la différence, fouriériste en somme; l'utopie (toujours maintenue) consiste alors à imaginer une société infiniment parcellée dont la division ne serait plus sociale, et, partant, ne serait plus conflictuelle.

(a pluralist philosophy... hostile to massification, aspiring towards the recognition of differences, in fact Fourierist; Utopianism (and it is still Utopianism) amounts then to imagining a society whose sub-divisions are infinite, and in which division is no longer social, no longer thereby the cause of conflict.)

(*Roland Barthes par Roland Barthes*, p. 81)

The vision is attractive but familiar. It is a social aspiration ('no longer...the cause of conflict') which is almost certainly shared by President Giscard d'Estaing. It tends also to confirm the impression that Barthes has, throughout his public career, tended to follow rather than lead the movement of ideas, which is not a reflection on his acuteness as a critic but casts doubt on his claims to be something more.*

* This book was already completed when news came on 26 March 1980 of the tragic death of Roland Barthes at the age of 64 following a car accident.

Chapter 5

THE CRITICISM OF F. R. LEAVIS

(1)

There is, of course, an institutional as well as an intellectual history to which the writings of Roland Barthes belong. To trace it one would, presumably, have to consider the rôle of the humanities in French education and the important place accorded even today to Latin and Greek in any school or university education in letters. One would have to take into account also the part that philosophy has played throughout the century and still plays today in secondary education: the creation in each *année de philosophie* before the *baccalauréat* of a public unafraid of ideas and eager for new ones, of which no equivalent exists in the English-speaking world. Then there is the highly organised and, even since 1968, centralised pattern of studies affecting students of every age: the tendency to send the better university graduates, those who pass the competitive *agrégation*, into the schools during at least the early stages of their career, while the aspiring university professor is at work, whether he is teaching in a school or in a university, on the massive *thèse d'état* and substantial *thèse complémentaire*, which, if they are accepted, will entitle him to a university chair. Neither of these theses, to which sometimes half a lifetime is devoted, can normally consist of mere literary criticism, even when their subject is literary. They are at their best – that is, where their length is justified – works of social as well as literary history in the tradition of Taine, Beljame, Jusserand and Mélèse; and they have tended to reinforce the assumption among educated Frenchmen that there are more serious topics of enquiry and debate than questions of mere interpretation or taste: that the competing claims of philosophical systems and the systematic accumulation of historical evidence are, even for the student of literature, of more serious concern. The close interpretation of texts – unless these are modern and arcane – is a matter for the classroom or the lecture hall. Discussions of taste belong to conversations among friends or to a declining literary genre, that of the essay as exemplified by Gourmont, Valéry or, occasionally, Barthes himself. Of course this is not to say that in general the French are, as critics, inferior. Traditionally, they have had the advantage, perhaps especially in conversation, of not taking criticism too solemnly and of enjoying a freedom and consequent deftness of insight which other nations, including the British might envy; though solemnity has unfortunately become more common in the last few decades with the growing prestige of what has come to be known as *la nouvelle critique*. With the vast expansion of university studies since the war and liberation many things have changed. The old-fashioned *thèse d'état* is now no longer the only road to promotion, and the l'Ecole des Hautes Etudes, in which Barthes taught for many years, has enjoyed for many years, and especially since the war, a freedom to innovate denied to the Sorbonne. None the less, many of the old assumptions about what is or is not worth-while remain and need to be taken into account by the English reader, whether or not he is attracted by the aspirations which Barthes and other leading intellectuals share.

Not only how different but how remote France is from the English-speaking world, as far as criticism and the study of literature are concerned – there is no lack of contact, one gathers, between mathematicians or scientists – may be seen if one considers the considerable prestige until recently of what was known as 'Cambridge English' and of its best-known representative, F. R. Leavis, and their almost total neglect in France. Here again, however, the historian may be a useful guide. To understand, if one is English, the prejudices and preferences of the French, one needs to know something of both their history and one's own.

The history of the teaching of 'English', not just in Cambridge but throughout the nation as a whole, has been traced recently by Margaret Mathieson in *The preachers of culture* and what Mathieson tells is a story very different from that of the teaching of French literature in France. Relevant, of course, is the fact that whereas English secondary education was in a state of decline for centuries and was revived in the nineteenth century in a form reflecting the division of social classes, the French *lycée* enjoyed a continuity of tradition and prosperity, almost unbroken and extending back to the early seventeenth-century Jesuit *collège*. The *collège*, like the *lycée*, moreover, catered for princes and young noblemen as well as the sons of lawyers and shopkeepers; and France, even before the

Revolution, according to Tocqueville, was the country in which 'men resembled each other most', 'had the same tastes...', read the same books and spoke the same language' (*L'ancien régime*, II, iii). The illiterate poor were numerous in France as in England but the English nineteenth-century educational reformers were trying to create what the French, none the less, had inherited. This is clear from the enormous admiration expressed by Matthew Arnold for the level of popular manners, the culture of the middle and upper classes and many of the educational and academic arrangements in France. 'Culture' was what the English lacked, and this despite the fact that in their own language they possessed a great literature. The teaching of English literature therefore came to be for Arnold and other reformers a major priority, not only in the primary and grammar school but in the public schools as well, where the study of Latin and Greek, unalleviated by the study of any other literature, had come to be regarded by its critics as a waste of valuable time to the extent that it was considered as an end in itself.[1]

What Mathieson illustrates at length is the remarkable moral fervour which inspired the early pioneers of English and the avowedly 'missionary' zeal with which it was once advocated. English, as Mathieson tells us, was during the nineteenth century in competition on the one hand with classics and on the other with science for the place of honour in the primary and secondary school syllabus, as compulsory and universal education got under way. Those who favoured the natural sciences pointed to the apparent success of scientific teaching in German schools – Germany already being seen as a serious economic rival – and also, as in the case of the headmaster of Clifton College, to its virtues as an intellectual and so a moral discipline. If the foremost advocate of English was Matthew Arnold that of science was his friend T. H. Huxley. Arnold and English, according to Mathieson, won; though the task of promoting English studies in universities and training colleges went on into the 1920s. The Cambridge English Tripos, for example, which Leavis was one of the first undergraduates to read, was not inaugurated until 1917. The arguments of Arnold, consequently, tended to be repeated with few variations over a period of half a century or more and with the same intensity of zeal. 'Poetry' especially for Arnold, we may recall, exemplifies 'culture' and among the reasons for which it may come to replace 'most of what passes for religion and philosophy' is that, like religion, it transcends all other interests, including the interests of class. To quote from *Culture and anarchy*, culture 'seeks to do away with classes; to make the best that has been thought and known in the world current everywhere; to make all men live in an atmosphere of sweetness and light... the men of culture are the true apostles of equality' (p. 70).

The very similar belief that the study of literature can ennoble and refine and inspire social harmony and national unity, as well as forestalling social revolution, is expressed in the Newbolt Committee's Report of 1921 on *The teaching of English in England*. English, it claims, could 'form a new element of national unity, linking together the mental life of all classes by experiences which hitherto have been the privileges of a limited section' (p. 15). The university professor of literature has therefore 'obligations not merely to students but still more to the teeming populations outside the university walls, many of whom have not so much as "heard whether there be any Holy Ghost". The fulfilment of these obligations means propaganda work, organisation and the building up of a staff of assistant missionaries' (p. 259).

However, two things may be obvious, looking back today on what the Newbolt Committee called the missionary work of the English teacher in universities and schools. Despite all the energy and conviction that went into this work, it was not an unqualified success – certainly, at least, by the standards of its instigators and inspirers. One need only think what Matthew Arnold would say if treated to a few minutes of *Tom and Jerry* or *Starsky and Hutch*. It would also be difficult today to find among the thousands of English teachers any unanimity with regard to the purpose of English studies comparable to that which seems to have existed half a century ago. There are few who would regard the idea of promoting social harmony through literature as anything other than a mischievous or naïve illusion; few also who would not be embarrassed at the idea of being thought of as 'apostles' or 'missionaries'. Some might be embarrassed only by the candour with which these terms express what is still their own idea of their function. The candour, however, is the candour of confidence and that confidence in a perfectly clear common purpose belongs almost certainly to the past.

Leavis's own earliest published writings reflect the optimism and quasi-political enthusiasm of Arnold and the original campaigners for English. This is nowhere more apparent than in *Culture and environment*, the textbook for schools which he and Denys Thompson

published in 1933 and which advocates a programme of studies
extending the 'English' syllabus to include the study of advertisements, newspapers and commercial fiction; the study, needless to
say, being one which was intended to be intensely critical and to
help young people resist conditioning by what we now call the
media. In explicitly political terms, the book is, however, to say the
least, neutral and does not see the promotion of 'equality' through
'culture' and the forestalling of revolution as one of its aims. On
the contrary, its hostility to commercial influences made it especially
congenial to readers on the Left. This was the period – a fairly brief
one – in which Leavis could pronounce in *Scrutiny* (i, 4, 1933,
p. 320) that he believed 'some form of economic communism to be
inevitable and desirable, in the sense that it is to this that a power-
economy of its very nature points; and only by a deliberate and
intelligent working towards it can civilization be saved from disaster'. Even in *Culture and environment*, the case for 'English' is
shown to be far less simple, if no less urgent, than it had appeared
hitherto. In Leavis's subsequent writings on the study of literature
and its relation to other interests and fields of interest, the case is
presented as both irrefutable and one that defies justification in terms
of any immediately recognisable social or ethical benefits or any
equivalent of the sociologist's or ethical philosopher's expertise. It
would be impossible to understand the extraordinary appeal Leavis
has exerted in the past and which his writings still hold for many
today unless one were to follow the implications of this professed
point of view and decide whether it is tenable.

(11)
     In trying to answer this last question I should like to begin
by making what may seem at first a paradoxical claim – paradoxical,
that is, in view of the extent to which he has commented explicitly
and earnestly on social issues. My claim is that, unlike Barthes,
Leavis has never pretended to be anything more than a critic. It is,
in fact, his reluctance even to set out the principles which his writings
on literature and society presuppose, which have contributed to his
neglect on the continent of Europe, while in the English-speaking
world, it has often been regarded as a disabling weakness or excessive
diffidence from which he needed to be rescued. 'Allow me', René
Wellek wrote in Leavis's journal *Scrutiny* (v, 4, 1937), 'to sketch
your ideal of poetry, your "norm" with which you measure every

poet: your poetry must be in serious relation to actuality, it must have a firm grasp of the actual, of the object, it must be in relation to life, it must not be cut off from direct vulgar living, it should be normally human, testify to spiritual health and sanity' (p. 376).

The picture of Leavis is recognisable and one might be tempted to agree with this and the rest of Wellek's account of the criteria implicit in Leavis's judgment of literature. However, Leavis's reply on this occasion is categorical. (It is also, as it happens, of the utmost relevance to the issues raised in the preceding chapters of this book.) 'That Dr Wellek should slip into this way of putting things', he wrote (see *The common pursuit*, p. 212), 'seems to me significant, for he would on being challenged agree, I imagine, that it suggests a false idea of the procedure of the critic. . . By the critic of poetry, I understand the complete reader: the ideal critic is the ideal reader. The reading demanded by poetry is of a different kind from that demanded by philosophy.'

Leavis's avowed inability to 'define the difference satisfactorily (though Dr Wellek knows what it is and could give at least as good an account of it as I could)' is obviously intended as a hint of caution to anyone else who thinks he might succeed where Leavis himself had failed. What he is claiming is that his reticence in this respect and with regard to the theoretical justification of his practice in general arises from an awareness of what is at issue rather than the opposite, and that it is the inevitable consequence of a certain type of thinking. This type of thinking, he maintains, can take the form of a distinctive discipline of thought. It can also be shown to be one of the characteristics of 'the ideal reader'.

Leavis's actual practice as a critic is, of course, the best clue to what he thought criticism was, and it will be generally agreed that as a critic he was uncompromising in that he judged all writing by what he understood as the highest possible standards. Much of the admiration he inspired and much of the anger can be attributed to this repeated lapse of what used till recently to pass, in British literary and academic circles, for ordinary good manners. What is not always appreciated, however, even by some of his warmest admirers, is that this way of judging, far from implying the application of some rigidly maintained 'norm' or 'ideal of poetry' (as Wellek, approvingly, explained to him), amounted to neither more nor less than an insistence on judging what he read by its own standards and on its own terms, a refusal to misrepresent.

This further paradoxical claim calls for a little explanation. To judge something by its own standards or on its own terms is usually taken to mean judging it with studied forbearance, with a kind of willing suspension, when necessary, of one's feelings of boredom or distaste, and such forbearance was, surely, beyond Leavis's powers. Studied forbearance is not, however, a surer guide in itself to understanding than instinctive admiration, boredom or disgust, and a willing suspension of the latter may entail merely sharing an author's own most flattering and hopeful view of what it is he thinks he has achieved. To be judged strictly on one's own terms and by one's own standards is something that many authors would dread. Almost anyone who has tried to write poetry will know that much of what is written, as he reminds us in *New bearings in English poetry*, is 'not so much bad as dead – it was never alive. The words that lie there arranged on the page have no roots: the writer himself can never have been more than superficially interested in them' (p. 6). The same effort of imaginative understanding, that is the same fidelity to actual intention, is apparent in what he says of poetry and prose in which we have every reason to believe that the words, which are alive, were and remain the focus of some intense interest.

The seeming paradox I have in mind may be clarified if we consider some of Leavis's earliest criticism, his discussion in *New bearings* of the explicitly religious preoccupations of Yeats and Eliot. 'Poetry matters', Leavis writes in the first chapter of *New bearings*, 'because of the kind of poet who is more alive than other people, more alive in his age' (p. 13). This is not to say that such a poet is nec:ssarily wiser than other people about economics or foreign affairs; and the fact that the poetry of Auden and Spender in the 1930s was overtly political did not, in itself, for Leavis, entitle it to be taken seriously.[2] 'Poetry matters' because of the kind of poet who is 'unusually aware, more sincere and more himself than the ordinary man can be. He knows what he feels and what he is interested in. He is a poet because his interest in his experience is not separable from his interest in words' (p. 13).

The phrase 'to know what one feels' is crucial and bears much of the weight of Leavis's argument. And it is further elucidated (p. 41) by a quotation from the *Autobiographies* of Yeats who remarks how many years it is 'before one can believe enough in what one feels even to know what the feeling is'. The section on Yeats in *New bearings* might be taken as showing how inseparable for Leavis are the poetry and the kind of life they express. They are also, I think, an example of the sophistication of his prose, the economy his respect for his reader's intelligence allows, and the swiftness and ease with which he is able to relate the different aspects of a poet's experience, his limitations and strengths, to the particular conditions of society and civilisation at a given point in history. It is a sophistication, arguably, which is stronger and more resilient in that it is less dependent on the indulgence of the reader than the sophistication of Roland Barthes. Yeats, according to Leavis, became a poet at a time when poetry seemed doomed, if it was to survive at all, to create an imaginary world set apart from reality or, if it were possible, constituting a higher reality. Yeats, however, Leavis writes,

> differs from the Victorian romantics in the intensity with which he seeks his 'higher reality'. This difference we have attributed to his being Irish; but it will not do to let this explanation detract from his rare distinction of mind and spirit... Indeed, his dealings with spiritualism, magic, theosophy, dream and trance were essentially an attempt to create an alternative science. The science of Huxley and Tyndall he had rejected in the name of imagination and emotion, but he had an intelligence that would not be denied and less than the ordinary man's capacity for self-deception.   (p. 41)

The ordinary writer of verse is rarely more than 'superficially interested' in the words on that page. There is therefore no compelling reason which they communicate why anyone else should be interested in them. By contrast, the extraordinary conviction conveyed by Yeats in his creation of a world of magic and myth, in defiance of the Victorian conventional wisdom, is shared by Leavis to the extent that Yeats shares it himself. And Leavis is clearly convinced too by Yeats's own admissions of futility and failure:

> An aged man is but a paltry thing.
> A tattered coat upon a stick, unless
> Soul clap its hands and sing, and louder sing
> For every tatter in its mortal dress.

'This (though there is always an ironical overtone) is the voice of one who knows intellectual passion. He does not deceive himself about what he has lost, but the regret itself becomes in the poetry something positive. His implications, in short, are very complex; he has achieved a difficult and delicate sincerity, an extraordinarily subtle poise' (p. 46).

It is obvious that the seriousness with which Leavis is prepared to read poetry is due not only to what the poetry happens to reveal about the poet. His interest in the man goes with a rarely equalled attentiveness to the poetry as such, the attentiveness which makes Leavis write more perceptively about what is revealed by movement and rhythm than any other critic, any 'structuralist' critic, certainly. The best example of this gift is perhaps his commentary on Hardy's 'After a Journey' in *The living principle*. But take also his commentary on another poem by Hardy in *New bearings*: 'Woman much missed, how you call to me, call to me'. 'The voice', Leavis writes,

seems to start dangerously with a crude popular lilt, but this is turned into a subtle movement by the prosaic manner of the content, a manner that else-where would have been Hardy's characteristic gaucherie:

> Can it be you then I hear? Let me view you, then,
> Standing as when I drew near to the town
> Where you would wait for me: yes, as I knew you then,
> Even to the original air-blue gown!

Leavis goes on:

By the end of this second stanza, the bare matter-of-fact statement has already subdued the rhythm; the shift of stress on the rhyme ('view you then', 'knew you then') has banished the jingle from it.   (pp. 59–60)

For Leavis, 'movement' and 'rhythm' are not synonymous, though they are necessarily related, and related also to another key term in his criticism, 'direction'. It is these terms which are used to describe what is positively affirmed in Eliot's 'Ash Wednesday' (pp. 115–32), when contrasted with a poem like 'The Journey of the Magi': positively affirmed, even though so much of the poem is explicitly hopeless and even though the positiveness of the affirmation has nothing to do with an assertion of belief on Eliot's part or a demon-stration of logic.[3]

(III)

Not to believe or be interested in what one is saying amounts to saying little or nothing; though this may or may not be what one's listener or reader understands. The over-respectful reader or listener, of course, may well attribute a seriousness to the intention which was never there. To have a serious reason for using the words one uses is to command a certain kind of attention, to appeal for certain things to be understood about the world, if what one is saying is to be understood. It is Leavis's recognition that this must always be so that makes it impossible for him to accept René Wellek's idea of an abstract or abstractable norm by which to judge (in so far as judgment implies both interpretation and evaluation) the literature of the past or, for even more obvious reasons, that of the present and future. 'The ideal critic' could not, given the nature of criticism, write as a prescriptive moralist or as someone who is able to apply absolute aesthetic or linguistic rules.

Nor could he judge – that is, properly read – anything without some notion of what to expect, without some standards of judgment, though how these are acquired is a matter of the personal history of any critic, 'ideal' or otherwise, and of his place in history. 'Standards are formed in comparison and what opportunities had they for that?', he writes in *The great tradition* (p. 3) of the enthusiasm of Scott and Coleridge for *Tom Jones*. Scott and Coleridge, in other words, had no Dickens, George Eliot, Mark Twain or Conrad to compare with Fielding. One may disagree with Leavis's own judgment of *Tom Jones*; but implicit in the remark is the recognition that criticism is not, either primarily or ultimately, a prescriptive or regulative activity but a recognition of what has already been achieved. This is presumably why Leavis's primary concern in his writings on the study of English in the university is with the content of the programme of study, and why questions of critical 'method' and 'technique' take a secondary place in his earliest writings on the subject and are virtually absent from his later writings. The metaphor of the yard-stick is one he rejects in his reply to René Wellek when discussing the critic's procedure. Instead, he proposes that of a map or chart (a favourite metaphor):

The critic's aim is, first, to realize as sensitively and completely as possible this or that which claims his attention; and a certain valuing is implicit in the realizing. As he matures in experience of the new thing he asks, explicitly and implicitly: 'Where does this come? How does it stand in relation to . . . ? How relatively important does it seem?' And the organization into which it settles as a constituent in becoming 'placed' is an organization of similarly 'placed' things, things that have found their bearings with regard to one another, and not a theoretical system or a system determined by abstract considerations.   (*The common pursuit*, p. 210)

The chart is also an 'organization'. The metaphor is only a metaphor, testifying as such to the difficulties of definition (which Leavis admits), though the words 'not a theoretical system' (are un-

ambiguous. It is perhaps in another celebrated exchange, his disagreement with Quentin Anderson over the latter's reinterpretation
(in *Scrutiny*) of the later novels of Henry James, that the necessarily
unsystematic nature of criticism, as Leavis understands it, is most
clearly seen. Quentin Anderson, he claims, having discovered manifestations in these novels of James's own interest in his father's
philosophical system (deriving from Swedenborg and Fourier), is,
none the less, not 'actively enough a literary critic' (see *The common
pursuit*, p. 225). The literary critic

is concerned with the work in front of him as something that should contain
within itself the reason why it is so and not otherwise. The more experience –
experience of life and literature together – he brings to bear on it the better,
of course; and it is true that extraneous information may make him more
percipient. But the business of critical intelligence will remain what it was: to
ensure relevance of response and to determine what is actually *there* in the
work of art. The critic will be especially wary how he uses extraneous information about the writer's intentions. Intentions are nothing in art except as
realized, and the tests of realization will remain what they were. They are
applied in the operation of the critic's sensibility; they are a matter of his
sense, derived from his literary experience, of what the living thing feels like
– of the difference between that which has been willed and put there, or
represents no profound integration, and that which grows from a deep centre
of life.   (p. 225)

When what we understand appears to be said without conviction, it
affects us differently from what is said in earnest. Even if we dislike
what is said in earnest, we may say that it shakes us. This is what
Leavis has always recognised and it is why his own moral sense
(since the question of morality is here inevitably relevant), though
strong and unashamed, is neither dogmatic nor prescriptive. The
adultery theme in *The golden bowl*, 'the triangle or quadrilateral, of
personal relations', remains what it is, the question of James's
possible allegorical intentions apart, and:

We remain convinced that when an author, whatever symbolism he intends,
presents a drama of men and women, he is committed to dealing in terms of
men and women, and mustn't ask us to acquiesce in valuations that contradict our profoundest ethical sensibility.

The passage has been quoted more than once by critics who see this
as evidence of Leavis's inability to engage rationally with those who
cannot share his own highly specific and historically circumscribed
ethical point of view. What they do not go on to quote, however, is
the sentence which follows:

If, of course, he can work a revolutionary change in that sensibility, well and good, but who will contend that James's art in those late novels has that power?   (*The common pursuit*, p. 228)

The art that does have that power (and anyone familiar with Leavis's writing at all will realise that quotation is here unnecessary) is, pre-eminently in our own time and more than that of Yeats or even Eliot, the art of D. H. Lawrence.

(iv)

Leavis's writings on Lawrence, it might be said, more than any others, contradict my claim that, unlike Roland Barthes, Leavis has made no claim himself to being anything other than a critic. In endorsing so emphatically Lawrence's diagnosis of the diseases of modern industrial civilisation, Leavis has, surely, been writing not only as a critic but as a social historian and prophet. With Leavis, according to Perry Anderson, writing in *The New Left Review* ('Components of the national culture'),

literary criticism conceived the ambition to become the vaulting centre of 'humane studies and the university'... The claim was unique to England; no other country has ever produced a critical discipline with these pretensions. They should be seen, not as a reflection of megalomania on the part of Leavis, but as a symptom of the objective vacuum at the centre of the culture.
(p. 50)

The 'vacuum', according to Anderson, is caused by the absence in England of any intellectual activity concerned with 'totality': by the consciously unambitious nature, in this respect, of British philosophy, economics and history. Significantly, Anderson comments, there is no indigenous British sociology, no counterpart in England to what Durkheim has represented in France, Weber in Germany and Pareto in Italy. In literary criticism alone, as conceived by Leavis, 'the notion of totality found refuge... when philosophy became "technical", a displacement occurred and literary criticism became "ethical"' (pp. 50–1).

What Anderson does not mention is that, for Leavis, the great novelists, who include not only Dickens, George Eliot and Lawrence but Tolstoy, are also the great social historians:

Dickens was a great novelist, and, as such, an incomparable social historian. It is the great novelists above all who give us our social history; compared with what is done in their work... the histories of the professional social historian seem empty and unenlightening.   (*Nor shall my sword*, p. 81)[4]

It was not therefore for want of a contemporary British sociology or holistic philosophy that Leavis chose to write with the presumption Anderson commends. Lawrence, after all, Leavis regards as a contemporary. It was because of the nature, as he saw it, of the texts on which he was commenting.

This is something I feel S. H. Olsen also fails to take into account when he talks, in his *Structure of literary understanding*, of the tendency of Leavis and other critics to confuse 'truth-claims' in interpretations of works of literature and truth-claims about the world (pp. 66–72). The example he takes is of Leavis's discussion in *The great tradition* of *Hard times* and in particular his remarks (pp. 236–8) on the conversation between the Utilitarian Gradgrind and his daughter Louisa concerning her future marriage, which he urges her to accept, with Mr Bounderby. 'It is a triumph of ironic art', Leavis writes. 'No logical analysis could dispose of the philosophy of fact and calculus with such neat finality.' Leavis, however, Olsen comments,

in the arguments from which the above remarks are taken, does not in that place show that the work in question presents a true reflection. He does not there provide reasons for accepting the view of Victorian Utilitarianism which *Hard Times*, according to this interpretation, presents. He does, however, provide reasons in the interpretation of the novel, for accepting the proposition that *Hard Times* actually presents the view he says it does ... To put this objection briefly, reflections, if seen as general statements (i.e. as informative), would be controversial. But there is no *controversy* about the truth of reflection in literary debate.   (pp. 69 and 72)

A 'truth-claim' which amounted to 'information' offered by the critic in the guise of judgment would certainly indicate some confusion on the critic's part, whether or not he made any attempt to 'provide reasons' for believing that the information was true. However, Leavis's judgment of the Utilitarianism of Gradgrind (which he compares with that of James Mill, as described in the *Autobiography* of his son) is the very opposite of informative in intention. 'A judgment is personal or it is nothing', he writes in his Richmond lecture: 'you cannot take over someone else's. The implicit form of a judgment is: This is so isn't it?' (*Nor shall my sword*, p. 62). Olsen might legitimately have objected to Leavis's phrase 'neat finality', when applied to the presented conversation between Gradgrind and Louisa; especially to the idea that the finality was comparable to that which is possible in formal logic. But Olsen's assertion that critics should eschew truth-claims about the world if they are conducting critical debate puts impossible restrictions on criticism, which are not only practical but logical. 'The structuralist theory of language', he argues, 'fails to provide a basis for an acceptable theory of literature because it ignores the part played by context or setting in the interpretation of utterances' (p. 46). I would agree that this is true. But 'context' includes reference, and to read Dickens or Lawrence, who clearly refer in their novels to what they take to be the real as well as a fictitious world, without judging that intention is not to judge them at all. Judging the intention, moreover, judging the importance for the novelist of what is said, is possible only if one recognises the ways in which this resembles or differs from the ways in which it is important for oneself, 'importance' here including, inevitably, 'truth'. The truth of a judgment in *Women in love* is not the truth of a piece of information or fact. It has to be judged by totally different criteria from those called for by statements such as 'D. H. Lawrence was born in 1885', and cannot be taken on trust as such statements can be and have to be. We are talking here of what can only be seen and felt as real or unreal possibilities.

This is why there is no necessary inconsistency between Leavis's candid endorsement of the historical judgments of Dickens or Lawrence and his denial that 'the skilled reader of literature will tend, by the nature of his skill, to understand and appreciate contemporary social processes better than his neighbours'. This had been claimed by F. W. Bateson in *Essays in criticism* ('The function of criticism at the present time') and is quoted by Leavis in *Scrutiny* ('The responsible critic or the function of criticism at any time', p. 176). On the contrary, Leavis replied:

The business of the literary critic is with literary criticism. It is pleasant to think that, when he writes or talks about political or 'social' matters, insight and understanding acquired in literary studies will be engaged – even if not demonstrably (and even if we think it a misleading stress to speak of his special understanding of 'contemporary social processes'). But his special responsibility as critic . . . is to serve the function of criticism to the best of his powers. He will serve it ill unless he has a clear conception of what a proper working of the function in contemporary England would be like, and unless he can tell himself why the function matters.   (p. 178)

Telling himself why the function matters includes recognising the difference that is made by a proper understanding of what has been written or said. 'The ideal critic', as he replied to Wellek, 'is the ideal reader.' The world in which the critical function is in abeyance is a world in which people do not listen to each other; listening, as he makes clear in his observations on poetry, especially, being a matter of attention to the written as well as the spoken word. The attention in the case of attention to what is said by a 'really distinguished mind' is, moreover, by the very nature of the utterance, more than a mere constatation.

Really distinguished minds are themselves, of course, *of* their age; they are responsive at the deepest level to its peculiar strains and challenges: that is why they are able to be truly illuminating and prophetic and to influence the world positively and creatively.   (*Nor shall my sword*, pp. 42–3)

Not to take seriously Eliot's or Lawrence's response to the conditions of modern life would be either to dismiss them as self-deceived or to refuse to attend to what they are saying.

This is not, however, Leavis's own way of putting it. 'Poetry', he wrote in *New bearings*, 'matters because of the kind of poet who is more alive than other people, more alive in his age...But if the poetry and the intelligence of the age lose touch with each other, poetry will cease to matter much, and the age will be lacking in finer awareness' (pp. 13–14). The 'if' reminds us that *New bearings* was written almost half a century ago. Leavis himself, already in his added retrospect in the 1950 edition, saw the book as belonging to the past, and accused himself of having been too 'sanguine' in 1932 about the quality of the poetry that would be written as a result of the changes in expression brought about by Eliot and Pound. It is obvious too that by 1950 he regarded his fears concerning the relation between 'poetry' and 'the age' as having turned out to be justified. *New bearings* itself is still hopeful, and the hopefulness is indistinguishable from a seriousness which it is difficult to imagine in any criticism of contemporary verse today. Is there, after all, any critic today who is able to take any contemporary verse as seriously as Leavis took the poetry of Yeats and Eliot? Even if a successor to Yeats or Eliot were to emerge, is there any reader of contemporary poetry who could hope to convey to a large audience the differences it had made to our way of thinking?[5] I put the question rhetorically: it may be answered, but not by reference to the large numbers of people who buy poetry, attend poetry festivals or listen to it broadcast on the radio in Britain and the United States. A homogeneous educated public for poetry is not to be confused with groups of poetry fans. There have always, of course, been such groups and coteries, and Leavis himself in *New bearings* deplored the fact that poetry was becoming more specialised: 'the process is implicit in the process of modern civilization'. Yet to say this still implies a belief in the possibility of writing for an educated public which will normally read contemporary verse and be capable of responding to the poetry that really matters. It is this belief and the corresponding style and assumptions that make *New bearings* today read like something from another century.

The claim that 'poetry will cease to matter much' can be verified or falsified not by inspection of the sales of poetry but by a reading of the poetry itself, by an assessment of how genuinely or otherwise the poet appears to have been interested in the 'words on the page'. It can be further clarified also by making the obvious point that poetry is possible only when a relationship exists between the poet and a public which for the poet is real enough to make its presence felt at the very moment he writes, determining what can be said and assumed. The same is clearly true of the novelist and would-be dramatist. The nature of the relationship is examined at length by Leavis in his study of seventeenth- and eighteenth-century poetry in *Revaluation* and *The common pursuit*, and the consequences of isolation from a public shown (in his comments in the latter) on the later poetry of Blake.[6] The corollary, that 'if poetry and the intelligence of the age lost touch with each other' then the age itself will be 'lacking in finer awareness', cannot be proved in any scientific or legal sense to be either correct or false.

If Leavis *was* right, however, and if what we are witnessing today, in the age of automation and cybernetics, is not only a lack of 'finer awareness' but a failure of the collective human instinct for survival, this does not mean that the world can be saved by poetry and criticism. Nor is that what Leavis is saying. In forming his view of the modern world, Leavis was influenced not only by the testimony of Lawrence but also by that of George Sturt, the Farnham wheelwright and chronicler of the lives of the local craftsmen and cottagers in the years before his shop became a garage and Farnham a dormitory as distinct from a market town. Sturt's books were recommended for use in schools by Leavis and Denys Thompson in *Culture and environment*, though not, Leavis insists, 'in any nostalgic spirit'. Speaking years later of Sturt's evocation of a world in which the craftsmen knew where the wood they seasoned had grown and the roads and fields on which the wheels would turn, as well as the men who would drive them, Leavis wrote:

We didn't recall the organic kind of relation of work to life . . . as something to be restored or to take a melancholy pleasure in lamenting; but by way of emphasizing that it was gone, with the organic community it belonged to, not to be restored in any foreseeable future. We were calling attention to an essential change in human conditions that is entailed by the accelerating technological revolution and to the nature of the attendant human problems.

(*Nor shall my sword*, p. 85)

What Leavis draws attention to is something he regards as obvious to thinking people of his own generation, and both his diagnosis and remedy recall those of other advocates of 'English' in universities and schools, including Caldwell Cook, his own English master at the Perse School before the First World War.[7] The obliteration of folk memory and the exploitation by the penny press of the possibilities opened up by mass literacy, not to speak of later developments in the mass media, had placed the burden of responsibility for what he calls 'continuity' on the educated reading public[8] capable of keeping alive at least the works of inherited imaginative literature. The betrayal of the function of criticism by the intellectual weeklies and reviews made the survival of such a public something which the university alone and the university English school in particular might reasonably hope to ensure.

It may be asked, of course, whether such a public has ever existed, and the editor of *The Times Literary Supplement* has written a whole book disputing it; just as it may be questioned whether the 'organic community' was what it is made to seem in Sturt's and Leavis's writings.[9] Leavis himself, moreover, was perfectly conscious of the abyss separating the idea of the university as he saw it and the '*triste réalité*'. What I would suggest as not open to dispute is that the disappearance of a public conscious of its own existence and responsive to the 'really distinguished minds' of the past and the future would be disastrous not only in itself but in its consequences; and that 'literature' and 'criticism', if they are to be anything other than a self-indulgent or self-important hobby, matter in this respect alone.

(v)

To summarise thus far, one might say that Leavis's understanding of what we mean by criticism is that it entails a wholeness
of response: our judgment of what we read is a judgment of all that
is implied or revealed by a writer's use of words as well as of its
place in the world as we know it. To confine the rôle of the critic to
mere exegesis or to consider historical or ethical considerations as if
they were separate is to attempt the impossible. There is no such
thing as 'pure literary analysis' and there is no means of eschewing
what Olsen calls 'truth-claims' when these are made by the critic
because of the nature, as he sees it, of the piece of writing of which
he is offering an account. One may, of course, *pretend* to eschew
them, just as one may pretend to confine oneself to explanation as
distinct from judgment, but this is to give an unfaithful account of
what one has understood as a reader or else to read with only partial
understanding: 'By the critic of poetry, I understand the complete
reader' (see p. 150 above).

Judgment of this kind is inevitably heuristic as well and, since it
can never be taken by anyone else on trust, dependent for corroboration on the judgment of others, for 'a judgment is personal or it is
nothing'. This is not to say that the critic cannot substantiate a claim
he is making about what he has read, or that corroboration is merely
a matter of X's 'say so' coinciding with Y's. Factual corroboration
from the historian armed with statistics may be both relevant and
crucial. There is also often in Leavis's defence of his reading of a
passage of verse or prose an implicit appeal to the law of prob-
abilities (see pp. 65–6 above). The fallibility of the critic, none the
less, is seen by Leavis as without any final remedy: 'not dogmatically
but deliberately', he writes, quoting from Johnson's *Preface to
Shakespeare* at the opening of *The great tradition*.

The question of the critic's fallibility takes us to the heart of the
issues dividing Leavis from Barthes and the French structuralists;
not that Leavis ever publicly spoke of this himself or that his work
has been discussed from this point of view. Leavis, however, would
presumably be among those who are being got at in Barthes's contemptuous allusions to 'morality' and 'truth', the preoccupation,
that is, with such things (*Le plaisir du texte*, p. 102), and 'doxa',
the values and beliefs that are inherited and virtually inescapable in
so far as they are an intrinsic part of language (*Leçon inaugurale*,
pp. 12–14).

According to the earlier Barthes of 'Eléments de sémiologie' and *Critique et vérité*, there is a remedy for the fallibility of the mere critic: it lies in the Saussurean 'science of signs' and the 'anthropology' which could take as equally valid and revealing *all* readings of, for example, Racine. The notion of science invoked here is, however, positivistic (see p. 133 above) and, as such, repudiated in Barthes's later work where, much closer to Derrida in this respect, his attitude to 'truth' and 'morality' is also more Hegelian.

The widespread interest in Hegel in the last forty years in France may well derive from the course of lectures at the Ecole des Hautes Etudes in the 1930s by Alexandre Kojève, author of *Introduction à la lecture de Hegel* which concentrates especially on *The phenomenology of mind*. Sartre, who with Lacan was among those who followed the lectures, has complained that, earlier on, as a candidate for the *agrégation de philosophie* at the Ecole Normale Supérieure and the Sorbonne, he had been given almost no inkling of Hegel's existence. By contrast, a philosopher of the generation of Jacques Derrida, who has described Hegel as the first semiologist, is thoroughly at home with the Hegelian way of thinking and cast of mind.

To attempt to characterise Hegelianism as a system, even at length, would be a bold undertaking; but it can at least be said without fear of misrepresentation that it proposes, among other things, a solution to the problem of human fallibility with regard to the truth of things we say about ourselves or the world. The solution lies in seeing thought as dynamic and in a permanent state of evolution in which the 'dialectical' triad – what is asserted, then contested and as a result of this particular conflict, reasserted anew in a modified form – constitutes the very life of the mind. To think of 'truth' in any other terms is to indulge in a solemn delusion, to plunge even deeper into delusion than the mind which disputes its ability to know or to tell the truth. Often reading Hegel can be like reading Derrida himself or the later Barthes:

The honest soul takes each moment as a permanent and essential fact and is an uncultivated unreflective condition, which does not think and does not know that it is just doing the very opposite. The distraught and disintegrated soul is, however, aware of inversion: the conceptual principle predominates there, brings together into a single unity the thoughts that lie far apart in the case of the honest soul, and the language clothing its meaning is therefore full of *esprit* and wit (*Geistreich*).

The content uttered by spirit and uttered about itself is, then, the inversion and perversion of all conceptions and realities, a universal deception of itself and of others. The shamelessness manifested in stating this deceit is just on this account the greatest truth.   (*The phenomenology of mind*, VIB, 1a)

The writers who exemplify these virtues, for Barthes, are Sade, Bataille and the Flaubert of *Bouvard et Pécuchet*; for Hegel himself, the Diderot of *Le neveu de Rameau*.

An undeluded use of language is for Barthes, as for Hegel, necessarily self-critical. It is the use of language, according to Barthes, of which Balzac, for example, was incapable (see pp. 140–1 above). It implies a perpetual simultaneous acceptance and rejection of terms. This is in no way obviously dissimilar, however, from Leavis's view of language when it is used with the utmost intelligence and – a favourite Leavisian expression – 'poise'. Leavis also disliked Balzac's merely assertive use of language (see *The great tradition*, p. 29n.) and when he talks of the 'urbanity' of Jonson and Carew (*Revaluation*, p. 207) it is clear, as when Barthes compares Balzac with Flaubert, to the latter's advantage (see pp. 140–1 above), that he is referring to something more than mere irony.

The difference between Leavis and Barthes lies in what is meant by a self-critical or self-questioning use of language, and this takes us back to the different epistemologies which each writer can be seen to exemplify. Leavis is not, in any way, 'Hegelian' and though his view of the qualifications, the 'yes buts' which anything the critic says invites, may sometimes give this impression (see p. 67 above), the impression is not borne out by his writings as a whole or at any single stage of his career. The critic's fallibility is not, for Leavis, an inability to know or point out the truth. Nor is acceptance of such extreme fallibility, as far as he is concerned, the clue, as it was for Hegel, to 'the greatest truth', amounting, in the final analysis, to 'absolute knowledge'. He never, of course, says of himself as critic what Barthes once said of himself as semiologist, that he is someone 'who expresses his future death in the very terms in which he has named and understood the world' (*Système de la mode*, p. 293). Nor again does the self-critical use of language for Leavis mean necessarily a repudiation or 'inversion' of what has been previously affirmed. In his exchange with F. W. Bateson over some lines from Pope's *Dunciad* (quoted on pp. 65–6 above), he points out what he reminds us of frequently elsewhere: that familiar hackneyed expressions are often unavoidable and sometimes extremely apt. Pope's budding politician is

First slave to words, then vassal to a name,
Then dupe to party; child and man the same.

He has failed to realise, as Leavis comments, that 'Words should be servants – the servants of thought and the thinker; the badly educated child is made a "slave to words" (the cliché has its point as clichés usually have). Such a child, grown to political years, naturally becomes "vassal to a name". The felicity of this expression takes us beyond cliché.'

It is, however, when we read Leavis and Barthes together on the nature of language that the difference is most apparent. 'Language', for Barthes, is 'quite simply fascist.'

Language (*le langage*) is a legislation, a particular tongue (*la langue*) is the code. We fail to see the power which is in language because we forget that all language is a form of classification and that every form of classification is oppressive... In our French language (I am taking crude and obvious examples) I have no alternative but to present myself first of all as a subject, before enunciating the action which will be no more from then on but my own attribute: what I do is only the consequence and the consecution of what I am; in the same way, I am obliged to choose between the masculine and the feminine.   (*Leçon inaugurale*, pp. 12–14)

Resistance to this oppression consists in the 'cheating' with language, the 'permanent revolution', the 'traces' of which constitute, for Barthes, 'literature' (p. 16). The philosophical assumptions underlying this not uncommon view of language – though there are some who find the alleged oppression tolerable and even welcome[10] – have been discussed in an earlier section of this book (pp. 117–23 above). They are not assumptions which Leavis himself seems to share and his own account of language is different in the extreme. He is here reminding readers of C. P. Snow's *The two cultures and the scientific revolution* of the place of language even in the most successful science:

there is a prior human achievement of collaborative creation, a more basic work of the mind of man (and more than the mind), one without which the triumphant erection of the scientific edifice would not have been possible: that is the creation of the human world, including language. It is one we cannot rest on as something done in the past. It lives in the living creative response to change in the present.   (*Nor shall my sword*, p. 61)

The same assumption is to be found in a lecture of twenty years earlier addressed to an audience presumed to be mainly sociologists, and though the emphasis falls on 'literature', 'language' and 'literature' are clearly anything but mutually exclusive terms:

While you are in intimate touch with literature no amount of dialectics, or of materialistic interpretation, will obscure for long the truth that human life lives only in individuals: I might have said, the truth that it is only in individuals that society lives.   (*The common pursuit*, p. 185)

This is no less true for Leavis than – the complementary assumption – to say that there is 'a human nature, of which an understanding is of primary importance to students of society and politics' (*The common pursuit*, p. 184).

Leavis did not, of course, hesitate to say what he believed. It was his failure to do so in systematic terms that led some of his Marxist critics, such as Perry Anderson, to claim that there was 'a genuine impasse in Leavis's thought' ('Components of the national culture', p. 55) and that Leavis's 'refusal' in his exchange with René Wellek to defend his position more abstractly was the sign of a 'metaphysic which refused to justify itself' (p. 51). The reasons for Leavis's 'refusal' – I should like to think – can be explained as I have tried to myself. They amount to a refusal, for example, to bring to a poem, what Wellek calls an 'ideal of poetry' and a 'norm'; to an insistence on judging what one reads on the writer's terms, with all that this implies and consequently, where something new has been created, coming to terms with and identifying that which is new. This may, as in the case of T. S. Eliot's later poetry, amount to recognising what Leavis calls – borrowing the phrase from D. W. Harding – the 'creation of concepts'. At the same time, the critic's response to what he reads is that of an individual with a specific background and education living at a particular time. His account of what he reads is faithful to the extent that it derives from such a recognition. It is inevitably therefore evaluative and an expression of his 'ethical sensibility'. This, one might have thought, was an aspect of his thinking which would make him specially congenial to Marxists. To ask the critic to be something else is after all to ask him to deny his own historicity.

However, Leavis does not assume that because our judgments of what we read are personal, to the extent that they are authentic, they are therefore necessarily untrue and reflections merely of class interest, education and family background.

'The common pursuit of true judgment' and the understanding

of 'human nature' remain for him feasible as well as necessary aims. This may explain the other common Marxist charge, that of 'idealism', an idealism which, according to Terry Eagleton, he derives from D. H. Lawrence (see *Criticism and ideology*, p. 15). This is, of course, idealism not as Lawrence but as Marx understood it, and it consists, for the Marxist, in the hypostatisation of contingent historically determined and temporary aspects of human life into unchanging entities. Eagleton refers (p. 159), as if Leavis had made these his own, to Lawrence's reflections on the 'male' and 'female' principles.

The Marxist critique of Leavis can be compared in this one respect with the Marxist critique in France of the structuralism of Lévi-Strauss and all those who insist on seeing society, myth and language from a 'synchronic', i.e. non-historical, point of view. Jean-Paul Sartre, for example, who speaks in this respect from the Marxist point of view, once declared in an interview ('Sartre aujourd'hui', p. 93) that the structuralists were denying both history and human 'praxis' and described the rôle of 'praxis' in the following terms:

Man is for me the product of structure, but only in so far as he goes beyond it. If you like, there are static moments of history which are structures. Man receives these structures – and in this sense, one can say he is formed by them. But he receives them in such a way that he is unable not to destroy them, in order to constitute new structures which will condition him in their turn. As Marx puts it, 'the secret of the worker is the death of the bourgeoisie'.[11]

The term 'human nature' for Sartre, as for Michel Foucault and for Barthes, belongs, characteristically to the eighteenth-century Enlightenment, when the rising but not yet triumphant bourgeoisie identified its own interests, mistakenly, with those of mankind as a whole. According to Sartre, the myth of human nature was exploded by Marx himself who (Sartre quotes here approvingly) saw only 'workers, bourgeois and intellectuals' ('Sartre aujourd'hui', p. 93).

If there is a contrast with Leavis here it is, however, by no means simple. Sartre, while rejecting the term and the assumed reality corresponding to it, needs it in order to tell us (p. 91) that 'Man is...the product of structure.' And Leavis, while using the word deliberately, points out the difficulties, as well as the necessity, of using it with concrete application; in his discussion, for example, of a remarkable contemporary witness of the eighteenth-century Enlightenment.

Blake's genius was to be in the sense in which a great novelist necessarily is, a profound psychologist...He presents with clairvoyant penetration and compelling actuality the state – or rather the interacting energies, the disharmonies, the conflicts and the transmutations – of humanity as it is. When, however, he is faced with presenting the restored condition of the Eternal Man, the joyous resolution, he is at a loss. How can Man be brought before us unless as a man? It is true that the equivocal freedom from schematic, or logical, rigidity with which Blake uses personification and symbolism in general – a freedom that we find from time to time to be strikingly justified – enables him, in dealing with the condition of Eternity, to suggest that it is compatible with a familiar kind of human interplay between separate centres of sentience, so that the Eternal Man, the realized inclusive total harmony and unity, can be social life too. But it is only by being vague, general and boring that Blake escapes being arrestingly paradoxical...Love, we are made to believe, reigns in Eternity; but what can we make of the idea of love – human love – as belonging to a supremely human order (the Blakean eternal reality is essentially that) in which Man (or a man) is Woman (or a woman) too, and Woman Man, the sexes having ceased to exist?

(*Nor shall my sword*, pp. 17–18)

Leavis's discussion of Blake reveals him as also (despite his admiration for Morris's *News from nowhere*) explicitly anti-Utopian. Blake's Jerusalem is

a posited goal or τέλος – one that Blake constantly fails to make anything but posited. To say 'constantly' is to recognize Blake's awareness of his failure – failure by the criteria that as an artist he presents us with. The awareness is implicit in the way in which, over the years, he tried again and again in his poetico-mythopoeic explorations to arrive at a convincingly 'created' suggestion of what would succeed the reversal of the Fall.

(*Nor shall my sword*, p. 11)

The paradox, which Blake could not bear to leave as a paradox, by which intelligent activity and thought are directed to an end which determines and partially controls the acting and thinking and yet is unknown, became for Leavis, in his later writing, the most significant distinguishing feature of literary criticism and that which revealed its ultimate affinity with *all* creative exploratory thinking, including that of experimental science. The affinity was justified for Leavis by his reading of the works of Whitehead, Marjorie Grene and Michael Polanyi. It is possible that other philosophers and scientists would have provided similar corroboration, especially those who, following Sir Karl Popper,[12] point out the primacy of the hypothesis in scientific experiment and the necessarily unsystematic and unpredictable ways in which discoveries are made or, like Jacques Monod, who sees biological evolution itself as unpredictable, 'compatible certainly with first principles, but not deducible from them' (*Le hasard et la nécessité*, p. 55). For Monod, neither the dialecticism of Hegel nor that of Marx corresponds to what can be observed by the biologist or to experimental procedure (p. 194); though this is not to deny the place of human thought in human evolution. Language, for example, has contributed not only to the evolution of culture but 'in a decisive way to the physical evolution of man' (p. 150). The paradox of teleology is also, for Monod as for Leavis, fundamental to an understanding of the human condition.

Where Leavis stands in the history of ideas (and contrary to what is often supposed, was conscious of standing) is, in other words, fairly clear, if one thinks of his freedom either from a positivist view of his own activity, such as that which is implicit in Barthes's earlier writing, or from the Hegelian or Marxist theory or habit; and if one considers the epistemology he offers instead. This epistemology is, by its nature (as I have already argued), tentative and incomplete; it not only stands or falls by, it has its *raison d'être* in, the contribution it offers to our understanding of actual and immediate problems, the practical problems of understanding what is being said. 'Practical criticism', Leavis reminds us, 'is criticism in practice' (*The living principle*, p. 19). It is tentative and incomplete but it is also invulnerable to one of the commonest objections made to 'dialecticism' in general: that, as Merleau-Ponty puts it (*Le visible et l'invisible*, p. 229), once the dialectic itself becomes a thesis, i.e. is asserted by men at a certain point in history, it can no longer be asserted absolutely or if it is, 'is no longer dialectical'.

What is necessary in criticism is not only the recognition that what is studied is by its nature unpredictable, known and yet irreducible to what can be known in advance. Relevant too is the other (related) paradox that it is at the same time 'human' and 'individual'. This is what Benveniste (*Problèmes de linguistique générale II*, p. 68) calls 'the singular dialectic' by which language 'offers the speakers the same system of personal references which each appropriates through the act of language and which, in each instance of its use and as soon as it is assumed by its enunciator, becomes unique and unlike any other'. Leavis again sees in Blake an example of purposeful thinking about the implications of this (once stated) obvious enough paradoxical truth:

Blake's testimony is profoundly true: he lays such emphasis on art and the artist because the artist's developed creativity is the supreme manifestation of the creativity inherent in and inseparable from life – strictly inseparable, so that without it there is no perception. Except in the individual there is no creativity . . . But the potently individual such as an artist is discovers, as he explores his most intimate experience, how inescapably social he is in his very individuality. The poet, for instance, didn't create the language without which he couldn't have begun to be a poet, and a language is more than an instrument of expression.   (*Nor shall my sword*, p. 171)

To speak merely for oneself, merely as a member of a social class[13] (a worker, bourgeois or intellectual) or even merely as a member of a congenial group (as in Barthes's now increasingly actual as well as ideal Fourierist, i.e. pluralistic, society), would be to deny the possibility of understanding the grounds of one's separateness. 'As creative identity, the individual is the agent of life, and "knows that he does not belong to himself". He serves something that is quite other than his selfhood which is blind and blank to it' (*Nor shall my sword*, p. 172). Knowing this is to be conscious of responsibilities and also dangers. Like Derrida and Barthes, Leavis assumes in his reader some familiarity with the works of Nietzsche, though his admiration is somewhat more qualified than theirs. 'We didn't need Nietzsche to tell us to live dangerously', he writes, recalling the early days of the Cambridge English School, 'there is no other way of living' (*English literature in our time and the university*, p. 15).

(vi)

It would be absurd, of course, to pretend that no better vindication of the function of criticism, as Leavis understood it, could be found than the one he offers himself; or, for that matter, that one could ever be found that was known to be impregnable to any future objections; though a more perfect example of criticism in practice and greater fortitude in its defence I myself find hard to imagine. The fortitude lay especially in his resistance throughout his career to different forms of Philistinism, and in his readiness to seem ridiculous in the eyes of those who would not or could not see what was endangered in a world in which it was ceasing to matter very much whether we understood what other people were saying or, consequently, what we were saying ourselves:

The disturbing force of Polanyi's account of education[14] is illustrated by an exchange I had with a young man of research-student status in an Oxford Common Room. He was an American – inquiring and obviously nice; and, concluding that I was old enough to have been contemporary with the 1914 war, he asked some questions about the moral impact on the country, and referred in due course to the Somme. I replied that, yes, I supposed the country *had* been profoundly disturbed; speaking as one who had found himself trying to tot up from one casualty-list in the papers and odd reports, the sum of school-fellows dead in a morning, I didn't see how it could be otherwise. I added, still dwelling on a recalled particular sense of the general realization of disaster that shook the country, and not meaning in the least to imply irony – certainly not prepared for the response I drew, that those innumerable boy-subalterns who figured in the appalling Roll of Honour as 'Fallen Officers' had climbed out and gone forward, playing their part in the attacking wave, to be mowed down with the swathes that fell to the uneliminated machine guns. The comment, quietly sure of its matter-of-fact felicity, was: 'The death-wish!' My point is that I didn't know what to say. What actually came out was, 'They didn't *want* to die.' I felt I couldn't stop there but how go on? 'They were brave' – that came to me as a faint prompting, but no; it didn't begin to express my positive intention; it didn't even lead towards it. I gave up, there was nothing else to do.

('Elites, oligarchies and an educated public', p. 18)

'Criticism', like modern poetry, had become both respectable and fashionable by the time Leavis ended his academic career in Cambridge; and Joyce's *Ulysses*, Leavis's lectures on which had been attended in 1925 by plain-clothes policemen, is now a prescribed text in most universities. Leavis could easily have allowed himself to be lionised. Instead, one could say, he preferred to remain a man.

It is not only with the nature and presuppositions of Leavis's thinking, however, that the present study is concerned but with the alternative it offers to the now far more fashionable theory and practice coming from France and of which Barthes is the most distinguished representative. The difference between Barthes and Leavis is not merely one that can be noticed and that matters only if one pursues what each is saying to its remotest implications. It is a fundamental difference in the very habit of thinking and hence of style, despite the fact that each is in his own way allusive and sophisticated and sustained by what is recognisably, in certain respects, still the same humanist culture.

It may be appropriate therefore to conclude by comparing the ways in which Leavis and Barthes each thinks of sophistication and by quoting, to begin with, an instance in which Barthes has an advantage over Leavis in that he writes out of affectionate familiarity with a novel Leavis regarded as practically unworthy of comment, one of his blind spots, *Bouvard et Pécuchet*.[15] The subtlety and challenge of Flaubert's last novel, as Barthes sees it, lie in the fact that it refuses to be reduced to any satirical or misanthropic intention; whatever Flaubert himself may have said about it in his letters. However, this, for Barthes, amounts to saying that it can be read as if the words corresponded to no intention at all and had thereby attained the condition of authentic *écriture*. Flaubert does not, in the manner of Balzac, indulge in 'irony' at the expense of his two auto-didacts, and thereby assume a simple and unselfcritical form of solidarity with his readers. Not only is explicit judgment rare and, even then, not necessarily what it seems; there is no obviously superior intellectual or moral vantage-point to be found among the other presented characters in the novel. The text therefore which presents them

opens up a circularity in which no one (not even the author) has any advantage over anyone else: and this is, of course, the function of writing itself (*écriture*): to render derisory, annul the power (the intimidation) of one language over another, to dissolve, as soon as it is constituted, any meta-language   (*S/Z*, p. 105)

By 'metalanguage', presumably, we must understand any expressed viewpoint, direct or oblique, to which what is said in the text refers back, any equivalent of Balzac's simple sarcastic 'code'.

   This is certainly an interesting attempt to explain the profoundly disconcerting effect of Flaubert's humour and the beautiful reson-ance at every stage of the prose. It also, I find, leaves me asking whether, after all, Barthes might not be right to say that it is possible to read a text as if no one had written it. Yet is it true that 'no one (not even the author) has any advantage over anyone else'? The author has the advantage, at least, of his Sphinx-like elusiveness. Bouvard and Pécuchet themselves, at various points, and increasingly as the novel continues, have, if not an intellectual, an obvious moral advantage over their country neighbours. Morally, they are anything but contemptible, whereas the local representatives of the political Left and the Right, including the local priest, are morally sinister. If, by absence of 'metalanguage', Barthes means absence of anything like a paraphrasable moral to the novel as a whole, then what he is saying may be true.[16] This is however, a tribute to the novel's creative power or, to put it more neutrally, to the way it transcends moral commonplace. Without that power, the novel would not have been so clear, and at the same time so enigmatic, so plainly irreducible to the moral point of view of any one or more of its characters. Whether one calls this the power of the novel or the power of the author scarcely matters. It is a power that has all the characteristics of human thought.

Whether Barthes meant to say that Flaubert the novelist speaks to us with no more authority than, say, his village priest, his village schoolmaster or his bandit-like village revolutionary is by no means certain. And it may be that the critic was thinking more at this point of a familiar theory than of the novel itself. The regrettably short comments on Flaubert are made to show how different he is from Balzac in his treatment of 'stereotype' or cliché. Balzac, we are told, failed to realise that the condemnation of one kind of cultural stereotype is not in itself enough to guarantee the novelist who condemns it or refers to it ironically against the dangers of asserting another stereotype in his turn. Though Balzac doesn't see the problem, he, none the less, reveals it, and the problem remains: how can one escape from the 'vertiginous' and infinite repetition of distancing judgments, which any rejection of cliché entails, unless a circle takes the place of an infinite regression and judgment ends up by annulling itself? This is Barthes's solution to the problem and, so he claims, that of Flaubert as well. It has a number of clear theoretical advantages, in so far as the model proposed remains consistent with itself and, to this extent, is perfectly clear. It also suggests a way in which the admirer of such a novel may reconcile his present admiration for this achievement of the past with his belief in the inevitability of progress and of the normal supersession of the achievements of the past. Unfortunately, it doesn't work when it comes to an actual reading of *Bouvard et Pécuchet*, in which, if only temporarily (and Flaubert is good at reminding us that all human affairs are temporary), different characters and the viewpoints they represent have unmistakable advantages over others. To doubt this with regard to a novel which, in this respect, is so clear would be to doubt the possibility of making anything of it at all and hence even of finding it amusing.

The assertion of values and beliefs, whether or not it amounts to 'intimidation', is not in itself tantamount to cliché. To assert a stereotype is, on the contrary, to ask that something be taken on trust; that it should not, except superficially, be thought about at all or hence really valued or believed (see Leavis on what he sees as the clichés of C. P. Snow, p. 36 above). It is to assert authority rather than the grounds for that authority. The assertion of such authority tends, as commonly in Balzac, to declamation. But nor is declamation always or necessarily the same as cliché; tempted though one may be in our deliberately informal age to dismiss much of the declamatory writing of the past as merely this.

It is perhaps worth comparing therefore Barthes's account of the avoidance of stereotypes in Flaubert with Leavis's reading of two very different English writers, each apparently exploiting a conventional nineteenth-century vein:

> Cold in the earth – and fifteen wild Decembers
> From these brown hills have melted into spring:
> Faithful, indeed, is the spirit that remembers
> After such years of change and suffering!

'Cold in the Earth' by Emily Brontë is, Leavis accepts, a minor poem. The point is made by an extended comparison with Hardy's 'After a Journey', another poem of personal mourning and recollection, though one which has a 'reality' which, by contrast, makes Emily Brontë's, in a real but limiting sense, seem merely 'sincere'.

The poem does unmistakably demand to be read in a plangent declamation: in, that is, a rendering that constitutes an overt assertion of emotional intensity. If we ask why, nevertheless, the dangers such an account might suggest don't seem at any point disturbingly present, we can observe for answer that what is said in stanza seven:

> Then did I check the tears of useless passion

is more than *said*; it represents an active principle that informs the poem and is there along with the plangency. We have it in the movement, in the tough prose rationality, the stating matter-of-factness of good sense, that seems to play against the dangerous running swell: It makes us take the suggestion that some strength corresponding to 'those brown hills', which do not themselves melt, underlies the poem.

The Hardy poem begins (though it should really be quoted at length):

> Hereto I come to view a voiceless ghost;
>   Whither, o whither will its whim now draw me?
> Up the cliff, down, till I'm lonely, lost,
>   And the unseen water's ejaculations awe me.
> Where you will next be, there's no knowing,
> Facing round about me everywhere,
>   With your nut-coloured hair,
> And gray eyes, and rose-flush coming and going.

Unlike 'Cold in the Earth' this

is not declamatory. The point should in justice lead on to a positive formulation, and this may not come as readily; certain stylistic characteristics that may at first strike the reader as oddities and clumsinesses tend to delay the recognition of the convincing intimate naturalness. It turns out, however, that the essential ethos of the manner is given in

> Where you will next be, there's no knowing.

This intimacy we are at first inclined to describe as 'conventional', only to replace that adjective by 'self-communing' when we have recognized that even when Hardy (and it is significant that we say 'Hardy') addresses the 'ghost' he is still addressing himself.   (*The living principle*, pp. 126–8)

The commentary is quite long and I am assuming that the reader, if he is not familiar with it already, will read it through to the end. I have quoted just enough, I hope, to illustrate my own comparison.

This, no less than Barthes's account of Balzac and Flaubert, is one that can only be confirmed or refuted by the way the critic's reader finds himself reading the text under discussion. At the same time, it lacks what Barthes characteristically offers: a theoretical plausibility which may satisfy someone who has not read the text itself. The 'active principle' of which Leavis speaks is (audibly or not at all) within Emily Brontë's poem. The tentativeness of phrases like 'some strength' and 'running swell' is justified only by a reading of the poem. The argument entails an acknowledgment, deriving from Leavis's own first impressions or those of other readers, of the obstacles to recognition of what is being said and enacted in both poems and the adjustments of response and definition this compels. When I say that Leavis made no claim to be anything other than a critic, I am thinking not only of his freedom from the philosophical ambitions associated with structuralism, but of the human creativity which, as he understood it, criticism merely serves.

NOTES

1. Introduction. Reading as distinct from talking or writing about books

1. 'How the young man should study poetry', section 16. This obvious but often forgotten fact can be re-stated by pointing out what is also often overlooked: that the author and *persona* of a poem or narrator of a work of fiction are not the same, any more than the story is equivalent to the narrative. It would be absurd to pretend that we never need reminding of this.
2. A systematic enquiry into the effects and possible benefits of the study of literature in schools in England and abroad has been made and the results published in *Literature education in ten countries* by A. C. Purves. It seems to be nowhere assumed in this study, however, that the effects might be, in a number of cases, harmful from the point of view of a young person's development and in general detrimental to the growth of the kind of public on which worth-while literature depends.
3. On the other hand, there are some reasons for believing that the study of Latin literature in Jesuit colleges in the seventeenth century, which also offered free education to a large cross-section of society and emphasised written composition and the performance of plays as part of the normal curricular and extra-curricular activities, created the educated public without which there might never have been a Corneille, a Molière or a Racine.
4. If only there were more teachers like Raymond O'Malley, quoted by Margaret Mathieson in *The preachers of culture* (p. 118): 'It is of the utmost importance to perceive the possibility of unconscious meanings, to respect them and to leave them alone ... The good teacher develops an acute sense of the presence of deeper meanings. He knows what not to remark upon. He knows how to give oblique reinforcement, but he is scrupulous not to know too much. This extra sense gives the necessary blend of reticence and warmth that makes for good teaching.'

2. Benveniste and semiology

1. See Roland Barthes, 'Eléments de sémiologie' and *Système de la mode* (discussed in Chapter 3) and Claude Lévi-Strauss, *Anthropologie structurale, Le cru et le cuit*, etc.
2. Structuralist theory seems to have been influenced both by Husserlian

176

phenomenology and its search for a non-metaphysical realm of absolute (apodictic) certainty (see F. Wahl, 'Philosophie et structuralisme', in *Qu'est-ce que le structuralisme?*) and by Hegel. J.-M. Benoist, in *La révolution structuraliste* (p. 320), writes as follows: 'It should be noted, in fact, that in its local applications, structuralism reproduces, in combinatory fashion, the ambitions of what Hegel had called absolute knowledge.' The 'revelation to itself' of structure, to which structuralism aspires, is 'comparable to the reflexion on itself of absolute knowledge'. Jacques Derrida also sees Hegel as the first semiologist. (See *Marges de la philosophie*, pp. 79–127.)

3. 'Shaken us', that is, if we fall victim to the illusion that there is no problem or mystery in the attribution of authorship to a text. It would be an error, none the less, to suppose that before Benoist's revolution, there was no awareness of the problem or the mystery and it would be interesting, in this respect, to read, should one exist, a history of the idea of authorship.

4. The difficulty, Benoist argues, of breaking away from an 'anthropomorphic' view of the world is that the only alternative may appear to be one that is 'anthropocentric': 'Get rid of the anthropomorph and he comes back at the gallop' (pp. 16–23). Benoist is here echoing Michel Foucault's claim that Man, as we know him, is a fairly recent invention and destined fairly soon to disappear (*The order of things*, p. 387), a fairly unexceptionable statement if we accept that psychological and philosophical as distinct from zoological definitions of the human obviously vary from one time and place to another. A far more devastating account than Foucault's of the notions of humanity we have inherited from the eighteenth century is to be found in D. H. Lawrence's essay in *Phoenix I* entitled 'The good man'.

5. Compare the arguments of Benveniste, as summarised and quoted below, with the discussion in the opening chapter of Lévi-Strauss's *Le cru et le cuit* of signifying and non-signifying elements of music, painting and the spoken and written language. Benveniste's authority is called upon (p. 28) to justify the assertion that 'linguistic signs' in general are 'arbitrary' and that meaning or significance as such is '*cantonée sur un plan*', i.e. localised within and restricted to a pre-established scheme or design.

Compare too Julia Kristeva's contribution to *Langue, discours, société*, a collection of essays in honour of Benveniste of which he himself, through the generosity of the contributors, was to receive the royalties. Benveniste's last few years, after his retirement from the Collège de France, were spent in sadly reduced circumstances and he needed his friends. 'The two functions of predication noted by Benveniste', Kristeva writes, '(referential assertion and identifying cohesion) introduce "exteriority" into formality and, inversely, exteriorise the formality of the linguistic system' (p. 232). This leads to the notion that the interchangeability of the two terms amounts to an equivalence. Hence perhaps the inverted commas with which the word 'exteriority' is supplied. Hence too the assertion on the same page that 'predication constitutes a finitude', by which Kristeva seems to mean a closed system. However, her argument isn't easy to follow and I may easily have got this wrong.

Kristeva is, however, positively misleading when she refers to Benveniste's 'unique study as a linguist of language in Freudian discovery' (p. 231), all the more so in that she calls on the authority of Freud in support of the view that 'a repression (*Ausstossung*) or a negation are inherent in every affirmation...' Benveniste's 'Remarques sur la fonction du langage dans la découverte freudienne' (*Problèmes de linguistique générale*), far from endorsing Freudian views of negation, is a refutation of what Freud says about language. Freud's belief that primitive languages resemble the logic of dreams, in that they ignore the idea of negation and consist of numerous contradictory assertions, was inspired by his reading of Karl Abel, who had argued that the Old English *bat*, for example, meaning 'better', derived from *badde* meaning 'bad' and that *without* was a compound combining the notions of 'with' and 'out' and hence, virtually, amounting to 'with–without'. Abel's claims, Benveniste argues, are based on a series of simple howlers.

6. Alain used to ask his pupils to close their eyes, imagine the Parthenon and then see if they could count the columns. A similar point, with regard to the acoustic image, is made by Wittgenstein, *Philosophical investigations* (ii xi), 'I feel as if the name "Schubert" fitted Schubert's works and Schubert's face'.

7. This extreme view has also been contested by Roman Jakobson who maintains that the very sounds of a language are invariable and a change in any of the sounds is tantamount to a change in the entire linguistic system. See 'Phonology and Phonetics' (with M. Halle) in Roman Jakobson, *Selected writings*, vol. i, pp. 464-504.

8. Benveniste's distinction between the different 'levels' to which the phonemes, morphemes and sentence correspond is made from a strictly linguistic point of view. It's worth recalling here, none the less, the importance from the point of view of the philosophy of language of the distinction between the sentence and its constituent parts, as discussed by Frege, W. V. O. Quine and Michael Dummett. Professor Dummett, in his book on Frege's philosophy of language, argues that Quine misinterprets Frege when he claims that for the latter the unit of significance is 'not the word but the sentence'. Rather, Dummett suggests, if Frege's account 'is to be reduced to a slogan... in the order of *explanation* the sentence is primary, but in the order of *recognition* the sense of a word is primary... Since it is only by means of a sentence that we can perform a linguistic act – that we can *say* anything – the possession of a sense by a word or complex expression short of a sentence cannot consist in anything else but its being governed by a general rule which partially specifies the sense of sentences containing it. *If this is so, then on pain of circularity, the general notion of the sense possessed by a sentence must be capable of being explained without reference to the notion of the sense of constituent words or expressions*' (pp. 3-5). I have put in my own italics what, from Professor Dummett's viewpoint, corroborates entirely, as I see it, Benveniste's own definition of the sentence.

9. See 'Catégories de pensée et catégories de langue' (*Problèmes de linguistique générale*). Benveniste's argument here seems to me circular and – since he also maintains in the same volume ('Communication animale et langage humain') that animals, with the possible exception of bees, don't possess language – somewhat Cartesian. Benveniste, of course, wrote this before the remarkable experiments with chimpanzees learning human sign-language reported by, among others, Eugene Linden in *Apes, men and language*. For a fuller account of the relations between thought and language, see *Language learning and thought* (ed. J. Macnamara) and especially Professor Macnamara's own contributions. (See also pp. 117–23 above.)

10. See Benveniste (*Problèmes de linguistique générale*, p. 129), 'The phonemic level is that of the phoneme; there exist, in fact, concrete phonemes which can be isolated, combined and numbered. But categoremes? Do they exist? The predicate is a fundamental property of the sentence, it isn't the unit of a sentence. There are not several varieties of predication. And nothing would be changed, in this general constation, if for "categoreme" one substituted "phraseme".'

    For what seems to me a thorough and convincing account of where Greimas's system breaks down, see J. Culler, *Structuralist poetics*, pp. 75–95.

11. There is not, according to Derrida, any term that is not reducible to others, no logically simple terms, not even the word 'being'. In his critique of Husserl (*La voix et le phénomène*), Derrida denies even the possibility of knowing for certain one's own intentions when one speaks. This is a situation we must accept 'without *nostalgia*, that is, outside the myth of a purely paternal or maternal language, a lost homeland of thought. We should, in fact, *affirm* this, in the sense which Nietzsche lends to the word "affirm", through laughter, if you like and by taking a step into the dance' (*Marges de la philosophie*, p. 29). Derrida more than once recommends Nietzsche as an excellent guide to living with the absurd.

12. See Edmund Leach, *Lévi-Strauss* (pp. 112–13). 'When Lévi-Strauss tries to reach into the "human mind" (*l'esprit humain*) he is grasping at the structural aspects of the Unconscious. But Lévi-Strauss's approach is through linguistics rather than psychology. The linguistic model which Lévi-Strauss employs is now largely out of date. Present-day theoreticians in the field of structural linguistics have come to recognise that the deep-level process of pattern generation and pattern recognition that is entailed by the human capacity to attach complex semantic significance to speech utterances must depend on mechanisms of much greater complexity than is suggested by the digital computer model which underlies the Jakobson–Lévi-Strauss theories. Jakobson's schema of a limited set of binary distinctive features common to all human languages... is not necessarily false but it is certainly inadequate.'

13. For a bibliography of Jakobson's prodigious output, see *Janua Linguarum*, series minor, no. 134, Mouton, The Hague, 1971. At the time of writing, I know of no better collection of his essays on poetry than *Questions de*

poétique, 1973. Jakobson's essay on 'Linguistics and poetics' (in *Style in language*, ed. T. E. Sebeok) is, of course, of interest not only from the point of view of linguistics and poetry. Paul Ricœur in *La métaphore vive* (pp. 185–7, 223–5, 280–3), while differing from Jakobson in many respects, sees the central idea of this paper as of immense possible philosophical significance. The central idea (reminiscent of Sartre's definition of poetry in chapter 1 of *Qu'est-ce que la littérature?*) is that the poetic function is that which gives prominence to the message itself; that is, to the sign as signifier, and thus deepens the dichotomy between signs and objects. The paradigmatic axis of utterance, i.e. the implicit principle of selection of words deriving from their grammatical or phonological function, comes to determine strongly the syntagmatic, the normal meaningful sequence of words. Grammatical and phonic characteristics of language thus take on a positive semantic rôle, as in the poetry of Hopkins or the 1952 election slogan, 'I like Ike.' That this is a real phenomenon, of which countless examples could be found, would not be disputed; or that in a reading of Hopkins especially, it may be of profound linguistic, psychological or philosophical interest. The phenomenon is not, however, confined to poetry (cf. 'I like Ike') and Culler finds examples of it even in Jakobson's own discursive prose (*Structuralist poetics*, pp. 63–4). Moreover, there are many passages of what it would be difficult not to think of as poetry, e.g. parts of Wordsworth's *Prelude* or the non-rhyming poems of Edward Thomas, in which, while the 'message' is indeed of value in itself, there is no more obvious interplay of the two axes of selection and combination than can be found in ordinary prose.

14. Professor Riffaterre's attempts in *Semiotics of poetry* to characterise rigorously the poetic use of language comes no nearer, it may be argued, than Jakobson's to disproving Lawrence's claim that 'all speech is art speech'. What he says of the process of listening or reading is, none the less, an interesting corroboration of Hirsch's and Pettit's account, in so far as it stresses the restrictions imposed on freedom of interpretation by a proper understanding of the spoken and written word (see pp. 163–6).

15. Professor Pettit is interested in what has come to be known as implicational logic. I am too ignorant of this subject to know whether, taking as it does the logic of ordinary speech and of non-propositional as well as propositional utterance, it would ever provide the self-explanatory and totally inclusive account of human language envisaged by Saussure. Implicational logic has a lot to say about formal logic, i.e. about the assumptions underlying propositions. To what extent it could enable us to make predictions about the kinds of thing people could or could not meaningfully say I have no means of telling and Pettit does not make any ambitious claims in this respect.

16. See Barthes (*Leçon inaugurale prononcée au Collège de France*, p. 39): 'The semiologist would appear, in fact, to be an artist ... He plays with signs, as with some alluring and deceptive artifice, conscious and of which he is himself conscious, which he savours, wishes to make others savour and understand the fascination.' Barthes's thoughtful and helpful

chapter on criticism in *Critique et vérité* (pp. 63-75) makes the point
that the critic has a responsibility to his own language as well as that of
the author on whom it is commenting. And John Newton ('Leavis's new
book', pp. 367-9) has described Leavis's finest criticism as 'poetry'. Both
these thoughts are valuable but as long as it is remembered that criticism
– as distinct from poetry and whether or not it is also poetry – is a means
to an end, which is understanding of another text. Leavis's finest criticism
is often, in fact, incomprehensible or incoherent-seeming (see p. 175)
unless one reads it, as he repeatedly insists that one should, at the same
time as the text.

17. I am, of course, using 'language game' in the sense popularised by Wittgenstein. My no doubt presumptuous remarks on 'deep structure' are
justified only, as far as I know, by Noam Chomsky's own account of the
investigations he had inaugurated twenty years before in *Reflections on
language* (ch. 4) and the still tentative nature of the original hypotheses.

18. This now conventional requirement leads Jonathan Culler to compliment
'critics of every persuasion who have tried to be explicit about what they
are doing' (*Structuralist poetics*, p. 128). F. R. Leavis, who is notoriously
unforthcoming in this respect (see Chapter 5) usually gets a very bad press
as a result and is conspicuously absent from both Culler's *Structuralist
poetics* and Northrop Frye's *The anatomy of criticism*.

19. See R. Barthes: 'the semiologist is he who expresses his future death in
the very terms in which he has named and understood the world'
(*Système de la mode*, p. 293).

20. The late Jacques Monod claimed that biological evolution, as he understood it, in no way conformed to behaviour that Hegelian or Marxist
views of change would help us to understand. 'The thesis that I shall be
presenting here', he writes in *Le hasard et la nécessité* (p. 55), 'is that the
biosphere does not contain a foreseeable class of objects or phenomena
but constitutes a particular event, compatible certainly with first principles
but not *deducible* from these principles. Therefore essentially unpredictable' Benoist (predictably) upbraids him for 'un certain chosisme, un
certain être-là des choses' ('a certain thing-ism, a certain being-there-ness
of things') and describes *Le hasard et la nécessité* as a 'pre-Socratic poem'
(*La révolution structuraliste*, pp. 177-87).

3. Thoughts on how we read

1. See Sartre, *Qu'est-ce que la littérature?* (ch. 1). Sartre's account of how
poetry, especially French poetry since Rimbaud and Mallarmé, differs
essentially from discursive prose has had more influence on more recent
criticism and theory than is often realised. The whole of this chapter
(together with the qualifying footnotes in which Sartre admits that he is
making a relative and not an absolute distinction) deserves study, as does
also his later essay on Mallarmé (*Situations IX*). Julia Kristeva's account
of the linguistic revolution apparent in the poetry of Mallarmé and
Lautréamont corroborates in enormous detail Sartre's, though she does
not refer to it (*La révolution du langage poétique*). It is very long, shows

evidence of prodigious reading and is a book, I should confess, I have not been able to read through with sustained attention. I may be wrong therefore in suspecting that her discouragement of a close and focused reading – for all the detailed analysis – is here a form of deliberate 'mistreatment' of the texts, of the kind recommended by Barthes in *S/Z* (see pp. 138–9).

2. The account of intention I am outlining here is, I assume, familiar and, I hope, unexceptionable. It is not, as far as I can tell, at variance with Elizabeth Anscombe's far more perspicaciously argued *Intention*, which offers, for example, in sections 5–7, a more thoughtful and detailed version of my simple distinction between acts and accidents. Nor, I should like to think, is it at variance with a rather different view of intention from Professor Anscombe's, such as that of Gilbert Ryle in chapter 3 of *The concept of mind*. I take it that we can all assume that there is a difference between walking and falling downstairs, and that this is not just a difference of mechanics or physiology, in however many different ways we may account for the difference and whatever we claim we are able to know about it. I regard it as also philosophically uncontroversial that solving a problem is something one can do twice only if one has forgotten the solution or forgotten how one reached it; which is what I go on to argue here.

3. 'It is shameful for the human spirit', Voltaire wrote in his *Commentary* on Corneille (note on *Le Cid*, I, vi), 'that the same expression should be found good at one period of history and bad at another.' In *Le siècle de Louis XIV* (ch. 22), he comments also, 'It must not be thought that the great tragic passions and sentiments can be varied indefinitely in a new and striking way. There are limits to everything.' In Voltaire's literary criticism, Augustanism takes on a more rigidly conventional form than in Dr Johnson's, but it is remarkable, none the less, how close French assumptions and terminology are to English during this period. As far as literature and philosophy are concerned, Paris was far closer to London, Oxford and Cambridge in the eighteenth century than it is today. The citizens of the world today are the scientists and mathematicians.

4. How does one ever deceive *oneself*? The best introduction I know to discussion of how this common feat is possible is in H. Fingarette's *Self-deception* and *The self. Psychological and philosophical issues*, ed. T. Mischel.

5. I should not want to defend Grice's theory against the criticisms of John Searle in *Speech acts* or those of Chomsky in *Reflections on language*. Like Chomsky, I see no reason why 'meaning' should necessarily be equated with the 'use' made of words (pp. 55–77), a view often attributed to Wittgenstein; though, in fact, Wittgenstein argues (*Philosophical investigations*, I, 42, p. 20e) that 'the meaning of a word is its use in the language' in many but not in 'all cases'. Nor do I see why 'meaning' should always, as Grice and Searle both agree, be a matter of seeking, either overtly or virtually, to produce a certain effect in the listener or reader. There are many cases, as Chomsky says, where this may not be the case at all; as when he made a speech against the Vietnam War

which could only, towards the end, be heard by a group of soldiers who were advancing in full combat gear to clear the area where he was speaking. This is, of course, not a denial of the intentionality of writing or speech or of the possibility of understanding writers' or speakers' intentions. Hence, it does not, any more than Searle's critique, contradict the quotations from Grice I happen to find useful here.

6. Northrop Frye's view of the rôle of what he calls the 'ethical' or 'rhetorical' critic resembles somewhat Roland Barthes's view of the rôle of criticism as distinct from literary 'science' (*Critique et vérité*, part II). He is quite consistent in claiming that his avowed interest in taxonomy and formal definition precludes an interest in ethics, experience or historical fact. He is less consistent, however, in going on to claim that there are 'no definite positions to be taken in chemistry or philology and if there are any to be taken in criticism, criticism is not a field of genuine learning' (*Anatomy of criticism*, p. 19). If by 'definite', he means fixed and unbudgeable, obviously he is right but this is not what either he or 'definite' means. The scientist's and the serious scholar's concern for the truth, as distinct from what they would like to believe, is concern for truth both in general and in what is for them the all-important particular instance. This concern is (if anything, more than that of most other men) a 'definite position' and an ethical one too. Galileo would have had something to say about this, as would the Soviet geneticists who refused to pay lip-service to the theories of Lysenko. An excellent account of the confusions to be found in Frye's theoretical writings can be read in John Fraser's essay, 'Northrop Frye and evaluation'.

7. For the non-philosopher such as myself, the theory that 'P corresponds to the facts if and only if *p*', seems disconcertingly trite. The interest and immense originality of Tarski's theory within the context of previous philosophical debate are shown, from two somewhat different points of view, by Putnam (*Meaning and the moral sciences*) and by Sir Karl Popper in *Objective knowledge* (chapters 2 and 9). As usual, I prefer not to let my argument rest on a point of reasonable philosophical controversy if I can avoid it. I am therefore grateful for Putnam's suggestion that formal truth criteria may be invoked to explain the success of our understanding of others but that they in no way ensure this.

8.   Remettez-vous, monsieur, d'une alarme si chaude
       Nous vivons sous un Prince, ennemi de la fraude,
       Un Prince dont les yeux se font jour dans les cœurs,
       Et que ne peut tromper tout l'art des imposteurs.   (v, vii)

('Give yourself time to recover, Sir, from the frightening shock you've just had. We live under a prince who is the enemy of fraud, a prince whose eyes see clearly into men's hearts and whom all the wiles of imposters cannot deceive.')

9. There is an instructive parallel in this respect with the behaviour of the audience at the Paris opera as described by Stendhal: 'In Italy, it is not like Paris, where the first performance is rarely decisive and vanity prevents each one from expressing his personal opinion, for fear lest it

should not conform with that of the majority. On the contrary, in an Italian theatre people shout and stamp their feet with the utmost possible violence, to impose their own personal judgment of a new opera on others and to prove above all that this judgment is the only one which is exact or reasonable. For, strange though this may seem, there is no intolerance equal to that of a highly sensitive man. When you hear someone discourse calmly and methodically on the fine arts, change the conversation at once and talk to him about something else. Such a man may become an excellent magistrate, a good doctor, an enterprising merchant or a learned academician; in fact, anything you like, except a man capable of feeling the charms of music and painting' (*Courrier anglais*, 1, p. 284).

10. The 'true believer' is an expression that needs explaining or qualifying. There are of course degrees of faith and belief varying in the same individual from one moment to the next. Protestations of faith, like protestations of devotion to a political cause, are made all too easily; though this doesn't mean they are necessarily insincere. It is only, presumably, when the faith or devotion are made apparent or found wanting in an actual decision that one finds, sometimes to one's astonishment, what one really believes and what cause one is willing to serve. Archbishop Bloom has suggested that this is nowhere more obvious than in the story of the Apostles before Pentecost and especially of Peter, that 'rock', as Jesus (it is sometimes thought laughingly) called him, on whom he would build his Church. Peter's faith was found wanting: on the first occasion comically, on the last almost tragically. But this doesn't mean that he lacked faith or conviction entirely. Between total belief and total disbelief there are clearly many differences of kind and degree. Total belief is something that communicates itself even to those who don't share it through a person's behaviour, a glance or the spoken or written word. This was presumably the appeal of the historical Christ. It communicates itself for the reasons I am elaborating in this section: because we cannot understand what someone is saying unless we understand whether he is speaking facetiously, insincerely or in earnest. And if we realise that someone is speaking in earnest, it is because we realise that it is possible for someone to take this or that seriously or regard this or that as true. If we don't realise this, we haven't understood him.

11. *Courrier anglais*, v, p. 250. Stendhal is not, however, suggesting that this is the only reason for admiring Dante; and, though an avowed atheist, does not deceive himself that the power of Dante's art has nothing to do with Dante's religion. Note his remarks in this respect on Dante and Michelangelo in the *Histoire de la peinture en Italie* (Vol. II, pp. 362–3): 'In Michelangelo, as in Dante, one's soul is chilled by the excess of seriousness. The absence of any rhetorical device adds considerably to this impression. We see the face of a man who has just seen something which has filled him with horror... Possessed by divine fury like that of an Old Testament prophet, the pride of Michelangelo rejects all sympathy. He is saying to mankind: "Think of your own interest. Here is the God of Israel come to you in all his vengeance."'

12. The case of the Biblical scholar differs, however, it might be argued, from that of the literary critic whose reading of a modern novel leads him to conclude that its realistic intention is justified (see my discussion of Leavis on Dickens and Lawrence, pp. 157–9 above). The truth-claims made by such a critic are not claims about the truth of any particular historical fact or set of facts. Those of the Biblical scholar, in so far as he is more than a scholar and a believing Christian, *are*, presumably, claims about the historical facts: the immaculate conception, the resurrection and the ascension of Christ most notably.

13. Harding's account is entirely corroborated by Sartre who, in *Qu'est-ce que la littérature?* (ch. 2), writes of the act of reading: 'At each instant, I can wake up and I know it; but I don't want to: reading is a free dream (*un rêve libre*).' A fuller and extremely interesting account of the similarities and differences between sleepers' and readers' dreams is developed in *L'imaginaire* (Part iv, iv).

14. Flaubert's testimony is worth quoting in this respect. In the letter to Taine of November 1866 in which he tells him how, after describing the poisoning of Emma Bovary, he threw up his own dinner, he goes on: 'Do not mistake the interior vision of the artist for that of the genuinely hallucinated man. I am perfectly familiar with both of these states; there lies an abyss between them. In hallucination, properly speaking, there is always terror; you feel your personality escaping; you feel you are about to die. In poetic vision, on the other hand, there is joy.'

15.   Prince, l'unique objet du soin des Immortels,
         Souffrez que mon encens parfume vos Autels.
         Je vous offre un peu tard ces Présents de ma Muse;
         Les ans et les travaux me serviront d'excuse:
         Mon esprit diminue, au lieu qu'à chaque instant
         On aperçoit le vôtre aller en augmentant.
         Il ne va pas, il court, il semble avoir des ailes.
         Le Héros dont il tient des qualités si belles
         Dans le métier de Mars brûle d'en faire autant:
         Il ne tient pas à lui que, forçant la victoire,
                 Il ne marche à pas de géant
                 Dans la carrière de la Gloire.
         Quelque Dieu le retient: c'est notre Souverain,
         Lui qu'un mois a rendu maître et vainqueur du Rhin;
         Cette rapidité fut alors nécessaire:
         Peut-être elle serait aujourd'hui téméraire.
         Je m'en tais.

('Prince, the unique object of the Immortals' care, allow my incense to embalm your altars. I bring you, a little late, these offerings from my Muse; my years and my labours will have to be my excuse: my wits grow less, whereas yours, at every instant, one can see growing. They don't walk, they run, they seem to have wings. The hero from whom they inherit such fine qualities, burns to do as much in the trade of Mars. It is not he who is to blame if, forcing victory, he doesn't march with giant's steps in the paths of glory. Some god restrains him: it is our Sovereign, he whom a single month made master and conqueror of the Rhine; this rapidity was then necessary: perhaps today it would be rash. I say no more.')

The poem, addressed to the Dauphin's twelve-year-old son, compares two military campaigns: that of the Dauphin against the League of Augsburg in 1690 (not a conspicuous success) and either (here interpretations differ) the Dauphin's own more successful campaign of two years earlier or the much-celebrated crossing of the Rhine under Louis XIV himself in 1672. La Fontaine's own punctuation (or at least that which he would have seen in the first published texts of the poem), which I retain here, certainly suggests the latter. 'Lui', in line 14, would normally be in apposition to 'Souverain'. This reading is also borne out, I believe, by the rest of this superb and generally under-rated poem, which goes on to describe, with punctilious humility and deference, something rotten in the state of Versailles. The story that follows this prologue, taken from a favourite subject of court ballet, describes how the 'charms' of Circe 'metamorphosed' men into 'beasts'. Though the Pléiade and Garnier editions restore the original punctuation, which the *Grands écrivains* editor had changed by putting brackets round '*c'est notre Souverain*' in line 13, their notes assume an unironic intention on La Fontaine's part and do not discuss the possibility that a more daring and invidious comparison might have been intended. Their notes and introduction also say nothing to suggest that this poem is anything more than a piece of courtly homage folowed by moral commonplace. I owe my realisation that this is a very remarkable poem indeed to my friend Morris Shapira, who, on a long walk on a hot day in 1955 through Paris, countered, in a way only those who know him can imagine, my own conventional objections.

16. See Henri Marrou (*Connaissance de l'histoire*): 'when it was present, the past was like the present that we are living at this very moment, lacking cohesion, confused, multiform, unintelligible, a dense network of causes and effects, a field of forces infinitely complex that the consciousness of man, whether he be actor or witness, is unable to grasp in its authentic reality (there is no privileged observation point, at least not on this earth). We have to go back here to the example which has been classical ever since...Stendhal's Waterloo in *La Chartreuse de Parme*, or even better (for Napoleon himself, according to Tolstoy, is as lost as Prince Andrei or Pierre Bezuhov), the Austerlitz and Borodino of *War and Peace*' (p. 47).

4. The Utopianism of Roland Barthes

1. Barthes has acknowledged the strong influence of the then very fashionable Sartre on his early writings. Both, one might say, have sought constantly to justify the value they find in certain works of literature and in the writing of literature itself in a world which, for practical and philosophical reasons, seems inimical to literature; see note 12 below.

2. Readers of Camus's *L'étranger* will learn from the essay on Dominici,

the octogenarian peasant and presumed murderer of Sir Jack and Lady Drummond in 1952, that high-flown rhetoric of the kind used by the prosecutor and lawyers in Camus's novel was still in 1953 *de rigueur* in important trials. (This was also true ten years later during the trial of the Algerian settlers' leader General Salan.) Where is 'justice', Barthes asks (p. 51), in all this? 'Periodically, a trial and not necessarily a fictitious one, like the trial in *L'étranger*, happens to remind you that justice is always ready to lend you another brain to replace your own in order to condemn you without remorse, and that, in true Corneillean fashion, it depicts you as you should be and not as you are.' Barthes is less well alerted to Camus's own very literary prose and to that of his narrator, Meursault, at crucial moments in the story when he talks of the 'transparence' of *L'étranger* and its 'almost ideal absence of style' (*Le degré zéro de l'écriture*, Part II, iv).

3. The vices of Barthes's prose are similar in many ways to those of Paul Valéry, by whom he has also been much influenced. Both Barthes and Valéry transcend their vices, but it is necessary to know what these are; also to realise that they are not characteristic of French intellectual writing or conversation as a whole. Julien Benda's reminiscences of Valéry are worth quoting in this respect:

> Once when he was in the company of a group of psychiatrists, he expressed casually a number of views which aroused the attention and interest of his audience. When he was asked to express them in more detail, he could produce nothing but floundering assertions, verbal virtuosity, contrasts and comparisons based on appearances, metaphors where there should have been arguments; in short, general disappointment. When one reads the proceedings of the meetings in which the Société de Philosophie invited him to expand his ideas, one is struck by the authority with which they were thrown off and the feebleness of his replies when he was forced to defend them... None the less, it is easy to believe that Valéry had few illusions concerning his powers as a thinker. When he was dispensing his thoughts in the *salons*, it was always with a hunted look and hastily. He reminded me of a card-sharper looking from left to right to see whether the police are going to arrest him in the act. (*Exercice d'un enterré vif*, pp. 55–8)

4. Derrida objects that Saussure (like his fellow Genevan Rousseau in his *Essay on the origin of languages* a century earlier) 'accords an ethical and metaphysical privilege to the voice' and sees '*l'écriture*' ('writing') as exterior and inferior to the 'internal system of language' (*Marges de la philosophie*, p. 179, and the whole of the chapter on 'le cercle linguistique de Genève'). Saussure thus underestimates what is for Derrida the all-important and of course intrinsically problematical *letter* of whatever is written or said. Another version of this argument is to be found in one of the interviews in *Positions* (pp. 27–50).

5. Not that this is a crucial term in either system. The 'vesteme' is comparable to *both* a phoneme and a morpheme. 'It is a variant in the "matrix" formed by the vestimentary code whose "significance" is irradiated along

the item of clothing as written' (*Système de la mode*, p. 76). See too Lévi-Strauss, *Anthropologie structurale*, p. 99.

6. The most celebrated idea to emerge from this essay is that there is a fundamental distinction between what Barthes calls '*discours*' (discourse') and '*histoire*' ('history' or 'story') corresponding to the distinction between the French present and past historic tenses. Barthes acknowledges his debt here to Benveniste's essay, 'Les relations de temps dans le verbe français' (*Problèmes de linguistique générale*) in which Benveniste points out that in the past historic, there is no reference (as in the English perfect) to a time scale extending to the present and that, in this sense, there is no apparent present narrator: 'events seem to recount themselves' (p. 241). There is, of course, a difference here, which neither Benveniste nor Barthes mentions, between the English and French past tenses. The difference between the past historic and perfect in French is stylistic. The past historic is almost never used in conversation or informal epistolary prose. The distinction in English is purely functional: 'Did you see him?' 'No.' 'Have you seen him?' 'Yes.' An exchange of this kind cannot be translated directly into French. The English simple past is therefore less conspicuously distinct from other tenses than the French and less easy to identify with the ('timeless') Greek aorist. In the apparent autonomy of narrative in the French past historic, Barthes finds a reason for discounting intention.

7. The suggestion in *Sur Racine* (pp. 151-2) that a social history of the seventeenth-century theatre audience remains to be written is made, presumably, in ignorance of the work of Pierre Mélèse, John Lough and other historians of the French theatre.

8. I am grateful to Jan Horvat for drawing attention to this example and to the variations worked by Lacan on the original Freudian theme in his review of 'Lacan's *Ecrits*'.

9. The title of *Tel Quel*, the Parisian review which has published the work of Barthes and his associates since the early 1960s, is taken from one of Valéry's own collections of prose: Valéry's own impatience with the notions of intentionality, inspiration, emotion and sincerity and his desire to find some more intellectually rigorous way of accounting for the production of poetry and imaginative prose clearly anticipate structuralism. Despite the magnificent intelligence manifest in his poem, 'Le cimetière marin', there are, I think, good reasons for agreeing with Julien Benda that Valéry the sage has been much over-rated. Barthes's own boyhood worship of Gide (whom he never met but once saw at the back of the Brasserie Lutétia eating a pear and reading a book) was admiration not so much for the work itself as for 'the practices, the postures, a way of walking through the world with a notebook in his pocket and a phrase in his head'. He admired especially Gide's diary, that is, '*the writer without his work*: the supreme form of the sacred: the mark and the void'. *R. Barthes par R. Barthes*, from which this quotation is taken (pp. 81-2), has clear affinities with Gide's own diaries, as do Barthes's more recent *carnets* in *Le Nouvel Observateur*.

10. Barthes's essay of La Rochefoucauld in *Les nouveaux essais critiques* is

interesting in this respect, especially as Barthes sees in La Rochefoucauld many of the characteristics that are to be found in his own prose. In *R. Barthes par R. Barthes*, he confesses that he dislikes the 'maxim', associated as it is with 'the ideology of classicism and an essentialist idea of human nature', but he goes on writing maxims '*to reassure myself*' (p. 181).

11. The example he quotes is of the narrator's remarking of a piece of drawing-room conversation: 'These niaiseries, spoken with the witty mocking air which today characterises a society without belief'. There are, however, even better examples of Balzac's unintentionally comic sententiousness. One of my favourites is from *La cousine Bette* (ch. 19), where a courtesan who has left Le Baron Hulot for a lover who has installed her in what sounds like a miniature Louvre (with 'two paintings by Greuze, two by Watteau, two heads by Van Dyck, two landscapes by Ruysdael . . . a Rembrandt and a Holbein, a Murillo and a Titian . . . in fact two hundred thousand francs' worth of paintings, admirably framed. The frames were worth almost as much as the paintings') greets the dismayed Baron and calls him '*mon bonhomme*', 'a word which addressed to someone so highly placed in the civil service admirably conveys the audacity with which such creatures degrade men of the highest rank'.

12. This is again similar in feeling and theory to Sartre who, in *Qu'est-ce que la littérature?*, sees the freedom of the reader to follow or not, as he chooses, what the writer is saying, and the writer's recognition of this freedom, as a 'pact of generosity' and a realisation, in this one instance of mutual respect, of the Kantian 'kingdom of ends'. At the moment, Sartre claims, there is a dichotomy between the 'virtual public' for which any true writer writes and the 'real public' which, with few exceptions, is far too preoccupied by the distractions of labour, poverty and class division to participate in this or any other kingdom of ends. The writer, as such, therefore has a moral obligation to work politically to bring about an eventual identification of the virtual with the real through the creation of a classless society from which exploitation and alienation will have disappeared.

13. Charles Fourier (1772–1837) was a profoundly original and influential thinker and Barthes's novel tribute and commentary are very much to be welcomed. His prophecy of social evolution into a state of harmony in which all man's emotions would be freely expressed and society divided into co-operative *phalanges* was elaborated with a detail and voluptuousness which Barthes avowedly shares.

5. The criticism of F. R. Leavis

1. Leavis inherited from former propagandists for English the prejudice against Latin and Greek. It amounted especially to a sense of the dangers of reading a living language which is one's own as if it were a mere code; and hence seeing language as only ever decorative or instrumental. Robert Bridges was, for Leavis (see *The common pursuit*, pp. 62–3),

incapacitated by a classical education from reading and grasping the genius and originality of his friend Gerard Manley Hopkins. This doesn't mean that he ever advocated the abolition of classical studies and he might well have been appalled by their near-disappearance from the syllabuses of English schools by the end of the 1970s. He himself received an excellent classical training from the headmaster of the Perse School. W. H. D. Rouse, to whom he was once asked to explain in Greek, when he had a puncture in the tyre of his bicycle and 'observing quantity, stress and tonic accent', why he was late for school (see R. Hayman, *Leavis*, p. 1). In his last public appearance, a lecture at the Perse, he quoted Aeschylus in the Greek.

2. This is not, however, to be attributed to political prejudice. Reviewing Hugh Macdiarmid's *Second Hymn to Lenin and other poems*, Leavis wrote in *Scrutiny* ('Hugh Macdiarmid'): 'It is a great tribute to Hugh Macdiarmid to say that we find nothing either amusing or offensive in his characteristic attitude, which is that of the inspired Poet – the nobly indignant genius – of the Romantic tradition. But "Romantic" is an unfortunate word if it suggests the usual self-dramatising vanity, the petty egotism enjoying its *saeva indignatio*, the feminine gush of stoic pride and self-pity. Macdiarmid exhibits a truly fine disinterestedness and convinces us that we have here rare character if not rare genius' (p. 305). The respect seems to have been mutual. Macdiarmid addressed the Doughty Society of Downing College in 1960 and dined with Leavis in hall. 'He doesn't drink,' Macdiarmid told me afterwards, 'but I liked him. He's aggressive.'

3. 'Positively affirmed' needs, of course, considerable qualification, since Leavis himself returned continually, especially in his later years, to 'Ash Wednesday' and to the *Four Quartets* which, when *New bearings* was published, had still not been written. (It is arguable, incidentally, that Leavis's strong preference for 'Ash Wednesday' and 'Marina' in *New bearings*, to some of the Ariel poems, such as the 'Journey of the Magi', encouraged Eliot two years later when he wrote 'Burnt Norton', the first of the *Quartets*, to continue thinking and writing in the way Leavis had especially admired. It is possible, in other words, that this is a case of creative collaboration between poet and critic. However, I know of no written testimony to this effect, though Leavis was certainly a critic Eliot read closely.) Leavis's admiration for the *Four Quartets* when they were first published was almost unqualified, but he came increasingly to regard even this poetry, Eliot's finest, as that of a great poet paradoxically disabled by his 'fear of life and contempt (which includes self-contempt) for humanity' (*The living principle*, p. 205) from recognising the nature of his own (human) creativity. Leavis devoted much of the last years of his life to contemplation of and wrestling with Eliot's late poetry. (See *Lectures in America, English literature in our time and the university* and *The living principle*.) The implicit and often explicit contrast was with the achievement – literary and hence far more than literary – of Lawrence. It might be argued here that Leavis is indeed applying, as Wellek approvingly told him, a 'yard-stick' and that, as Michael Black

has argued ('F. R. Leavis: 1895-1978', p. 302), the comparison is 'tendentious'. And if this is so, my account of how Leavis's criticism works is, to that extent, invalidated. Leavis's writings on Eliot make arduous, as well as exhilarating and, I believe, deeply rewarding reading. The reader will obviously decide for himself whether I am right to claim that, far from confining Eliot within a yard-stick, they exemplify Leavis's adventurousness, his ability, that is, to go as far as the poetry takes him.

4. This judgment may sound presumptuous in the sense of implying that Leavis was capable of writing better social histories, but I don't think this follows, or that Leavis thought that it followed. In *Nor shall my sword*, he calls on the authority of Harold Perkin's *The origins of modern English society 1780-1880* to justify his belief that Sir Charles Snow was wrong to pronounce ('breezily sweeping aside the sentimentalists') that 'with singular unanimity, in any country where they have had the chance, the poor have walked off the land into the factories as fast as the factories could take them'. The history, as Leavis and Perkin both argue, has been a good deal more complex than that. In this connection, it is worth remarking that, though Leavis himself read Part I of the History Tripos at Cambridge and strongly recommended to undergraduates reading English the study of social and political history (e.g. Halévy's *Rise of philosophic radicalism*), he never pretended that the two disciplines were anything other than mutually complementary.

5. In saying this, I have to ask whether the very considerable claims that John Newton has made for the poetry of Ted Hughes (in *The Cambridge Quarterly*, II, iv; v, iv; vi, iv; and vii, iv) don't have the same seriousness as Leavis's criticism in *New bearings*, or, at least, an equivalent kind of seriousness. I feel they don't, and this is partly because of the extent of Newton's claims on Hughes's behalf. Newton has been shaken and exhilarated by Hughes's poetry and is admirably bold in saying this. I find it difficult, however, to agree with him that any *new world* is thereby revealed or that there is any sustained movement of thought corresponding to the initial impact of Hughes's poetry on the nerves or his undoubted ability to tear the scales momentarily from our eyes. That a poet of Hughes's obvious gift and power should write in this way – suggestive of a constant violent movement away from any living centre of awareness – seems to me, if anything, symptomatic of what has happened to poetry since Eliot's *Four Quartets*. None the less, I would certainly agree that Hughes's poetry and Newton's account of it offer a perfect test-case for deciding whether my observations of poetry, criticism and the reading public today are or are not without foundation.

6. '*The Tyger* is a poem... But again and again one comes on the thing that seems to be neither wholly private nor wholly a poem. It seems not to know what it is or where it belongs, and one suspects that Blake didn't know. What he did know – and know deep down in himself – was that he had no public: he very early gave up publishing in any serious sense. One obvious consequence, or aspect, of this knowledge is the carelessness that is so apparent in the later prophetic books. Blake had ceased to be

capable of taking enough trouble. The uncertainty I have just referred to is a more radical and significant form of the same kind of disability. In the absence, we may put it, of adequate social collaboration (the sense, or confident prospect, of a responsive community of minds was the minimum he needed) his powers of attaining in achieved creation to that impersonal realm to which the work of art belongs and in which minds can meet – it is as little a world of purely private experience as it is the public world of the laboratory – failed to develop as, his native endowment being what it was, they ought to have done' (pp. 187–8).

7. Caldwell Cook, author of *The play way* (see Margaret Mathieson's *Preachers of culture*, pp. 61–3 and 86), shared the common view among propagandists for English that English should replace classics as the centre of humane studies, and anticipated Leavis's and Thompson's *Culture and environment* by seeing in the study of literature, and especially creative work in the classroom, a means of countering the degrading influences of commercialism. How direct his influence was on Leavis it is probably too late to know; though it is worth noting that he directed Leavis in the rôle of Macbeth in a production of the play in 1912 (see R. Hayman, *Leavis*, p. 1).

8. Leavis, one might say, was an unashamed and, I would add, wholly rational élitist. He was, as such, a champion of the English grammar school, at a time when schools were being compelled to go 'comprehensive' or 'independent'. Typical of the misunderstandings to which Leavis's views of individual superiority have given rise is Raymond Williams's objection to the use by Leavis and others of the word 'mass': 'nobody feels himself to be only the man in the street; we all know more about ourselves than that. The man in the street is a collective image, but we know all the time our difference from him. It is the same with "the public" which includes us, but is not yet us. "Masses" is a little more complicated yet similar' (*Culture and society*, p. 299). The words can obviously, as Williams says, be used in an offensive and patronising way, but, when I am talking to a physicist, a Hebrew scholar or an economist, I am very conscious that I talk only as 'the man in the street' and that when I am enjoying the monologues of Al Read on the radio, I am part of the mass audience.

What, I would agree, can be insulting is a certain kind of pedagogic zeal with regard to 'the masses', the zeal, for example, of the Newbolt Committee on the Teaching of English in England (see p. 148 above) who talk explicitly of the teacher as a 'missionary' or of Arnold Wesker's heroine in *Roots*. Leavis's advocacy of English, even in his early writings, is not naïve in this way. He did not regard its benefits as either direct or self-evidently beneficial (see *English literature in our time and the university*, pp. 28–30). Leavis disliked thinking of himself as a 'teacher' and, as a Director of Studies at Downing, treated his students, as I can personally testify, with the courtesy with which one addresses an intellectual equal. The nearest I ever got to a ticking off from him was when he strongly disputed my claim that *The Waste Land* offered a realistic picture of contemporary English life.

9. See John Gross, *The rise and fall of the man of letters*, especially pp. 270–1, and Raymond Williams, *The country and the city*. Obviously either view of the past can be presented crudely and implausibly. But, to take the first, there is a difference between the kind of relation to contemporary literature and thought of the Victorian reviews with their wide circulation or of the *Nation and Athenaem* during the all-too-brief period of Middleton Murry's editorship and that of any journal or newspaper today. This is partly, of course, because the intellectual world is over-populated but this is not to dispute the reality of the change. As for the danger of over-valuing the past, Sturt, I would claim, certainly doesn't do this and in *Change in the village* saw social improvement as something long overdue. (It was not only a realisation of the value of craft industry that he gained from his reading of Morris and Ruskin.) Nor did Leavis think of himself as a 'Luddite'. In *Nor shall my sword* (pp. 77–99), he quotes enthusiastically from those passages in which both Dickens and Lawrence welcome the advent of the machine. As for the disputed reality of the 'organic community', see John Fraser's 'Reflections on the organic community' in *The Human World* or even Jane Jacobs's *Death and life of the great American cities*. The reality is not something that can be determined only in terms of the classic Weberian distinction between *Gemeinschaft* and *Gesellschaft*. It is a matter of recorded experience and actual memories such as as those which both Sturt and Fraser provide.

10. I have in mind especially a critic I admire, one of Leavis's warmest champions, Ian Robinson, in *The survival of English*. Robinson in his reaction against the common view that words are merely the clothing of thought, beliefs and feelings which remain what they are whether or not they are expressed in words, seems to adopt the very opposite view (discussed on pp. 117–23 above) that thoughts, beliefs and feelings are wholly and invariably determined by language. 'In the beginning', he writes on page 1, paraphrasing St John, 'was language. That was the true light which lighteth every man that comes into the world.' He also quotes on page 12 from J. L. Austin's famous essay, 'A plea for excuse': 'Our common stock of words embodies all the distinctions that men have found worth drawing, and the connections they have found worth making, in the lifetime of many generations.' (*All* the distinctions? *All* the connections? one is naturally inclined to ask.) Both the left-wing Barthes, revolting against the fascist oppression of language, and the far more conservative Ian Robinson who welcomes it, deny, in effect, that it is possible for men to be the masters of words. This, I think, prevents Robinson from fully understanding, as Leavis himself complains (*The living principle*, pp. 59ff.), what Leavis means when he talks of human creativity. Robinson attempts to apply Leavis's criticism of Blake (quoted on page 168): that Blake tried to know the unknowable – to give substance and form to the goal or τέλος to which creativity purposefully strives – to Leavis's own criticism. Leavis writes, he claims, 'sometimes movingly, of "human need"; but "need" is bound to demand the kind of satisfaction that can be prescribed. And that is not the kind that can

be offered by the great poet or critic – as Leavis, most of the time, is well aware' (p. 239). I don't see why 'need' has to be like that at all. Something which is unexpected in one's discovery of a work of art is that it can lead one to recognise needs of which one had hitherto been unaware; and in the process be rewarded by new and fresh thoughts, feelings and even beliefs.

11. This argument is developed in *L'idéologie structuraliste* by Sartre's admirer, the sociologist Henri Lefebvre, whose seminars on Sartre's *Critique de la raison dialectique* were attended by Daniel Cohn-Bendit, the leader of the May '68 'revolution'. Lucien Goldmann is said to have been delighted by the slogan, '*Le structuralisme ne descend pas dans la rue*' ('Structuralism doesn't go in for street fighting') which appeared on a wall in Paris during the student riots. Lefebvre, incidentally, bases a great deal of his case on the arguments of Benveniste, summarised in Chapter 2 above, concerning the irreducibility of the two domains of the 'semantic' and 'semiotic'.

12. There is a danger of over-hasty assimilation of very different kinds of argument, but it is worth noting all the same that Popper himself agrees that there may be a 'close similarity' between what he calls the world of 'objective knowledge', distinct from the physical and the 'subjective' worlds, and what Leavis refers to as the 'third realm' in his lecture on C. P. Snow. (See Popper, p. 73n.) Leavis writes: 'It is in the study of literature . . . that one comes to recognise the nature and priority of the third realm (as, unphilosophically, no doubt, I call it talking with my pupils), the realm of that which is neither merely private and personal nor public in the sense that it can be brought into the laboratory or pointed to' (*Nor shall my sword*, p. 62).

13. See the chapter on 'Lawrence and class' in *D. H. Lawrence, novelist*. I say 'merely as a member of a social class', but Leavis never denies, of course, that he writes from a particular historical and social standpoint and is sometimes ridiculed for this. Eagleton sees in his 'élitism' a characteristic trait of the petty bourgeoisie (*Criticism and ideology*, pp. 13–14) and a correspondent in *The Spectator* after the publication of the lecture on Snow wished that one could simply 'leave him in his lower middle class critical Bethel'. Leavis's criticism might be taken as exemplifying the truism, expounded at length by Althusser (see p. 119 above), that it is only by speaking from a specific (social and historical) point of view that one can speak as a representative human witness to the truth; and that the only alternative is to pretend to speak from the clouds. Those critics, such as Eagleton, who complain of his refusing to make 'his assumptions explicit' fail to realise that there are more important forms of candour; and also that the ability to transcend the possible limitations of one's point of view is what makes it impossible to predict what one may learn to value and perceive.

14. This passage appears in the first published version of the essay in *The Human World*. Leavis omitted it when the essay reappeared in *Nor shall my sword* a year later. Polanyi's 'account of education', to which Leavis refers, is taken from his 'Logic of tacit inference', in *Knowing and*

being (p. 148): 'We may say that when we learn to use language, or a probe, or a tool, and thus make ourselves aware of these things as we are of our body, we *interiorize* these things and *make ourselves dwell in them*. Such extensions of ourselves develop new faculties in us; our whole education operates in this way; each of us interiorizes our cultural heritage.'

15. Leavis, for all his breadth of imaginative understanding, tended, I believe, to under-rate Flaubert. He tended to take too readily and even too literally the adverse judgments of Henry James and Lawrence. There is an interesting discussion of this in *Flaubert and Henry James* by David Gervais (pp. 89–119).

16. There is, of course, something of *Don Quixote*, which Flaubert immensely admired in *Bouvard et Pécuchet*. There is also perhaps some point in trying to see what Ezra Pound was trying to say when he made the comment (preposterous if one takes it literally) that, unlike Henry James, Flaubert 'gives us in each main character: *Everyman*' (*Literary essays of Ezra Pound*, p. 300). My own remarks on *Bouvard et Pécuchet* in *Stendhal: the education of a novelist*, pp. 81–2, now seem to me to miss the point completely.

BIBLIOGRAPHY

I should again mention that quotations from French authors are given in my own translation, even where the page reference is to the original French text.

Althusser, Louis, *Pour Marx*, Maspero, Paris, 1965.
Anderson, Perry, 'Components of the national culture', in *New Left Review*, 50, 1968, pp. 3–57.
Anderson, Quentin, 'Henry James, his symbolism and his critics', in *Scrutiny*, xv, 1, 1947, pp. 12–19.
Anscombe, G. E. M., *Intention*, Blackwell, Oxford, 1963.
Arnold, Matthew, *Culture and anarchy*, ed. J. Dover Wilson, Cambridge University Press, 1960 (first published 1869).
    Essays in criticism, second series, Macmillan, London, 1935 (first published 1888).
Austin, J. L., *Philosophical papers*, ed. G. Warnock, Clarendon Press, Oxford, 1961.
Bachelard, G., *La formation de l'esprit scientifique*, J. Vrin, Paris, 1967.
Ballard, M. (ed.), *New movements in the study and teaching of history*, Temple Smith, London, 1971 (reviewed anonymously in *The Human World*, 5, 1971, pp. 62–76).
Barthes, Roland, *Le degré zéro de l'écriture, suivi de Nouveaux essais critiques*, Seuil, Paris, 1972 (first published 1953).
    Mythologies, Seuil, Paris, 1970 (first published 1957).
    Sur Racine, Seuil, Paris, 1963.
    Essais critiques, Seuil, Paris, 1964.
    'Eléments de sémiologie', in *Communications*, 4, 1964.
    Critique et vérité, Seuil, Paris, 1966.
    'Introduction à l'analyse structurale des récits', in *Poétique du récit*, R. Barthes, W. Kayser, W. Booth, etc., Seuil, Paris, 1977 (first published 1966).
    Système de la mode, Seuil, Paris, 1967.
    L'empire des signes, Seuil, Paris, 1970.
    S/Z, Seuil, Paris, 1970.
    Sade, Fourier, Loyola, Seuil, Paris, 1971.
    'Ecrivains, intellectuels, professeurs', in *Tel Quel*, Paris, 1971, pp. 3–18.
    Le plaisir du texte, Seuil, Paris, 1973.
    Roland Barthes par Roland Barthes, Seuil, Paris, 1975.
    Fragments d'un discours amoureux, Seuil, Paris, 1976.
    Leçon: leçon inaugurale prononcée au Collège de France, Seuil, Paris, 1978.

Bateson, F. W., 'The function of criticism at the present time', in *Essays in Criticism*, III, January 1953.

Benda, Julien, *Exercice d'un enterré vif*, Trois-collines, Geneva, 1944.

Benoist. J.-M., *La révolution structuraliste*, Grasset, Paris, 1975.

Benveniste, Emile, *Problèmes de linguistique générale*, including 'Les niveaux de l'analyse linguistique', Gallimard, Paris, 1966.

Le vocabulaire des institutions indo-européennes, Minuit, Paris, 1969.

Problèmes de linguistique générale II, including 'Sémiologie de la langue', Gallimard, Paris, 1974.

Black, Michael, 'A kind of valediction: Leavis on Eliot', in *The New Universities Quarterly*, Winter 1975, pp. 78–93.

'F. R. Leavis: 1895–1978', in *The New Universities Quarterly*, Summer 1978, pp. 293–304.

Bloch, Marc, *The historian's craft* (trans. Peter Putnam), Manchester University Press, 1963.

Boileau (Nicolas Boileau-Despréaux), *Œuvres complètes*, Gallimard, Bibliothèque de la Pléiade, 1966.

Bouhours, Le Père, *Entretiens d'Ariste et d'Eugène*, Bossard, Paris, 1920 (first published 1671).

Brooks, Cleanth, *The well wrought urn*, Harcourt Brace, New York, 1947.

Bultmann, Rudolf, *Jesus Christ and mythology*, S.C.M. Press, London, 1958.

Chomsky, Noam (with M. Halle), 'Some controversial questions in phonological theory', in *Journal of Linguistics*, I, 1965, pp. 97–138.

Aspects of the theory of syntax, M.I.T., Cambridge, Mass., 1965.

Language and mind, Harcourt Brace, New York, 1968.

Reflections on language, Fontana/Collins, London, 1976.

Collingwood, R. G., *The principles of art*, Oxford University Press (paperback), 1963 (first published 1938).

The idea of history, Oxford University Press (paperback), 1961 (first published 1946).

Conrad, Joseph, *Typhon* (trans. from the English by André Gide), Gallimard, Paris, 1917.

Croce, Benedetto, *Aesthetic as science of expression and general linguistic* (trans. Douglas Ainslie), Macmillan, London, 1909.

Culler, Jonathan, *Structuralist poetics*, Routledge, London, 1975.

Derrida, Jacques, *La voix et le phénomène*, P.U.F., Paris, 1967.

De la grammatologie, Minuit, Paris, 1967.

L'écriture et la différence, Seuil, Paris, 1967.

Marges de la philosophie, Minuit, Paris, 1972.

Positions, Minuit, Paris, 1972.

Dummett, Michael, *Frege: philosophy of language*, Duckworth, London, 1973.

Eagleton, Terry, *Criticism and ideology*, Methuen, London, 1976.

Marxism and literary criticism, New Left Books, London, 1976.

Eliot, T. S., *Selected essays*, Faber, London, 1949.

Empson, William, *Seven types of ambiguity*, Chatto and Windus, London, 1930.

The structure of complex words, Chatto and Windus, London, 1952.

Fingarette, H., *Self-deception*, Routledge, London, 1968.
Foucault, Michel, *The order of things* (trans. from the French), Tavistock, London, 1970.
    The archaeology of knowledge (trans. A. M. Sheridan), Pantheon Books, New York, 1972.
Fraser, John, 'Northrop Frye and evaluation', in *The Cambridge Quarterly*, II, 2, 1967, pp. 97–116.
    'Reflections on the organic community', in *The Human World*, 15–16, 1974, pp. 57–74.
Freud, Sigmund, *Psychopathology of everyday life* (trans. anonymously), Penguin Books, Harmondsworth, 1938.
    Character and culture (intro. Philip Rieff), (collected papers, trans. anonymously), Collier Books, New York, 1963.
Frye, Northrop, *Anatomy of criticism*, Princeton University Press, 1957.
Fubini, Mario, *Racine e la critica delle sue tragedie*, Sansoni, Florence, 1925.
Gervais, David, *Flaubert and Henry James*, Macmillan, London, 1978.
Goldmann, Lucien, *Le Dieu caché*, Gallimard, Paris, 1955.
    Pour une sociologie du roman, Gallimard (Collection Idées), 1964.
Greimas, A.-J., *Sémantique structurale*, Larousse, Paris, 1966.
    (ed.), *Essais de sémiotique poétique*, Larousse, Paris, 1971.
Grice, H. P., 'Meaning', in *The Philosophical Review*, 1957, pp. 377–88.
Gross, John, *The rise and fall of the man of letters*, Weidenfeld and Nicolson, London, 1969.
Harding, D. W., 'Psychological processes in the reading of fiction', in *The British Journal of Aesthetics*, II, 2, 1962, pp. 133–47.
Harré, H. R. (Rom), *The principles of scientific thinking*, Macmillan, London, 1970.
    Philosophies of science, Oxford University Press, 1972.
Hayman, Ronald, *Leavis*, Heinemann, London, 1976.
Heath, Stephen, *Le vertige du déplacement*, Fayard, Paris, 1974.
Hegel, Friedrich, *The phenomenology of mind* (trans. J. M. Baillie), 2 vols., Swann, Sonnenschein and Co., London, 1910.
Hesse, Mary, *Models and analogies in science*, Sheed and Ward, London, 1963.
Hirsch, E. D. Jr, *Validity in interpretation*, Yale University Press, 1967.
    The aims of interpretation, Chicago University Press, 1976.
Hjelmslev, Louis, *Prolegomena to a theory of language* (trans. J. Whitfield), rev. edn, University of Wisconsin Press, Madison, 1961.
Horvat, Jan, 'Lacan's *Ecrits*', in *The Cambridge Quarterly*, VII, 4, 1978, pp. 346–57.
Husserl, Edmund, *Logische Untersuchungen*, 3 vols., Niemeyer, Halle, 1929.
Jacobs, Jane, *The death and life of great American cities*, Random House, New York, 1961.
Jakobson, Roman, *Selected writings*, Mouton, The Hague, 2 vols., 1962 and 1971.
    Questions de poétique, Seuil, Paris, 1973.
Jasinski, René, *Vers le vrai Racine*, Armand Colin, Paris, 1958.
Johnson, Samuel, *Johnson on Shakespeare*, including *Preface to Shakespeare*,

intro. Walter Raleigh, Oxford University Press, 1949 (first published 1908).

Lives of the English poets, 2 vols., Dent, Everyman's Library, London, 1950.

Kant, Immanuel, *The critique of judgment* (trans. and intro. James Creed Meredith), Clarendon Press, Oxford, 1964.

Kojève, Alexandre, *Introduction à la lecture de Hegel. Leçons sur la phénoménologie de l'esprit*, réunies et publiées par Raymond Queneau, Gallimard, Paris, 1947.

Kristeva, Julia, *La révolution du langage poétique*, Seuil, Paris, 1974.

(ed.), *Langue, discours, société: pour Emile Benveniste*, Seuil, Paris, 1975.

Lacan, Jacques, *Ecrits*, Seuil, Paris, 1966.

Lawrence, D. H., *Phoenix*, Heinemann London, 1936.

Studies in classic American literature, Doubleday Anchor Books, New York, 1953.

Leach, Edmund, *Lévi-Strauss*, Fontana/Collins, London, 1970.

Leavis, F. R., *New bearings in English poetry*, Chatto and Windus, London, 1932.

(with Denys Thompson), *Culture and environment*, Chatto and Windus, London, 1933.

'Restatement for critics', in *Scrutiny*, I, 4, 1933, pp. 315–23.

'Hugh Macdiarmid', in *Scrutiny*, IV, 3, 1935, p. 305.

Revaluation, Chatto and Windus, London, 1936.

The great tradition, Chatto and Windus, London, 1948.

The common pursuit, Chatto and Windus, London, 1952.

'The responsible critic or the function of criticism at any time', in *Scrutiny*, XIX, 3, 1953, pp. 162–83.

D. H. Lawrence, novelist, Chatto and Windus, London, 1955.

'Anna Karenina' and other essays, Chatto and Windus, London, 1967.

English literature in our time and the university, Chatto and Windus, London, 1969.

(with Q. D. Leavis), *Lectures in America*, Chatto and Windus, London, 1969.

(with Q. D. Leavis), *Dickens the novelist*, Chatto and Windus, London, 1970.

'Elites, oligarchies and an educated public', in *The Human World*, 4, 1971, pp. 1–22.

Nor shall my sword, Chatto and Windus, London, 1972.

The living principle, Chatto and Windus, London, 1975.

Lefebvre, Henri, *L'idéologie structuraliste*, Editions Anthropos, Paris, 1975.

Lepschy, Giulio, 'Osservazioni sul termine "struttura"', in *Annali della Scuola Normale Superiore di Pisa*, Serie II, vol. xxxi, 1962, pp. 173–97.

La linguistica strutturale, Einaudi, Turin, 1966.

Lévi-Strauss, Claude, *Anthropologie structurale*, Plon, Paris, 1958.

La pensée sauvage, Plon, Paris, 1962.

Le cru et le cuit, Plon, Paris, 1964.

Du miel aux cendres, Plon, Paris, 1966.

Lyons, J., *Structural semantics*, Blackwell, Oxford, 1963.

Macnamara, J. (ed.), *Language learning and thought*, Academic Press, New York, 1977.
Marrou, Henri, *Histoire de l'éducation dans l'antiquité*, Seuil, Paris, 1948.
Connaissance de l'histoire, Seuil, Paris, 1954.
Mathieson, Margaret, *The preachers of culture*, Allen and Unwin, London, 1975.
Medawar, P. B., *The art of the soluble*, Methuen, London, 1967.
Merleau-Ponty, Maurice, *Le visible et l'invisible* (texte établi par Cl. Lefort), Gallimard, Paris, 1964.
Mischel, T. (ed.), *The self. Psychological and philosophical issues*, Blackwell, Oxford, 1977.
Mishan, E. J., *Making the world safe for pornography*, Alcove Press, London, 1973.
Monod, Jacques, *Le hasard et la nécessité*, Seuil, Paris, 1970.
Montgomery, Stuart, *Circe*, Fulcrum Press, London, 1969.
Moore, G. E., *Philosophical papers*, Allen and Unwin, 1959.
Murry, J. M., *The problem of style*, Oxford University Press (paperback), 1960.
Newbolt, Sir Henry (chairman), *Report to the Board of Education on the teaching of English in England*, H.M.S.O., London, 1921.
Newton, J. M., 'Ted Hughes's metaphysical poems', in *The Cambridge Quarterly*, II, 4, 1967, pp. 395–402.
'Leavis's new book', in *The Cambridge Quarterly*, III, 4, 1968, pp. 354–69.
'Literary criticism, universities, murder', in *The Cambridge Quarterly*, V, 4, 1971, pp. 335–54.
'A book on Ted Hughes', in *The Cambridge Quarterly*, VI, 4, 1975, pp. 371–5.
'Hughes's *Gaudete*', in *The Cambridge Quarterly*, VII, 4, 1977, pp. 335–45.
Olsen, S. H., *The structure of literary understanding*, Cambridge University Press, 1978.
Pannenberg, Wolfhart, *Faith and reality* (trans. John Maxwell), The Search Press, London, 1977.
Pettit, Philip, *The concept of structuralism*, University of California Press, Berkeley, 1975.
Piaget, Jean, *Biologie et connaissance*, Gallimard, Paris, 1967.
Le structuralisme, P.U.F., Paris (Collection 'Que sais-je?'), 1968.
Picard, Raymond, *Nouvelle critique ou nouvelle imposture*, Pauvert, Paris, 1965.
Plutarch, 'How the young man should study poetry', in *Moralia*, vol. I (trans. F. C. Babbitt), Heinemann, London, 1927.
Polanyi, Michael, 'The structure of consciousness', in *Anatomy of knowledge* (ed. Marjorie Grene), Routledge, London, 1969.
Knowing and being (ed. Marjorie Grene), Routledge, London, 1969.
Popper, Karl, *Objective knowledge* (3rd edn), Clarendon Press, Oxford, 1974.
Pound, Ezra, *The literary essays of Ezra Pound* (intro. T. S. Eliot), Faber, London, 1954.

Purves, A. C., *Literature education* (*sic*) *in ten countries: an empirical study* (with contributions by other authors), Wiley, New York, 1973.

Putnam, Hilary, *Meaning and the moral sciences*, Routledge, London, 1978.

Quine, W. V. O., *Word and object*, M.I.T. Press and Wiley, New York, 1960.

Richards, I. A., *The principles of literary criticism*, Routledge, London, 1924.

Ricœur, Paul, *La métaphore vive*, Seuil, Paris, 1975.

Riffaterre, Michael, *Semiotics of poetry*, Indiana University Press, Bloomington, 1978.

Robinson, Ian, *The survival of English*, Cambridge University Press, 1973.

Ryle, Gilbert, *The concept of mind*, Hutchinson, London, 1949.

Sartre, Jean-Paul, *La nausée*, Gallimard, Paris, 1938.

  L'imaginaire, Gallimard, Paris, 1940.

  Qu'est-ce que la littérature?, Gallimard, Paris, 1948.

  'Sartre aujourd'hui', in *L'Arc* (*numéro spécial*), Paris, 1966, no. 30.

  Situations VIII/IX (2 vols.), Gallimard, Paris, 1972.

Saussure, Ferdinand de, *Cours de linguistique générale* (3rd edn), Fayot, Paris, 1967.

Schlumberger, J., *Plaisir à Corneille*, Gallimard, Paris, 1936.

Searle, John, *Speech acts*, Cambridge University Press, 1969.

Stendhal (Henri Beyle), *Histoire de la peinture en Italie*, 2 vols., Champion, Paris, 1924.

  Mélanges de littérature, vol. iii, Le Divan, Paris, 1933.

  Courrier anglais, vol. i, Le Divan, Paris, 1936.

Stephen, Leslie, *English literature and society in the eighteenth century*, Methuen, University paperbacks, London, 1963 (first published 1903).

Strickland, G. R., *Stendhal: the education of a novelist*, Cambridge University Press, 1974.

Sturt, George, *Change in the village*, Duckworth, London, 1912.

  The wheelwright's shop, Cambridge University Press, 1923.

Tarski, Alfred, *Logic, semantics, metamathematics: papers from 1923 to 1938* (trans. J. H. Woodgear), Clarendon Press, Oxford, 1956.

Tocqueville, Alexis de, *L'ancien régime et la révolution*, 2 vols. (ed. J. P. Mayer), Gallimard, Paris, 1952 (first published 1856).

Trier, Jost, 'Das sprachliche Feld. Eine Auseinandersetzung', in *Neue Jahr. f. Wiss. u. Jugenbildung*, 10, 1934, pp. 428–49.

Trubetzkoy, N., *Principes de phonologie*, Klincksieck, Paris, 1949.

Turnell, Martin, *The novel in France*, Penguin Books, Harmondsworth, 1958 (first published 1950).

Ullmann, Stephen, *The principles of semantics*, Blackwell, Oxford, 1951.

Veblen, Thorstein, *The theory of the leisure class*, Allen and Unwin, London, 1957 (first published 1899).

Wahl, François (ed.), *Qu'est-ce que le structuralisme?*, Seuil, Paris, 1968.

Wellek, René, 'Literary criticism and philosophy: a note on *Revaluation*', in *Scrutiny*, v, 4, 1937, pp. 375–83.

  (with Austin Warren), *Theory of literature*, Cape, London, 1949.

  Concepts of criticism (ed. S. J. Nichols), Yale University Press, 1963.

Williams, Raymond, *Culture and society*, Penguin Books, Harmondsworth, 1961 (first published 1958).

The country and the city, Frogmore/Paladin, London, 1973.
Wittgenstein, Ludwig, *Philosophical investigations* (trans. G. E. M. Anscombe), Blackwell, Oxford, 1953.
   On certainty (ed. G. E. M. Anscombe and G. H. von Wright, trans. Denis Paul and G. E. M. Anscombe), Blackwell, Oxford, 1969.

INDEX

Abel, Karl, 178n.5
academic study of literature, 3–4,
    4–6, 9, 25, 58–60, 66–7, 88–9,
    92, 103, 108, 109–17, 136,
    145–9, 156, 176n. 2, 3 and 4
Academy, French, 66
acoustic image, 15–16, 178n.6
aesthetics, study of, 101–2
Alain (Emile Chartier), 178n.6
Althusser, Louis, 119–21, 194n.13
ambiguity, 25, 39
analysis, literary, 6–8, 79–80, 162
analytic propositions, 55–6
Anderson, Perry, 156–7, 166
Anderson, Quentin, 155
Anscombe, G. E. M., 182n.2
Aquinas, St Thomas, 83, 94
Aristotle, 56
Arnold, Matthew, 5, 100, 147–8
Auden, W. H., 151
Austen, Jane, 6, 49
Austin, J. L., 193n.10

Bachelard, Gaston, 20, 119
Ballard, M., 117
Balzac, Honoré de, 49, 50, 104, 107,
    164, 172, 173, 174, 189n.11
    La cousine Bette, 189n.11
    Illusions perdues, 50
    Sarrasine, 138–9, 140
Barthes, Roland, 3, 5, 6–7, 11, 13,
    29, 37, 39–40, 41, 76–80, 104,
    127–44, 145, 146, 149, 152,
    156, 162–75, 176n.1 (ch. 2),
    180n.16, 181n.19, 186n.1–
    189n.13
    on *Bouvard et Pécuchet*, 140–1,
    172–5

comparison with F. R. Leavis, 149,
    152, 156, 162–75
on James Bond, 135–6
on language as oppressive, 165,
    172, 193n.10
on Racine, 41, 76–80
and Saussurean semiology, 13, 19,
    127–37, 163
on the study of literature as a
    form of science, 131, 133, 136,
    137, 138, 163, 183n.6
Bataille, Georges, 140
Bateson, F. W., 65–6, 158, 164
Baudelaire, Charles, 25, 63
beauty, as a critical term, 101, 108
belief (and critical judgment), 92–5,
    184n.10
Beljame, A., 145
Benda, Julien, 187n.3, 188n.9
Bennett, Arnold, 9
Bennett, E. K., 107
Benoist, J.-M., 14–15, 30, 177n.4,
    181n.20
Benveniste, Emile, 10, 15–19, 25, 26,
    54, 121, 132, 134, 137, 169,
    177n.5, 179n.9, 188n.6, 194n.11
on the acoustic image, 15–16
on *histoire* and *discours*, 188n.6
on semantic and semiotic levels of
    language, 18, 19, 134, 177n.5,
    178n.8, 194n.11
on the sentence, 17–18, 178n.8
Vocabulaire des institutions indo-
    européennes, 19, 23, 29–30
Black, Michael, 190n.3
Blake, William, 49, 102–3, 160, 168,
    169–70, 191n.6, 193n.10
Bloch, Marc, 112, 114, 115, 116

Bloom, Archbishop Antony, 184n.10
Boileau (Nicolas Despréaux), 52, 102, 111
Bond, James, 135–6
Borges, J. L., 118
Bouhours, Le Père, 101, 102
Bridges, Robert, 189n.1
Brontë, Emily (quoted), 174–5
Brooks, Cleanth, 39
Bultmann, Rudolf, 74–5, 95

Campbell, Thomas
'The burial of Sir John Moore at Corunna', 73
Camus, Albert, 186n.2
canons (of sacred and profane texts), 4–5, 95, 96, 99–100
Carew, Thomas, 164
Carroll, Lewis
Through the looking-glass, 121
Castries, General de, 129
categoremic level (of language), 17, 134, 179n.10
censorship, 95, 96, 98, 99
certainty, 55–67, 162–4, 168–70
Cervantes, M. de
Don Quixote, 195n.16
Chesterton, G. K., 140
Chiang Kai-Shek, 113
Chichester, Sir Francis, 42–3
chimpanzees (communicating with human beings), 179n.9
Chomsky, Noam, 26, 54, 80, 181n.17, 182n.5
on deep structure, 26, 181n.17
on intentionality, 54, 182n.5
Clare, John, 6
Clément, J.-M., 78
clichés, 36–7, 48–9, 65, 129–30, 140–1, 165, 173–4
Cohn-Bendit, Daniel, 194n.11
Coleridge, S. T., 89, 154
Collingwood, R. G., 100, 115–16
Comte, Auguste, 133
conceptual fields (in semantic theory), 22–3
Conrad, Joseph, 63–4, 154
Typhoon, 63–4

conventionalist view of language, 19, 117–18, 120–3, 165, 193n.10
Cook, Caldwell, 161, 192n.7
Corneille, Pierre, 66, 176n.3, 182n.3, 187n.2
Cratylus, 121, 140
Croce, Benedetto, 101–2
Culler, Jonathan, 123, 179n.10, 180n.13, 181n.18

Dante, 62–3, 72, 80–1, 83, 92–5, 112, 184n.11
day-dreaming (as part of imaginative reading), 105–8, 185n.13 and 14
deep structure, 26, 28, 181n.17
Derrida, Jacques, 20–1, 22, 23, 26, 47, 118, 120, 121, 132, 137, 138, 163, 170, 177n.2, 179n.11, 187n.4
on *différance*, 20, 118
on *écriture*, 21, 137, 187n.4
on Saussurean linguistics, 20–1, 132, 137, 187n.4
Descartes, René, 58, 179n.9
dialectic, Hegelian and Marxist, 31, 163, 166, 169, 181n.20
Dickens, Charles, 4, 88, 107, 117, 154, 156, 157–8, 185n.12, 193n.9
Hard Times, 117, 157–8
Diderot, Denis, 42, 138, 164
differential semantics, 25–6
Dilthey, W., 10, 115
discours (as contrasted with *histoire*), 188n.6
DNA, 23
Dominici, Gaston, 129, 186n.2
Donne, John, 5, 89, 91
Donskoi, Mark, 89
Dostoevsky, F. (Freud on), 51
'double-perspective' in reading, 70
Douglas, Gavin, 63
Drouet, Minou, 129
Dummett, Michael, 178n.8
Durkheim, Emile, 156

Eagleton, Terry, 167, 194n.13

Ecole des Hautes Etudes, 146
écriture, 21, 137, 139, 140, 141,
    142–3, 172, 187n.4
Eisenstein, Sergei, 89
Eliot, George, 107, 154, 156
Eliot, T. S., 80–1, 92–5, 101, 151,
    153, 156, 159, 166, 190n.3,
    192n.8
  on poetry and belief, 92–5
  poetry of, 151, 153, 156, 159, 166,
    190n.3, 192n.8
Empson, William, 25, 39, 70–1, 101
Epicurus, 138
'episteme' (as defined by Foucault),
    118–19
evidence in criticism, internal and
    external, 110–11
explication littéraire, 8
explicit inference, 29

fallibility of criticism, 29–31, 55–67,
    162–70
Fielding, Henry
  Tom Jones, 89, 154
Fingarette, H., 182n.4
Flaubert, Gustave, 4, 43, 104, 105,
    129, 135, 140, 164, 172–5,
    185n.14, 195n.15 and 16
  Bouvard et Pécuchet, 140, 164,
    172–5, 195n.16
  Madame Bovary, 104
Fleming, Ian
  Goldfinger, 135–6
foreclosure, 143
Foucault, Michel, 118–20, 121, 167,
    177n.4
Fourier, Charles, 138, 143, 144, 155,
    170, 189n.13
Fraser, John, 183n.6, 193n.9
Frege, Gottlob, 178n.8
Freud, Sigmund, 10, 51–2, 55, 103,
    120, 138, 144, 178n.5, 188n.8
  Psychopathology of everyday life
    (quoted), 51–2
Frye, Northrop, 56, 181n.18, 183n.6
Fubini, Mario, 137

Galileo, 30, 183n.6

Gervais, David, 195n.15
Gide, André, 63–4, 78, 83, 118, 139,
    188n.9
  as translator of Conrad, 63–4
Giscard d'Estaing, President, 144
Goldmann, Lucien, 12, 112–14,
    194n.11
Gombrich, E. H., 27
Gorki, Maxim, 8, 89
Gospels, 9, 37, 53, 73–5, 91, 95, 116,
    184n.10, 185n.12, 193n.10
Gourmont, Rémy de, 104, 146
Gracchus, Tiberius, 117
grammatikoi, 4, 7, 99–100
grammatology, 21
Greimas, A.-J., 19, 179n.10
Grene, Marjorie, 168
Grice, H. P., 53–5, 60, 182n.5
Gross, John, 193n.9
gustemes, 135, 187n.5

Halévy, Elie, 191n.4
Halle, M., 178n.7
Harding, D. W., 106–8, 166,
    185n.13
Hardy, Thomas, 7, 153, 174–5
  'After a Journey', 7, 174–5
  'The Voice', 153
Harré, R. M. (Rom), 23–4
Hawthorne, Nathaniel, 41, 49
Hayman, Ronald, 190n.1, 192n.7
Heath, Stephen, 129
Hegel, G. W. F., 21, 53, 120, 163,
    164, 169, 177n.2, 181n.20
  Phenomenology of mind (quoted),
    163–4
Heidegger, Martin, 27, 74, 95
hermeneutic circle, 74–5
hermeneutic code, 139
hermeneutics, 9–10
Hesse, Mary, 24
heuristic judgment, 58–60, 162
Hirobuni, Ito, 117
Hirsch, E. D., 4, 6, 9–10, 27, 28, 54,
    68, 70, 75, 97–8, 109–10, 120,
    121, 180n.14
  on double perspective, 70
  on the hermeneutic circle, 75

Hirsch, E. D. (*contd*)
on meaning and significance, 10, 68, 120
on value judgment, 97–8
Hitler, Adolf, 84, 98, 99
Hjelmslev, L., 16
Homer, 23, 29–30, 41
Hopkins, Gerard Manley, 72, 180n.13, 190n.1
Horvat, Jan, 188n.8
Hughes, Ted, 191n.5
Husserl, Edmund, 21, 47–8, 176n.2, 179n.11
Huxley, T. H., 147, 152

indeterminacy of translation, 69–70, 75
intention, 3, 9–10, 36–55, 60–2, 83–9, 109–10, 122–3, 155, 158, 182n.2, 188n.6
and subject-matter, 54, 109–10
unconscious intention, 51–2, 70–2
irony, 39, 140–1, 164, 172

Jacobs, Jane, 193n.9
Jakobson, Roman, 15, 25, 38, 178n.7, 179n.12 and 13
James, Henry, 195n.16
on Flaubert, 195n.15
The Golden Bowl, 155–6
Jansenists, 12, 113, 114
Jasinski, René, 136
Jerome, St, 100
Jesuit colleges, 146, 176n.3
Johnson, Samuel, 47, 62, 63, 89, 91, 162, 182n.3
Jones, Ernest, 51
Jonson, Ben, 164
Joyce, James, 123, 171
judgment, subjective and objective, 85–100
and belief, 91–5
Jusserand, 145

Kant, Immanuel, 55–6, 96–8, 109–10, 189n.12
Keats, John, 45, 105

Kojève, A., 163
Kristeva, Julia, 177n.5, 181n.1
Kuomintang, 113

Lacan, Jacques, 137–8, 188n.8
La Fontaine, Jean de, 110–11, 185n.15
language games, 28
La Rochefoucauld, François, Duc de, 188n.10
Lautréamont (Isidore Ducasse), 181n.1
Lawrence, D. H., 9, 41, 49, 64, 91, 111, 156, 158, 159, 160, 167, 177n.4, 180n.14, 185n.12, 194n.13, 195n.15
on critics, 9, 111
on Flaubert, 195n.15
'idealism' of, 167
Leavis on, 156, 159, 185n.12, 190n.3, 193n.9
'Never trust the artist, trust the tale', 41, 49
Lawrence, T. E., 64
Leach, Edmund (quoted), 179n.12
Leavis, F. R., 3, 5, 7, 36–7, 47, 48–9, 58, 65–7, 88, 89, 100, 102–3, 105, 112, 146, 148–75, 181n.16 and 18, 185n.12, 189n.1–195n.15
on cliché, 36–7, 48–9, 65, 165, 173–4
on language, 47, 165–6, 170
on literature and history, 156–61, 191n.4, 193n.9
rejection of prescriptive criteria in, 150–1, 154, 166, 190n.3
Lefebvre, Henri, 194n.11
Lepschy, Giulio, 19
Lévi-Strauss, Claude, 13, 19, 24, 128, 135, 167, 176n.1, 177n.5, 179n.12, 187n.5
on binary structures, 24, 179n.12
and Saussurean semiology, 13, 19, 176n.1, 177n.5
lexemes, 17, 18, 134
lexical fields, 22–3
Linden, E., 179n.9

literature
definition of, 8–9
and history, 109–23, 156–61
see also academic study of litera-
ture
Longfellow, H. W., 41
Lough, John, 188n.7
Louis XIV, 87, 110–11, 114, 185n.15
Lowell, Robert, 81
Loyola, St Ignatius, 141
Lyons, John, 21–3, 26, 47
Lysenko, T. D., 183n.6

Macdiarmid, Hugh (C. M. Grieve),
190n.2
Macnamara, J., 179n.9
Mallarmé, Stéphane, 181n.1
Malraux, André, 113–14
Marrou, Henri, 186n.16
Marvell, Andrew, 89, 117
Marx, Karl, 20, 55, 119, 120, 128,
167, 169
Marxism, 12, 20, 55, 92, 93, 95–6,
119, 144, 166, 167, 169,
181n.20
Mathieson, Margaret, 146–8, 176n.4
Maurois, André, 64
meaning, 37
'natural' and 'non-natural', 53–5,
60
and significance, 10, 44–5, 120
and subject-matter, 54, 109–10
Medawar, Sir Peter, 28
Mélèse, Pierre, 145, 188n.7
Merleau-Ponty, Maurice, 169
metaphysical presuppositions, 20–1,
118, 121
method, critical, 6, 7, 8, 154
see also analysis, literary
Michelangelo, 184n.11
Mill, James, 157
Mill, John Stuart, 157
Milton, John, 88
Mishan, E. J., 98
models, in science, 23, 24, 26
Molière, 87–8, 100, 176n.3
Tartuffe, 87–8, 183n.8
Monod, Jacques, 169, 181n.20

Montaigne, Michel de, 50
Montesquieu, C. de Secondat, Baron
de, 55
Montgomery, Stuart, 38–9
Circe (quoted), 38
Moore, G. E., 56, 57, 61–2
morphemes, 17, 18, 19, 134, 178n.8,
187n.5
Morris, William, 168, 193n.9
movement in poetry, 80, 153
Murry, John Middleton, 104–5,
193n.9

Newbolt, Sir Henry
Newbolt Committee's report on
*The teaching of English in
England*, 148–9, 192n.8
Newton, John, 5–6, 181n.16, 191n.5
Nietzsche, Friedrich, 10–11, 21, 103,
118, 120, 170
Barthes and, 138
Derrida on, 21, 179n.11

Oates, Titus, 117
obscene jokes, 108
Obscene Publications Act, 98–9
Olsen, S. H., 157–8, 162
O'Malley, Raymond, 176n.4
organic community, 160–1, 193n.9

Pannenberg, Wolfhart, 75
paradigmatic principle of structure,
19, 132, 180n.13
paramorphs, 23–4, 26
Pareto, V., 156
Pascal, Blaise, 12
perception, psychology of, 86
Perkin, Harold, 191n.4
Peter, St, 184n.10
Petrarch, 82
Pettit, Philip, 23–5, 27, 180n.15
Philo, 53
phonemes, 17–18, 19, 134, 136,
178n.8, 179n.10, 187n.5
phonology, 15, 17–18, 19, 132, 134
Piaget, Jean, 27, 28, 119
Picard, Raymond, 29, 41, 76–8
Plato, 22, 109–10, 121

Plutarch, 4, 176n.1
Pobedonostsev, K., 117
poetry, nature of, 25, 38, 47, 72, 82, 92–3, 112
Polanyi, Michael, 28, 29, 168, 171, 194n.14
Pope, Alexander, 39–40, 46–7, 65–7, 164–5
Popper, Sir Karl, 28, 56, 59–60, 67, 168–9, 183n.7, 194n.12
pornography, 98–100
Poujade, Pierre, 129
Pound, Ezra, 63, 159, 195n.16
Powys, T. F.
    Mr Tasker's gods, 107
practical criticism, 29, 169
    see also analysis, literary; and method, critical
praxis, 20, 95–6, 167
proaïretic code, 139
probabilistic criteria, 65–6, 162
puns, 39–40
Purves, A. C., 176n.2
Putnam, Hilary, 61, 69–70, 183n.7

quantum physics, 24
Quine, W. V. O., 69–70, 75, 178n.8

Racine, Jean, 4, 8, 12, 37–8, 40, 41, 51, 76–80, 113, 114, 130, 163, 176n.3
    Barthes on, 37, 41, 76–80, 136–7, 163
    Goldmann on, 12, 113–14
    quoted, 40, 76–7
Read, Al, 192n.8
Régnier, H. de, 110–11, 186n.15
Revel, Jean-François, 64
rhythm, 73, 81–2, 153
Ricardo, D., 120
Richards, I. A., 101
Ricœur, Paul, 10, 180n.13
Riffaterre, M., 180n.14
Rimbaud, Arthur, 142, 181n.1
Robinson, Ian, 98–9, 193n.10
Ronsard, Pierre de (quoted), 82
Rouse, W. H. D., 190n.1
Rousseau, Jean-Jacques, 21, 187n.4

Ruskin, John, 193n.9
Ryle, Gilbert, 182n.2

Sade, Marquis de, 138, 164
Salan, General, 187n.2
Sartre, Jean-Paul, 38, 68, 128, 130, 137, 140, 144, 163, 167, 186n.1, 189n.12, 194n.11
    on imaginative reading, 185n.13
    on poetry, 38, 180n.13, 181n.1
    on structuralism and praxis, 167
    La nausée, 128, 143–4
Saussure, Ferdinand de, 12–21, 22, 23, 26, 123, 127–37, 139, 163, 180n.15, 187n.4
    influence of, 12–13, 127–37, 139, 163
    langue and parole, 123
    on semiology, 13–14, 26, 127–9, 163, 180n.15
    on the signifier and the 'acoustic image', 15–16, 22, 187n.4
scepticism, weak and dynamic, 56–7
Schleiermacher, F., 9, 75
Schlumberger, Jean, 66
science, experimental, 23, 24, 59–60, 67, 119, 133, 165, 168, 169, 183n.6
Scott, Walter, 89, 154
Searle, John, 182n.5
Selby, Hubert, Jr
    Last exit to Brooklyn, 99
semantic level of language, 18, 19, 20, 31, 134, 194n.11
semiology, 10, 13–19, 26, 127–37, 180n.15
    see also Saussure on semiology
semiotic level of language, 18, 19, 134, 194n.11
sentences
    Benveniste on, 17, 18
    Frege, Quine and Dummett on, 178n.8
Shakespeare, 4, 8, 25, 47, 62, 103–4
    Hamlet, 51, 87, 104–5
Shapira, Morris, 186n.15
Shelley, Percy Bysshe, 8, 102
Siger of Brabant, 93–4

Snow, C. P.
  Leavis on, 36–7, 48–9, 67, 165, 174, 191n.4
Solzhenitsyn, Alexander, 44, 108
Spender, Stephen, 151
Starsky and Hutch, 148
Stendhal (Henri Beyle), 50–1, 52, 53, 95, 100, 103, 135, 183n.9, 184n.11, 186n.16
  La chartreuse de Parme, 50–1, 103, 186n.16
  quoted, 183n.9, 184n.11
Stephen, Leslie, 112
Strickland, Geoffrey, 195n.16
structuralism, 10–11, 12–31, 40, 68, 112–14, 123, 127–37, 153, 158, 162–3, 167, 175, 176n.1–181n.20, 187n.4–188n.6, 194n.11
  deriving from Saussurean semiology, 12–15, 19, 20, 127–37, 163, 194n.11
  and discussion of rhythm and movement, 153
  genetic structuralism, 12, 112–14
  and *praxis*, 167
  and theory of 'open' or 'polyvalent' texts, 68, 79–80, 136
structure, history of term, 19–20
Sturt, George, 160–1, 193n.9
Swedenborg, E., 155
synonymity, 121
syntagmatic principle of structure, 19, 132, 180n.13
synthetic propositions, 55–6

Taine, Hippolyte, 29, 145, 185n.14
Tarski, A., 61, 183n.7
taste, 88–90, 145–6
Thomas, Edward, 180n.13
Thompson, Denys, 3, 148, 160
Times Literary Supplement, 66, 161
Tocqueville, Alexis de, 23, 147
Tolstoy, Leo, 156, 186n.16

Tom and Jerry, 148
Trier, Jost, 21–2
Trubetzkoy, N., 15, 132
truth-claims in literary criticism, 95, 157–8, 162, 185n.12
truth-conditions, 61, 183n.7
Turnell, Martin, 103
Twain, Mark (Samuel Clemens), 88, 98, 100, 154
Tyndall, J., 152

Ullmann, Stephen, 22
unconscious motivation, 43, 51–2, 70–2, 101–2, 178n.5, 179n.12
unconscious
  Freudian, 51–2, 70–2, 178n.5
  structure of, 179n.12

Valéry, Paul, 139, 146, 187n.3, 188n.9
value judgments, 11, 83–108, 149–56
Veblen, Thorstein, 132–3
Verlaine, Paul, 8
vestemes, 135, 187n.5
Villon, François (quoted), 81
Voltaire, 9, 52, 182n.3

Wahl, F., 177n.2
Weber, Max, 156, 193n.9
Wellek, René, 97, 149–50, 154, 159, 166, 190n.3
Wesker, Arnold
  Roots, 192n.8
Whitehead, A. N., 168
Williams, Raymond, 192n.8, 193n.9
Wilson, Sir Harold, 8
Wittgenstein, Ludwig, 49, 56, 57, 61, 61–2, 178n.6, 181n.17, 182n.5
word-counts, 6, 28
Wordsworth, William, 70–3, 102–3, 180n.13
  The Prelude (quoted), 70–1
Wyatt, Sir Thomas (quoted), 82

Yeats, W. B., 151–2, 156
  Sailing to Byzantium (quoted), 151